THE REAL
McCOY

ISBN 978-1939710-147

Orange Frazer Press
P.O. Box 214
Wilmington, OH 45177
Telephone: 937.382.3196 for price and shipping information.
Website: www.orangefrazer.com

Book and cover design: Alyson Rua and Orange Frazer Press
Cover photo: David Kohl
Flap photo courtesy of Hank Green
Photos on pages 9, 53, 97, 138, 151, 170, and 223 courtesy
    of the *Dayton Daily News*
All others courtesy of Hal McCoy

Library of Congress Cataloging in Publication Data Pending

THE REAL

McC⚾Y

My half-century with the Cincinnati Reds

Hal McCoy

ORANGE *frazer* PRESS
Wilmington, Ohio

CONTENTS

To my best friend, to the love of my life, to my guardian angel, and to the most important person in my life—all of whom happen to be the same person, my beautiful wife, Nadine.

ACKNOWLEDGEMENTS

For years, everywhere I went, people would ask, "When are you going to write your book?" And I would say, "What book?" They would say, "About your many, many years of covering sports and baseball. You have to have so many stories, told and untold." My wife, Nadine, would be there listening and pretty soon, she picked up the mantra.

As do most wives, she began nagging me, always with the same question, "When are you going to start your book?" This went on for a couple of years. She promised me a new laptop if I would get started. She came through. I didn't. The laptop stayed in the box for more than a year, and she finally gave it to her brother, Dr. Rod Tomczak.

Then I promised her again that I would write the book. She bought me another new laptop. Then I finally sat down, mostly on a dilapidated couch in my garage, the man cave, and began writing and writing and writing. A book has a lot of words in it. When I retired as a traveling beat writer after the 2009 season I received a note from John Baskin of Orange Frazer Press saying they were interested in publishing a book, if I would write it. I tucked the note back into its envelope and placed it in a drawer in my desk. And forgot about it.

After I wrote a couple of chapters in late 2013, I realized, "Hey, if you write a book, you need a publisher." I contacted Baskin and Orange Frazer Press publisher Marcy Hawley. They asked me to lunch. I was immediately impressed with both. Within a couple of weeks we had a deal.

And I thank Marcy Hawley for taking a chance on a grizzled old sports writer who is a neophyte book author. For certain I thank John Baskin, an editor who should be working for a big publishing house in New York. Without his guidance the project would never have been finished, and as

I wrote I kept in mind his suggestion, "Details, details, details." It was his constant encouragement as I wrote that kept me going. As an accomplished writer himself, he knows how fragile egos can be on those who write and he always knew just how to assuage mine with the right words and the right encouragement. As he told me, "I can't be in your house looking over your shoulder, you have to do it yourself." But he was always looking over my shoulder as I wrote, even though he wasn't physically present.

Even though I lived everything I wrote about, the old memory isn't always so good. Many stories and incidents in the book came because free-lance writer Gary Schatz and Associated Press sports writer Joe Kay jogged my memory of incidents and stories. Both have been around the Reds a long time and I thank them for their help. I wrote a few chapters while sitting at a table in a house in Buckeye, Arizona, during spring training of 2014. I shared the house with Schatz. I would tell him what or whom I was writing about and he would say, "Remember the time…" And I would remember. But I wouldn't have remembered without his reminders. And it was the same with Joe Kay, who has shared many of the good times and a few bad times covering the Reds.

As a beat writer for forty-two years, I have touched shoulders and exchanged words with thousands of baseball players, managers, coaches and other sportswriters. Without them, of course, there would be no stories. I was just there to absorb them and chronicle them.

Along the way, covering sports for more than half a century, I missed many important dates and accomplishments of my sons, Brian and Brent, and my stepson, Chad. I missed their baseball games and other important events in their lives. They never complained, never asked me to be a stay-at-home dad. For that, and all their life-long support, I thank them and apologize for all I missed. And I'm still missing things. I missed my grandson Eric's high school baseball career at Centerville High School, and now I'm missing my other grandson's tee-ball games.

In January of 2004, I was at the New York Baseball Writers Association of America awards dinner at the New York Hilton, there to receive a "Ya Gotta Have Heart" award for continuing as a beat writer despite my vision problems. A young pitcher named Josh Beckett of the Florida Marlins was at the dais with me and other baseball dignitaries and we had a nice conversation and became acquainted. That season when the Marlins came to Cincinnati, my daughter-in-law, Tammy, was in a bar with some of her friends when Beckett walked in. She stopped him and asked, "Do you know Hal McCoy? He's my father-in-law." He acknowledged that he did and took time to answer her questions and be a genuinely nice guy. She never forgot it. When she gave birth to her son, she named him Beckett.

During spring training one year when Beckett was then with the Boston Red Sox, I stopped by his locker in the clubhouse in Fort Myers, Florida. I told him the story and how my daughter-in-law named my grandson after him. He threw up his hands and said, "I didn't do it. Honest, I didn't do it." And we both laughed.

In 2013, my granddaughter, Staci Taylor, gave birth to a son, Liami. I became a great-grandfather. Right then, right there, I knew it was time to get busy on this book. Time is running out. Everything in this book is mine, as I lived it and remember it. Any errors or mistakes are mine and for those I apologize.

THE REAL
McCOY

01 | SEEING IS BELIEVING

COMEBACK FROM A MAJOR-LEAGUE INJURY

For thirty-one years I watched baseball games with perfect clarity, perfect eyesight. As the baseball writer for the *Dayton Daily News*, I was performing a job that wasn't a job. I always told my wife, Nadine, "Some day I'm going to have to get a real job." But I never did.

I love baseball. I love writing. I love to travel. I was getting to do all three, and I was getting paid. What could be better? There were no problems in my world as I covered more than seven thousand games and wrote more than twenty-five thousand baseball stories.

And then my world came crashing down, or so I thought.

It was August 16, 2001. Why would I specifically remember that date? Because it is a date forever lodged in my memory bank. Because it is the date when my world began to go dark and fuzzy, although I did not know it at the time.

As I walked toward my seat in the Busch Memorial Stadium press box, preparatory to covering a Cincinnati Reds–St. Louis Cardinals baseball game, my right eye began itching, as if something was in it. I rubbed it, believing I would dislodge the foreign object. The blurriness did not go away.

It was the last game of a road trip, a Thursday. As I packed Friday morning to return home, my right eye still felt as if something was in it and I called Nadine. She decided it best to go see my ophthalmologist when I returned to Dayton that afternoon.

Dr. Jay Kelman, always chatty with me when I sat in his chair, liked to quiz me about the Reds. And that Friday was no different when I sat in the chair and he began his exam as I described my symptoms—blurriness in my right eye, as if something was in it.

As he flashed his light in my eye he became quiet, unusually business-like. Something was wrong. When he covered my left eye and had me read the chart, I not only couldn't see the letters, I couldn't see the chart. I fudged. Isn't the first letter always "E?" I couldn't see it, but I said, "E." I couldn't read anything. He did more testing without saying a word. Finally he delivered the news.

"You have Non-Arteritic Anterior Ischemic Neuropathy," he said.

"Okay," I said with a shrug. "What's that?"

"It's rare," he said. "It's a stroke of the optic nerve. The bad news is that there is no cure and the hope is that it doesn't get much worse. The good news is that it only happens in both eyes in 15 percent of the cases." He prescribed some eye drops for both eyes in an attempt to prevent swelling of the orbital nerves, which caused the stroke.

I adjusted. My left eye, always my dominant eye, took over. I didn't even notice that my right eye was nearly useless. I still drove, I still played my beloved tennis nearly every day and didn't lose any efficiency. I finished the baseball season and all was right with my world.

On January 27, 2002, my world literally crashed. My left eye had given me a reprieve, but now it was blurry. Everything was blurry. Everything was dark. I knew instantly what had happened. As I walked down the stairs from the bedroom, I said to Nadine, "Honey, I just hit the big 15 percent lottery. My left eye is gone, too."

That night, the Cincinnati Reds had a celebration for my election as winner of the J.G. Taylor Spink Award and inclusion into the Baseball Hall of Fame in Cooperstown, New York. It was at the University of Dayton Arena as part of the Reds annual winter baseball caravan. I said nothing to anybody about it, but as I sat at a table, about twenty feet from the first row of fans, I could not recognize faces, even though they belonged to close friends.

Spring training was only two weeks away and I thought my career was over. How can you cover baseball when you are legally blind, when everything is dark and fuzzy?

I tried to drive after that, even though my peripheral vision was zero, and as I looked through my glasses it appeared as though they were fogged over and dirty. I wrecked the car. I turned into the side of a car that was sitting directly to my left at an intersection. No more driving.

Three days later, it was confession time. I gathered up all the charts from my eye examinations, which showed I could barely see, and visited Frank Corsoe, my sports editor at the *Dayton Daily News*. I told him what had happened and the diagnosis, no cure. I told him I was finished.

We both had a good cry, but he looked me in my faltering eyes and said, "No, you're not. You are going to give it a try. You are going to spring training and we'll see how it goes."

I packed my black suitcase in mid-February and flew to Sarasota, Florida, spring home of the Reds at the time. I was by myself in a dark and fuzzy world and worried beyond comprehension as I sat on the airplane, unable to make out the faces of the passengers seated next to me.

When I got to the baggage carousel at the Sarasota airport, I was befuddled. Nearly everybody's luggage is black. I couldn't find mine. I waited until nearly every passenger claimed their luggage before I could find mine.

I took a cab to my rented condominium at the Palm Bay Club on Siesta Key and after checking in, dropped my luggage in my bedroom. It was time for The Big Test. I took another cab to Ed Smith Stadium and walked toward the familiar clubhouse. When I walked through the double doors and around a large wall that was covered with a huge photograph of Johnny Bench, I stopped short as I looked around the room.

I recognized nobody. The faces were blurry; faces I'd known for years. I thought about turning around right then and heading home, my career over. Reds third baseman Aaron Boone spotted me standing with a perplexed look on my face and came over to say hello.

When he got very close and I recognized him, I said, "You are probably seeing me for the last time. I'm going home. I'm quitting." And I told him why.

He grabbed me by the elbow and led me to his locker, pointed to his chair and said, "Sit down. You are not going to quit. I don't ever want to hear you say the word 'quit' again. You love what you are doing and you are good at it."

That turned me around. To this day Boone doesn't remember much about that conversation, doesn't take much credit for what he did, but he helped save my career. He also sloughs aside what he did for me and not long ago he said this to somebody who asked him about it: "Sometimes God uses people in different ways and maybe I was his tool. I wasn't doing anything overwhelming. I wasn't going out of my way. It wasn't any skin off my back, I just saw a friend who was obviously down and I remember being quiet and a little bit sad. He told me a story and I just simply said, 'Come on, dude. That's not a good enough reason,' and it turned out to mean a lot to him and hit home with him, and here we are several years later and he's still having a significant impact with the Cincinnati Reds. Given all he's done with the *Dayton Daily News* and the history of Reds baseball, the fact he got to continue it, continue it at a high level, and that everyone rallied around him and I helped make it possible is a tribute to everyone else involved."

Hal and Aaron Boone on Hal McCoy Day at GABP, 2009.

First baseman Sean Casey was in the room that day and overheard the conversation. He jumped to his feet and said, "We'll give you all the help you need."

So I stayed, although there were many nights in the condo when the tears flowed and I remained skeptical about how I could continue. There was another problem. How do I get around, especially when the exhibition games began and the Reds played games all over south Florida?

My peers stepped up. My competition. Tony Jackson of the *Cincinnati Post* offered to pick me up every morning and deliver me back to the condo every late afternoon. When Jackson left the *Post*, Marc Lancaster, his replacement, did that same thing. Then it was Mark Sheldon of *MLB.com*, C. Trent Rosecrans of the *Cincinnati Post* and freelance writer Gary Schatz.

That first week was the most difficult, and even after Boone's speech I thought about going home. Then Bob Nightengale of *USA Today* came to camp and did a story about what happened to me. When the story appeared, my e-mail box filled up. My telephone never quit ringing. They were all words of encouragement, telling me to persevere. A person dying of leukemia e-mailed me and told me not to give up. A military man serving on a ship off the coast of Iraq e-mailed me and told me, "You are my hero. Keep at it." I e-mailed him back and said, "No, my friend, *you* are the hero."

Nightengale's story and the response was all I needed. It was then I decided there were millions of people in this world a lot worse off than I was and I should quit feeling sorry for myself and do my job to the best of my ability.

It was time to make adjustments. I tried to watch batting practice but couldn't see the ball after it was hit. From the press box I discovered I could see the pitcher deliver. I could see line drives and ground balls, but I couldn't see fly balls. I haven't seen a home run since 2001.

But after covering baseball for thirty-one years, I made a discovery while watching Ken Griffey Jr. take batting practice. I noticed that after he hit the ball, he always looked in the direction where he hit it. I watched other players. They all did it. So I watched the batter's head to see where he was looking. Then I looked that way, too, and could pick up the ball.

It wasn't easy. There were some pratfalls. Boone became a comedian. He told people he once saw me talking to a Coke machine. I probably was. He also jumped up and down and waved his arms when I came into the room and shouted, "Hal, I'm over here."

Road trips were tough, especially going through airports, although I had been through most of them so often I knew their layouts. And it was the same with the ball parks. The worst incident happened in New York on Times Square. I was carrying a Starbucks Venti nonfat latte in my left hand and a bag of expensive cigars in my right hand. Normally when I walk I have to look down to watch for curbs, cracks in the sidewalks, and protruding objects like steps. But I was in Times Square at noon and it was shoulder-to-shoulder people. I had to watch them. As I neared the Marriott Marquis Hotel, I stumbled over a curb and went to my knees.

I was so proud. I didn't spill a drop of the latte and I didn't break a single cigar. But as a kind pedestrian helped me to my feet (without trying to remove my wallet), I discovered some pain in my left knee. I had torn the meniscus. I didn't realize the seriousness of the injury because there wasn't a lot of pain at the time. My wife, Nadine, joined me in Miami when the Reds were there to play the Marlins and we walked South Beach, enjoying the sights and frequenting the shops.

But as the days went by the knee began to ache and after a while I began to drag my left leg. Reds broadcaster Chris Welsh asked me if I was imitating Amos McCoy, actor Walter Brennan's character on the TV show *The Real McCoys*. He walked with an exaggerated limp.

Finally I visited Dr. Tim Kremchek, the Reds medical director, and he discovered the tear in the knee and said surgery was necessary. The Reds were to leave the next day for a trip to Washington, Pittsburgh, and Chicago. I said, "I'll wait until after the trip. I haven't missed a single trip in my entire career and I'm not going to do it now." Dr. Kremchek and Nadine overruled me. I could get away with saying no to the doctor but not to Nadine. The surgery was performed while the Reds were in Washington.

But I didn't miss the entire trip. And it was a foolish move. I decided to join the team in Chicago, even though I was on crutches. It is the worst ballpark in America for a beat writer on crutches. The press box is atop the stadium and there is no elevator. To get there requires a long trip up a series of long ramps. And the clubhouses are located at the bottom of those ramps, which meant walking, on crutches, down those ramps to the clubhouses, accompanied by thousands of fans leaving the game.

It was a painful learning experience.

After the Montreal Expos moved to Washington, I had to cover games in an unfamiliar stadium. The press box configuration in D.C. Stadium was difficult for me. To reach the elevator to take you to the clubhouse, you had to leave the press box and cut through a private box that had some steps. The press box was often occupied by former Washington, D.C., mayor Marion Barry, who was arrested while in office by the FBI on drug charges after he was videotaped smoking crack cocaine.

After one game in the stadium, I left the press box to head for the clubhouse and started up the stairs in the private box. I missed a step and went down hard, my notebook flying one way and my digital recorder the other.

As I got up, one occupant of the box said, "Don't feel bad. Mayor Barry used to do that all the time."

Pete Rose once asked, "How can you cover a baseball game when you can't see?" I can see enough, Pete, and there are always large-screen TVs in the press boxes so I can watch replays. And the main part of the job is getting the story after the game, doing interviews. You don't have to see; you have to listen.

Who wants a baseball signed by a journalist? With a fan base like Hal's, just about everybody.

I was interviewing Reds pitcher Mat Latos one day and he was barefoot. Unbeknownst to me, I stepped on his toes and he moved back. I took a step forward and stepped on his toes again.

"Damn, Hal, are you stepping on my toes on purpose?" he asked. Somebody told him I was legally blind and he laughed and said, "Well, that explains a lot."

It is the best compliment I receive when a player discovers my vision problems and says, "I didn't know that."

The major part of covering a baseball team seventy miles from your home is getting there and back when you can't drive. For the first five years, the *Dayton Daily News* furnished a driver for me. First, it was sports department clerks and interns, mainly Elizabeth Rossi. Then they located a permanent driver, Larry Glass, a retired school executive and a long-time amateur baseball coach around the Cincinnati area. He did it because he loved the game, and he did it without pay. But after the 2012 season he encountered medical difficulties and couldn't continue.

I was in a panic. How would I get back and forth to games? I decided to put a notice in the blog I do for the *Dayton Daily News*, believing maybe somebody out there had the time to do it. The blog informed anybody interested that they would accompany me to all eighty-one home games and get a free seat next to me in the press box. The downside is that it is an all-day affair—pick me up at my home at 1:30 in the afternoon for night games and drop me back home after midnight. I hoped I might get nine or ten offers.

For the next week, my e-mail inbox filled up. I had 485 offers. Some were for weekends only. Some were offers for part-time duty. I received offers from men, women, firemen, lawyers, teachers, professors, retirees, student journalists who wanted to pick my brain. One man offered to come home from Dubai if he could be my driver. Another said he had an RV in Florida and would drive it to Ohio and take me to games.

I read as many as I could and one jumped out. It was from a retired Air Force loadmaster. He had recently lost his wife and his e-mail said, "I wake up at six every morning, read the paper, drink my coffee and say, 'Now what?'"

His name was Ray Snedegar. I called him and invited him to lunch. It was only five minutes into the ride to the restaurant when I decided, "This is the guy." We were the same age and we quickly discovered we had many similar interests. I offered him the job and he quickly took it. The Major League Baseball Network sent a crew to follow us around for two days— starting at my house, accompanying us to the ball park to film us, and returning home with us. It was a big hit and has been played over and over.

The last week of his first season as my driver, I asked him, "Well, you tired of it yet?"

"No," he said. "I'm having the time of my life."

"You want to do it next year?" I asked.

"I thought you'd never ask," he said, smiling broadly.

It is now twelve years after I hit the 15 percent lottery and I am still pounding the keyboard, ever thankful for the day Aaron Boone said, "I don't ever want to hear you say the word 'quit.'" And to make certain I don't consider it, I have a placard in a prominent place in my home office on which there is a quotation from former North Carolina State basketball coach Jim Valvano that says, "Don't quit. Don't ever quit."

I won't quit. I won't ever quit. I am into my forty-second season of covering the Reds, into my fifty-second year as a sports journalist. When people ask when I will give it up, I tell them, "As long as somebody will pay me to write, I'll do it until my head hits the laptop—probably in the bottom of the ninth in Great American Ball Park."

MY FIRST FLY BALL

OR PASSION AT A YOUNG AGE

Baseball is in my blood. Baseball is part of my DNA. Baseball dropped into my lap. Literally. It plopped into my baby carriage when I was less than a year old.

When I was born in 1940, my father, Harold, was a hard-throwing semi-pro baseball pitcher/outfielder for the Akron Sahara Dry and Canton Road Furniture. My mother, Hazel, took me to games that next summer and parked the baby carriage in the grass next to her behind the screen. During a game, a batter lifted a pop foul over the screen, and the baseball landed in my carriage, right between my legs. The game stopped, my dad told me later, when I was able to appreciate a good story, and players from both teams surrounded me, fearful that I had been skulled. But I was smiling, looking up with my baby browns, the ball snuggled in the carriage with me. That's when everybody knew: Baseball would always be close to me.

That was my formative moment, although my love affair began in earnest when I was four and my father came back from World War II after serving with the U.S. Army in the Philippines with another Irishman, General Douglas MacArthur. Dad was a Cleveland Indians fan, enamored with a young pitcher named Bob Feller, and my dad told me, "This kid throws the baseball 110 miles an hour." So Dad wanted me to be pitcher.

We had no indoor plumbing and the outdoor facility was a wood-slatted outhouse shed. Not even a two-holer, it was an all-purpose one-holer. For our game of catch in the backyard, Dad decided it would be our backstop, but my arm was so scattergun that I put a few holes in the rotten, decaying wood, leaving embarrassing peepholes in our bathroom.

So we concentrated on making me an outfielder, although I had suffered a minor case of polio when I was a year old, forever making me run two steps behind a snail.

I was Harold Stanley McCoy Jr. because my mother, Hazel, went against my father's wishes and named me after him. To make certain I wasn't called Harold, my dad began calling me Bubby. So for the first eleven years of my life I was Bubby McCoy, the tousle-haired, freckle-faced waif who loved baseball.

As a scraggly-dressed, pre-teen kid in east Akron, I played baseball every day, all day, all summer, on a vacant lot off Seiberling Street. The neighborhood was called the Seiberling Terrace, a strip of streets on which wood-frame houses lined crumbling sidewalks where weeds grew up between the cracks. Not far away were the belching smokestacks of the Goodyear Tire & Rubber Company, where most of the neighborhood men earned their wages turning out tires. This being the age before air conditioning, we slept with the windows open and by morning the white sheets were a dull gray with specks of rubber covering the room like an army of ants.

Hal with his little league team in 1952.

Our games began in early morning and concluded when it got dark and we couldn't find the baseballs, particularly when they rolled down the sewers. We used our baseballs until the covers came off, then we covered them with black electrician's tape and their lifespan continued until the sewer swallowed them into its murky bottom.

There was a gigantic billboard in center field and behind it was Nick the barber's box-shaped cinder block hair emporium. We never knew Nick's last name, but we assumed it ended in a vowel. When somebody cleared the billboard—a home run—it plopped with a thud on the flat tarpaper roof of Nick's establishment. At that same moment, we also assumed, Nick lived up to his name by nicking a patron with his straight razor. For Nick came running out of his shop, brandishing his razor and shouting at us, presumably in Italian, but since it was an Irish neighborhood none of us knew what he was saying, although it was clearly a threat.

Being a dead-pull hitter, and one with not enough power to ever clear the twenty-five-foot high billboard—our own Green Monster—I never hit a home run. But because my father was the only dad who patronized the barber, Nick would—at least once a week after locking up shop—walk the four houses down Hobart Avenue and climb the fourteen steps to our front porch. He pounded on the screen door, although the screen was so full of holes that flies laughed at even the thought of being kept out of the house.

Dad would come to the door and Nick would shout, "Your kid is putting dents in my roof again!" Dad would tell Nick that he'd take care of it, but he never said a word to me because he thought baseball was a religion and he loved my daily worship at the shrine of home plate.

My own Pesky Pole—the nickname for the right field foul pole at Fenway Park in Boston—was down the right field line, a short distance to Seiberling Street. Across the street was Helsel's Square Deal grocery, a small establishment with a dark orange sign across the front and a metal container the size of a steamer trunk up front where Helsel kept glass gallon jugs of milk. At times, my mother interrupted my baseball game to send me to Helsel's for a pound of bologna and a loaf of bread for my lunch, both of which were less than fifty cents, and I usually had a nickel or so left for a twelve-ounce bottle of Royal Crown Cola.

Unlike Nick, Helsel was a baseball fan and when nobody was in his store, he would come out to sit on his gray metal milk case and watch us play. He didn't mind when I, being the only left-handed hitter in the neighborhood, pulled one across Seiberling Street, a ground rule double, and one-hop bounced it off his storefront. Fortunately, I never shattered his picture window. I did once break out a headlight on a 1950 Packard when it had the misfortune to be passing just as Jim Ankeney threw an inside pitch, which I drilled into the car's headlamp. The guy kept on going and didn't make a trip to my father's front door, baseball in hand. Dad would have been proud—another ground rule double.

Helsel the grocer was a big fan of mine, probably because I spent so much time in his store buying baseball bubblegum and Royal Crown Cola with any loose change I found around the house, which wasn't much. He told my dad, "That kid of yours can really play baseball. He has a future in the game." I'm sure Helsel meant that I might some day wear a major-league uniform, but, of course, that never materialized. And it is a certainty that Nick the barber never thought I'd come to anything worthwhile.

Little League came to Akron in 1951, but there were only eight teams in the entire city, which at the time was still the Rubber Capital of the World, a thriving place of nearly three hundred thousand. The teams were divided into sections of the city and tryouts for east Akron were held at Reservoir Park where I would later play first base for Akron East High. On the day of tryouts at Reservoir Park, three hundred kids showed up to compete for fifteen spots on the Hoskins Olds Giants—five ten-year-olds, five eleven-year-olds, and five twelve-year-olds. I was eleven. The outfield was covered with so many kids you couldn't see the grass.

I showed up wearing my yellow baseball cap with the block blue 'O' on it, a hat I received for being a safety patrol boy at Thomastown grade school when I was elected to make a trip to Washington, D.C. The 'O' stood for Ohio. I decided I was an outfielder. A coach, Dinky Barnes, told all outfield candidates to spread out in the outfield. About 150 kids ran to the outfield.

How do you get noticed among 150 kids? You become selfish. Very selfish. Every fly ball that Dinky hit, I pushed aside shy kids who stood their ground. I ran after every ball, I tried to snag every one I could. After I caught nine or ten, Dinky called me in, and I made the team. But it was quickly determined that I had a spaghetti arm and could barely throw the ball from the outfield to second base. So they converted me to a first baseman.

That first year we won our first seventeen games and had the National League title clinched. In our final game, against the Dodgers, we trailed, 2–1, going into the bottom of the last inning. We had a runner on second with two outs when I came to bat.

Do I drive the first pitch on a rising line over second base?

Is it a home run, and we win?

Perhaps only a double, but we tie the game?

Nope.

The second baseman made a leaping grab. Game over. We lose.

I was devastated. Our perfect season was ruined because of me. I cried. That was before Tom Hanks ever said, "There is no crying in baseball." Dinky Barnes took me aside and put an arm around me. "Bubby," he said. "If the second baseman doesn't make that great catch, the ball goes over the fence, and we win." That didn't appease me. But his next words did: "Now let's go get some ice cream."

Even though we lost our last game to the Dodgers, we finished 17–1, the best record in the Akron National League. That qualified us to play the American League champions, the Indians, for the Akron Little League World Series. We beat the Indians two games to one, and the highlight for me was hitting an inside-the-park home run. Well, it *should* have been an inside-the-park home run. Instead, it was the third out of the inning. In my exuberance to circle the bases while the outfielders chased the ball in deep left center, I missed first base and was called out.

"Don't get too upset, Bubby," our manager, Dinky Barnes, told me. "You also missed third base." The irony of our win over the Indians was that two years later, in the big leagues, the New York (Hoskins Olds) Giants defeated the Cleveland (Kenmore Lumber) Indians in the real World Series. It was the World Series in which Willie Mays made the incredible back-to-the-infield catch on Cleveland first baseman Vic Wertz, who was my hero because I, too, played first base.

I also made the Akron Nationals All-Star team that would play in the tournament, a team trying to get to the Little League World Series in Williamsport, Pennsylvania.

The West Chevrolet Dodgers had a first baseman, Tom Fiocca, who hit a lot of home runs. I hit none. I was a singles and doubles hitter. So they stuck me in center field. Our first game was against the Ellet Little League, a suburb of Akron. We led late in the game by a run when one of their hitters, Gerry Glinsky, drove one to deep center. I ran to the wall, stuck up my tattered, well-used glove that my father bought second-hand for me. It was on my backhand side and I snagged it. Saved that game. I also had two hits and we won.

A few days later, we played the Canton All-Stars and we trailed, 3–2, in the last inning and had the tying run on second base. Same situation as the last game of the regular season. I was due up. This time it began raining. It rained for a long time, the field became unplayable, and it was decided to resume play the next day. The game lasted exactly two pitches. I hit the first pitch to the left center gap for a game-tying double. On the next pitch, our shortstop, Frances Rollins, drove one to right center and I scored the winning run.

Ah, sweet redemption. But we lost the next game, just a couple of wins short of making it to Williamsport.

The *Akron Beacon Journal*, amazingly, wrote stories about all our games that year and there was a photographer at a pre-season premier game. He took a post-game photo of me and the kid who hit the home run—the kid was flexing his muscles and I was told to feel his biceps while the photographer snapped the shot. Home run hitters get the girls, singles hitters get to feel their muscles.

He then asked my name for the cutline under the picture. Not wanting the world, or at least the readers of the *Beacon Journal*, to know that my name was Bubby, I shyly mumbled, "Harold McCoy." He misunderstood and thought I said, "Hal McCoy," and that's how it appeared in the cutline.

So Bubby was buried and Hal McCoy was born.

From Little League it was on to Pony League (ages thirteen to fourteen), and I played for the Rempel DeeGees. The team was named after the sponsor, D.G. Rempel, a company that made those hideous, politically incorrect, tomahawk-wielding Indians (Native Americans was not a term then) with the big noses.

Again we had a first baseman better than I, so I was exiled to left field. My coach, Paul Rife, kept instilling in me, "Don't let a ball get past you. Always keep it in front of you." During one game, my best friend and pitcher, George Neilsen, had a no-hitter going into the last inning. The first batter lofted a shallow fly ball to left field. I started in, then stopped. The ball crash-landed just in front of me, a cheap hit, a ball I should have caught.

When Mr. Rife asked me, "Why didn't you dive for that ball and save George's no-hitter," I said softly, "Because I didn't want to let the ball get past me." On *that* day, George Neilsen cried.

After one year in the Pony League, I was asked to play for the prestigious American Legion Post 209 team that traveled all over the state, sometimes staying overnight on weekends to play three-game series in places like Newark and Bryan and Bucyrus.

One Saturday, we were invited to play the prison team at the Mansfield Reformatory. The prison team received special privileges—extra practice time—so the team was not popular with the prison population. We were told they always rooted for the outsiders. And it was fun watching them bet cigarettes on the outcome of each at-bat.

On my second at-bat, I fouled one over the screen and through a window of the mess hall, shattering the glass. I was given my first (and only) standing ovation as a baseball player.

We made the state American Legion finals against the legendary Cincinnati Bentley Post, the perennial state champions. We had a 2–1 lead late in the game when Bentley put runners on second and third, one out. They put on the suicide squeeze, and the batter bunted the ball to me up the first-base line. The runner from third easily scored to tie the game. I casually fielded the ball and turned to toss the ball to the second baseman, who was covering first. I wasn't thinking that the runner on second would try to score, but he did. He never stopped until he crossed the plate, and I never saw it. We lost, 3–2.

Baseball was my passion but I loved basketball, too, even though for most of my life I was a shrimp. When I was in the sixth grade, my father tacked up a backboard on the back of our garage because there was an empty lot behind the garage. It was the only basketball court in the neighborhood, so during most of the fall there were pick-up games every late afternoon after school. Because I was only 5-foot-4, I developed a little left-handed hook shot so I could shoot over my taller friends. And I seldom missed.

I was a star in gym class in the seventh grade at David Hill Elementary School, so I decided to try out for the school team. That's when I discovered that size *does* matter, especially in basketball. At the tryouts, the final spot came down to me and Delmar Eisle. I was confident because in gym class I played rings around Delmar Eisle. But he was 5-foot-8 and I was, at the time, 5-foot-5. He made the team. I didn't.

So I shelved my basketball career until my sophomore year at Akron East High School. By then, I was 5-foot-8 and could shoot long shots. Once again at the tryouts it came down to two players for one spot, me and Don Glidden, who was six feet. The assistant coach wanted to keep me, but when he pointed to me I saw head coach Russ Estey shake his head no. He kept Glidden and I was cut.

Hal with his Akron East High basketball team in 1957.

This time I didn't give up. Between my sophomore year and my junior year I grew six inches—from 5-foot-8 to 6-foot-2, and I made the team. After my senior season, during which we finished second in the City Series, we had an awards assembly in the school auditorium. Coach Estey said something nice about each player and when he came to me he said, "When McCoy was a sophomore he was so short he could walk under the sink in the boys bathroom."

Never mind that during a game against Akron St. Vincent, the school that produced LeBron James (no, he wasn't playing), I scored my career high, 21 points. St. Vincent wasn't very good then. Never mind that I hit a free throw with eleven seconds left to beat Akron South, even though my second free throw was an air ball and we only won because South missed a shot at the buzzer. But I was carried off the floor on the shoulders of the student section anyway, even though that one point was the only one I scored.

Never mind also that I scored 11 points in the City Series semifinals when we beat Akron Kenmore. Never mind that on the next night I hit a shot from the corner to tie the game, 49–49, against Akron Central, a team that had future NBA stars Nate Thurmond and Gus Johnson. Okay, so my man, Brian Gump, did drive around me to score the winning layup at the buzzer to win the City Series championship. Never mind that in a game on a snowy night at Kent State High School I scored the game's first 12 points. Then my dad, delayed by work and the snow, arrived early in the second quarter, and I didn't score again. He was not convinced I'd scored 12 points until he saw the box score the next morning in the *Beacon Journal*.

Never mind that in a game at Massillon High School I scored three quick long-range baskets to start the game, baskets that would be three-pointers in today's game. After making those three shots, I was taking the ball out of bounds near mid-court. The seats were close to the floor and as I prepared to throw the ball inbound I felt a stabbing pain in my right buttocks. It was a stabbing pain because a female Massillon fan stuck me with a hatpin. I never suffered pain like that playing baseball.

My sons, Brian and Brent, love to taunt me about my basketball career, asking me, "Hey, Dad, tell us about your basketball days when you wore those tiny shorts and the key was really shaped like a key." They both played Division III basketball, Brian at Ohio Northern University and Brent at Thomas More College. They were both just like their dad, only much, much better. Both could shoot from long range but, unfortunately, they had their dad's genes—slow and couldn't jump.

Baseball, though, was my passion because, well, in baseball, size really doesn't matter. We had a good baseball team at Akron East High, a city championship team, with many of my Little League teammates now playing for the Orientals—and how is that for a politically incorrect nickname, a nickname the school changed just a few years ago?

We were a good team because we had good players. Our coach, Dominic Patella, was the football coach, his passion. He spent a lot of time during our baseball games drawing football plays in the dirt in front of our bench. During my senior season I struck out only eight times all year, but one guy struck me out four times. His name was Dean Chance.

I felt awful, even though Chance was 52–1 (we didn't beat him) for Northwestern High School in West Salem, and in 1959 he pitched every inning in leading his team to the Ohio State Class A championship. Then he won the Cy Young Award with the 1964 Los Angeles Angels while teaming up with fellow pitcher Bo Belinsky to chase Hollywood starlets as efficiently as throwing shutouts. And he threw eleven of them in 1964. He also pitched a five-inning, rain-shortened perfect game for the Minnesota Twins in 1967 and a nine-inning no-hitter that same year against the Cleveland Indians.

Then I didn't feel so bad.

One of our pitchers, Don Kyser, was offered a scholarship to Kent State University. I had decided to go to Kent, too, so when Kyser reported for an open practice, I tagged along. I impressed them enough that they offered me a partial scholarship and I accepted.

When I was in high school, our shortstop my sophomore year was Gene Michael, who went to Kent State and was drafted by the Pittsburgh Pirates. He played one year with the Pirates and one year with the Los Angeles Dodgers, then played most of his career with the New York Yankees. The stadium at Kent State is named Gene Michael Field. His nickname was "Stick" because he was so skinny. He never hit much but was a wizard with the glove. I proudly told people that I hit better than he did in high school and that I had the clippings to prove it. He always graciously acknowledged that but with a caveat: "Tell them how good I was in basketball."

So true, so true. He probably was a better basketball player than a baseball player. And he made the majors, so you know how good he was on the basketball floor. We both played guard, and my job was to get him the ball and stay the hell out of his way.

My baseball career at Kent State was a dust speck. I didn't play much my freshman year and I never learned the mysteries of hitting sliders and curve balls, let alone ninety-mile-an-hour fastballs. Before my freshman year at Kent, I did receive a letter from legendary Philadelphia Phillies scout Tony Lucadello, inviting me to a tryout camp. I did well enough that they asked me about signing to play Class D (low Class A at the time) in Clearwater, Florida. I chose college instead and until the day he died my father thought I made the wrong choice, that I could have made it to the majors. Fathers are that way.

I saw the handwriting on the dugout wall very early and wondered, "How can I stay in baseball?" There was only one choice. Journalism. My major at Kent State was journalism and the light clicked on: "If you can't play it, write about it." I decided I wanted to be a baseball writer.

From baby carriage to baseball press box.

03 SPORTSWRITING ON THE WALL

FROM KENT TO THE DAYTON WOODSHED

For some reason, I know not why, I took a typing class my senior year in high school, perhaps because I knew I'd be the only male in the class. And it was only good fortune that I was seated next to Patsy Walling, head majorette and the most gorgeous girl in Akron East High School.

One late fall day, the typing teacher, Rose Piciotti, asked me to stop at her desk after class. I thought maybe it was because Patsy Walling and I giggled too much in class or maybe I made too many errors in the sentence we had to type over and over and over: "The quick brown fox jumped over the lazy dog's back." If you check that sentence, it contains every letter of the alphabet and we had to type it over and over as fast as we could.

It was neither. "Don't you play on the basketball team?" Mrs. Piciotti asked. I shyly shifted on both feet and with my eyes focused on the floor I said, "Yes," somewhat proudly. "Well, I'm the advisor for the school newspaper and I don't have anybody to write a story about the basketball team's upcoming season. Would you write it?"

I'd never written a story in my life. I did love reading baseball writer Jim Schlemmer in the *Akron Beacon Journal*. And sometimes I played mock games with my baseball cards, then designed the front page of a sports section on notebook paper and wrote something about the baseball card games. But I never showed them to anybody, not even my father.

But I agreed to give it a try, for both dear ol' East and dear ol' Mrs. Piciotti. I turned it in a few days later and once again she approached me and asked me to stop by her desk. I expected her to throw the story in my face and say, "Uh, you better try again."

Instead she stunned me by asking, "Have you considered writing as a profession? Have you considered journalism in college?" Well, no, not really. In fact, not at all. I hadn't even considered *college*.

When the baseball opportunity at Kent State arose, I had to declare a major and remembered what Mrs. Piciotti said. So I declared journalism as my major. Rose Piciotti knows not what she did for me, and I have no idea what I would have done with my life. She unknowingly steered me into a life-long passion.

I signed up to work for the *The Daily Kent Stater*, where the first things I learned was how to smoke cigars and drink coffee, just like they did in newspaper movies. I spent every extra minute on campus in *The Kent Stater* office, soaking up the atmosphere, mostly with a cigar in one hand, a cup of coffee in the other, and my feet on the desk.

I was named sports editor my senior year and wrote a column called "Sideline Sidelights." It was abysmal. It was mostly rah-rah Kent State stuff with lots of fluff and no substance. One day, the editor of the paper approached me and said, "When are you going to write something of substance?"

The Kent State basketball team was almost as abysmal as my columns. Under Coach Bob Doll they were 2–19 my junior year and 3–18 my senior year. And to think I tried to make the team as a walk-on and couldn't make it. I thought I was a decent basketball player. So I sat down in front of the typewriter and penned a column with the headline: "Doll Should Be Fired."

In the early 1960s, student newspapers didn't have the journalistic freedom they have now, and censorship was heavy. But our advisor, Professor Bill Fischer, permitted the column to run. And I was so proud the next day when editor Tom Suchan walked up and handed me a coffee cup with the inscription: "Journalist of the Week." I'd never won it, never come close, and he said, "Finally, you wrote something with substance." But that afternoon the glow on my face turned to dripping perspiration.

I received an invitation—actually a demand for a command performance—in the office of school president George A. Bowman. I'd never been in his office and was immediately intimidated by the size of the room, the size of his desk, and the size of his right hand as he ordered me to sit.

"I want you to know, young man, that I am the person who makes the determination of who is fired and who is not fired on this campus, not some student wannabe newspaper writer. I suggest that you print a retraction or find your education elsewhere."

The retraction appeared the next day, with humble apologies to Coach Doll, probably congratulating him on his five wins over the past two seasons. But I was permitted to continue my education at Kent, graduated with honors from the School of Journalism, and was named Journalism Student of the Year. It is not known how President Bowman reacted to that.

It was time to go out into the journalistic world, and I had twelve job offers. I wanted sports. But there was nothing solid. The *Christian Science Monitor* offered me a job in its Chicago bureau, but the *Monitor* didn't have a sports page. The *St. Petersburg Times* offered me a position on the news side, but it was on a trial basis. I don't like trials.

I settled on the *Fort Wayne News-Sentinel* as a general assignment reporter for $100 a week. A week later, Ritter Collett, sports editor of the *Dayton Journal Herald*, called and offered me a sports job for $105 a week. I quickly called Fort Wayne and backed out of that job. They were not pleased, but I had my sports job.

My first assignment in Dayton was covering high school sports, the Dayton City League. In 1964, Dayton Belmont High School put together what I still believe is the best high school team ever in the state of Ohio. The stars were Don May and Bill Hosket, but all five starters went to college on basketball scholarships, as did the sixth man.

May went to the University of Dayton and made All-American, the best 6-foot-4 rebounder I ever saw. He led the Flyers to the 1967 national championship game, where they lost to UCLA and Lew Alcindor (Kareem Abdul Jabbar) and May was the MVP of the 1968 NIT, which UD won when the NIT meant something. Hosket went to Ohio State and made All-American, captaining the 1968 Buckeyes to the Final Four. He also played on the gold medal U.S. Olympic team in 1968. Later, May and Hosket were reunited as bench-warmers for the 1972–'73 New York Knicks team that won the National Basketball Association championship with Willis Reed as the star.

The other Belmont players were Tim Kenner (Ohio State), Harry Culberton (Kent State), Ray Ridenour (George Tech) and sixth man Ralph Jukkola, who captained an LSU team with Pistol Pete Maravich as the star, which meant Jukkola got about two shots a game.

That 1964 season was incredible as the Belmont team overwhelmed the Ohio prep scene en route to the Class AA (big school) state championship. The team was coached by John Ross, who later started the basketball program at Wright State University in Dayton. Belmont was 26–1, averaging 82.9 points a game (32-minute games) and there were no three-point shots. Opponents averaged 55.3 points against a blanketing 1-3-1 zone that Ross employed.

The Bison scored more than 100 points four times and scored in the 90s five times. They won their nine tournament games by an average of 22 points. They crushed Urbana, 90–64, in the regional finals. They destroyed Canton McKinley, the No. 2 team in the state, in the state semifinals, 80–56, and annihilated Cleveland East Tech, 89–60, in the state finals.

Of those twenty-seven games, I covered twenty-six. I did not cover the one game they lost, an overtime defeat to Dayton Chaminade when both May and Hosket fouled out. Why did I not cover that game? We had two prep writers at the *Dayton Journal Herald* and Bucky Albers was the other. Every week, sports editor Ritter Collett, Albers, and I convened in Collett's office to put together the weekly *JH* rankings. Albers covered the valley/suburban schools and never covered Belmont. Collett decided that since we all had input into the ranking that Albers should at least see Belmont play one game. So he was assigned to cover the Belmont–Chaminade game.

Well, Belmont lost that game and the team, including Coach Ross, never forgave me. It was my fault that they lost because I wasn't there. But they hold a reunion every year in Dayton over the Christmas holidays and I get invited every year—so they can heap abuse on me.

That's not all the abuse they dump on me. They accuse me of participating in an infamous event that occurred on a trip to Portsmouth in mid-January. Portsmouth was another state power and that year's team included two future Major-League baseball players, Al Oliver and Larry Hisle.

Hal's mug shot for the *Dayton Journal Herald*, 1963.

Every January I make a trip to Portsmouth for a baseball dinner and Oliver is always there, always gives the invocation. I always bring up the Belmont–Portsmouth game, won by Belmont, 79–60, after Belmont led at halftime, 55–21. "Those dudes were unbelievable," said Oliver. "We thought we were good. Nobody beat us at home, especially a bunch of white guys. And the officials were always ours, if you know what I mean. Well, they destroyed us."

That's not all the Belmont team destroyed that night. They were staying overnight at the Portsmouth Holiday Inn. After the coaches went to bed, the team slipped out of their rooms. I was not long out of college so I was only five years older than most of the team, and I slipped out with them. It started innocently enough with a snowball fight in the parking lot and, yes, I was involved.

When the players became bored with snowball fighting, things got crazy. Somebody found a storeroom full of towels, linens, pillows, a baby bed, a playpen, even a baby carriage. Most of the stuff in the storage room ended up in the swimming pool. The coaches popped out of the hotel during the melee and I dove under the team bus and was not spotted. As the years progress, my limited involvement grows and grows from the boys-will-be-boys incident. There was, of course, considerable monetary damage. The team later took up a collection among themselves to pay for the damages and turned the proceeds over to Coach Ross. The collection was $12.

When the team returned to Dayton, Ross told them, "Next practice there will be no basketballs used. They'll stay locked up. There will be nothing but wind sprints and running up and down the steps of the school." I was brave enough to show up for that practice and as the team ran killer sprints up and down the floor, with me watching from the sidelines, guard Tim Kenner yelled, "Why isn't McCoy out there running sprints with us?" Not only did I not run sprints, I never printed a word about the after-the-game pool party.

After the prep beat, I moved onward and upward. I covered Miami University football and basketball. Bo Schembechler, later of University of Michigan fame, was the football coach and once permitted me to go into his locker room at halftime. His teams seldom lost, but they were behind at halftime in this particular game and I was witness to one of Bo's scream-ing, paint-peeling outbursts. They won.

I also covered the Cleveland Browns of the NFL in 1964, led by fullback Jimmy Brown, quarterback Dr. Frank Ryan, and wide receiver Gary Collins. They beat the Baltimore Colts, 27–0, in the NFL title game, the last cham-pionship won by the Browns. I still have the silver tiepin the Browns gave the media. As a young reporter, I was in awe of Jimmy Brown, as were most defensive backs on other teams who were steam-rollered by the greatest of all running backs. Not once that season did I approach Brown for an interview, or even for one question. I just stood and stared at him after games.

That was the year I boarded an airplane for the first time in my life. I was going to New York to cover a Browns–New York Giants game. There were no security issues then and I walked from the ticket counter at the Dayton airport, down a hall, and out a door onto the tarmac where I froze in my tracks. The TWA Constellation, with four propeller-driven engines, was the biggest passenger vehicle I had ever seen. With trepida-tion, I climbed the portable stairway to the interior. For the next couple of hours I stared out the circular window, wondering how a behemoth like the Constellation could stay in the air.

Nate Wallach, as kind and as pleasant a man who ever walked the earth, was the publicity director of the Browns. On Saturday night, before Sunday's game, he took all the writers covering the team out to dinner. He took us to Toots Shor's. I didn't know Toots Shor from Dinah Shore, un-aware that it was, at the time, the most famous celebrity/athlete restaurant in New York. It was the first time I had even been inside a real restaurant. The Browns beat writer for the *Cleveland Plain Dealer* was Chuck Heaton, father of Patricia Heaton, "Debra Barone" on the TV comedy series *Every-body Loves Raymond*. On the show, Ray Barone is a goofy-acting sports-writer and I felt as dumb as he sometimes acts as I looked at the menu. I didn't know what to order. I waited until Heaton ordered and ordered the exact same thing, right down to, "Cook the New York strip steak medium, but tinge the edges (whatever that meant)."

The proprietor, Toots Shor, was always there and made the rounds, talking to all the famous people that frequented his restaurant. When Wal-lach introduced us he treated me as if I was Red Smith of the *New York*

Herald Tribune rather than Hal McCoy of the *Dayton Journal Herald*. The guys back in the sports department didn't believe I had eaten at Toots Shor's, let alone met the man, until I produced a matchbook with his autograph inside the cover. (Yes, I unashamedly asked for his autograph.)

I was also permitted to cover home games played by the old Cincinnati Royals in the NBA, a team led by Oscar Robertson and Jerry Lucas. If Robertson isn't the best all-around basketball player in the history of game, he is in the top two and I don't know who the other guy is. One of the first games I covered was between the Royals and Philadelphia, led by 7-foot-2 center Wilt "The Stilt" Chamberlain. He had about 50 points that night and I went into the locker room to interview him. He was not at his locker but soon sauntered out the shower, buck naked.

When he approached his locker, I stuck out my hand and said, "Hi, I'm Hal McCoy of the *Dayton Journal Herald*." He politely shook my hand.

I was mesmerized. The next day I went into the office to tell my story to deskman Jerry Howe, a man who edited my copy and taught me more in one month than I learned in four years of journalism school. Howe was editing copy when I walked in and said, "Guess what? I interviewed Wilt Chamberlain. He came out of the shower, stark naked, and I shook hands with him."

Without looking up, Howe said, "Are you sure you shook hands with him." To this day I still wonder about that.

Even though I didn't know a duck hook from an eagle or a birdie, *Journal Herald* sports editor Ritter Collett assigned me to the golf beat in 1964. On the rare occasions that I wasted four hours of my afternoon chasing a white ball into terrain never before seen by homo sapiens, I never broke 100, even if I conveniently encountered memory lapses when it came to counting shots on each hole.

But like most sports, covering golf was covering people, and I could write about people. I did that for three years, covering local golf tournaments. The reward was getting to cover the Masters at Augusta National Golf Club, the U.S. Open, and the National PGA tournament for three consecutive years. The first time I drove up the driveway at Augusta National between its magnificent magnolia trees, goosebumps sprouted from my forehead to my toes. I had only seen its magnificence on television, and encountering it in person was breathtaking.

It was the era of Arnold Palmer, Jack Nicklaus, and Gary Player and I wanted to interview Nicklaus before the tournament because he was from Ohio. The first time I walked into the ornate men's locker room, Nicklaus was seated on a three-legged stool in front of his locker, lacing up his white golf shoes. I stuttered when I introduced myself, and he reacted as if I was the famous golf writer, Herbert Warren Wind. He answered all my dumb questions with expansive, in-depth replies, accompanied by a smile.

It was at the '64 Masters that I discovered how well Scotch and I went together. I had never sipped Scotch, ever, but at a pre-tournament party I partook of several rounds with some of my fellow writers. After I returned to my motel, the night went by slowly because much toilet-hugging was involved. I haven't had a sip of Scotch since that day, sticking to my preferred Yuengling Lager beer and Grey Goose vodka.

Palmer won the tournament, beating Jack Nicklaus and Dave Marr by six strokes. When *Sport Magazine* came out that month, there was a photo of Palmer putting out on the 18th green to finish his conquest of the Augusta lady, shooting a first-round 70 and three straight rounds in the 60s. I proudly told my parents, "My picture is in *Sport Magazine*." Oh, yeah, it sure was. All you could see of me was the top of my porkpie hat as I stood in the third row of fans gathered around the green.

The media is permitted to play Augusta National on Monday after the final round and I boldly gave it a try. After I finally reached the first green, about fifteen feet from the pin, my first putt whizzed breezily past the pin and off the green. The greens at Augusta National are like pool table tops, certainly nothing like the high-grassed muni goat runs I played on once in a while. Suffice it to say, I did not break 100, probably not even on the front nine.

The 1964 National PGA tournament was held at the Columbus Country Club and it was won by Bobby Nichols, the only tour championship of his career. I don't remember a single shot because I hardly ventured out of the media tent. My seat assignment was next to my writing hero, Jim Murray of the *Los Angeles Times*. I wrote fast, so I'd write my feeble stories then sit and surreptitiously watch Murray work slowly, crafting each sentence, spending a lot of time staring at the walls. I read his stuff and said, "I know all those words. I just can't put them together the way he does."

Murray was famous for one-liners, a sports writer/comedy writer. His columns usually were strings of one-liners, one after another, all of them hilariously funny. He loved to make fun of cities, picking on foibles. When he made a visit to Cincinnati, he saw construction sites surrounding old Riverfront Stadium, with no construction equipment in sight. So he wrote, "It must have been Kentucky's turn to use the cement mixer." One of my favorite Murray lines was when he described the California Angels' double play combination in their expansion year. He wrote, "You've heard of the famous double play combination of Tinkers to Ever to Chance, right? Well, the California Angels have a double play combination of Fregoso to Aspromonte to Avalon Boulevard."

Hal "hard at work" at the *Detroit Free Press*, 1966.

Murray and I do have one thing in common. During the later stages of his career he lost most of his eyesight. He, too, needed a driver and his driver escorted him around ball parks and stadiums. Even though he could barely see beyond his nose, he always said to everybody, "So nice to see you." After he died and my eyesight faded, his widow read stories about it and sent me a couple of his books (I already had both, but the thought was nice). Her maiden name? Linda McCoy.

In 1966, the *Detroit Free Press* offered me a job to cover Big Ten football—Michigan State and Michigan. I accepted only to rue the day. I lasted only ten months. I loved the job and loved the *Free Press*. But I hated Detroit. I covered the famous–infamous Michigan State-Notre Dame game in '66 in Spartan Stadium. Michigan State was 9–0 and No. 2 in the country. Notre Dame was 8–0 and No. 1, and the two teams were coached by legends—Duffy Daugherty and Ara Parseghian. The game ended in a 10–10 tie when Notre Dame ran out the clock on its final series rather than try to win the game. And Parseghian took torch-like heat for it. *Free Press* columnist Joe Falls wrote, "For Christmas, Ara Parseghian will receive a black tie with a yellow stripe down the middle."

After the game, I froze—and it wasn't that cold out. The game was monumental, an all-time classic. And I sat in front of my typewriter with numb fingers. I tore up lead after lead until I finally began writing. *Free Press* sports editor George Puscas sat down next to me and read what I had written. He was not happy. He hustled me out of my chair, sat down at my typewriter, and quickly punched in a five-paragraph lead, then said, "Now you take it from there." I was mortified, but never again froze in front of a typewriter or computer.

Not long afterward, Puscas approached me at my desk in the office and said, "I have an assignment for you. A boxer is coming to town and he's going to ride around the city in a car to visit the ghetto. I've arranged for you to ride with him."

His name was Cassius Clay and I knew nothing about this young boxer who would later be heavyweight champion of the world under the name of Muhammad Ali. He stopped the car at nearly every intersection and as crowds gathered he screamed, "I am the greatest. I am the greatest and the prettiest."

Nobody argued the point. Almost nobody. We stopped near a playground where several adults and children were gathered. Clay scrambled out of the car and began his "I am the greatest" mantra. A girl of about twelve approached and said, "You are the greatest what?"

"I am the greatest at everything," he said.

"No, you're not. Only God is the greatest," she said.

He put his arm around her shoulders and said, "But he didn't have much of a left hook. Now you stay in school and study hard," a message he delivered several times that day.

One day, the elevator doors near the sports department opened and a short, fat guy emerged. He, too, proclaimed, "I am the greatest and I can whip anybody in this town." But he didn't do it with fists, he did it with a pool stick. He said his name was Rudy Wanderone, better known as Minnesota Fats, self-proclaimed best pool player in the world. He invited me to accompany him to a pool emporium—okay, a pool hall—in a seedier side of a very seedy town. He hooked up with another legendary pool hustler,

Billy Burge, known as Cornbread Red. I watched them play for hours and ended up with a front page story.

Another story enraged a certain moneyed portion of the population. This time Puscas sent me out to do a story on a horse show and wanted a feature on a nationally known horse. I could never figure out why horse shows were part of the sports pages, but I trudged my way to the show. What to do, what to do. So I decided to interview the horse. I made up an imaginary interview with the star attraction and quoted him liberally. One quote was, "I don't understand why I have to do this stuff, why I have to parade around in front of people. Can't they just let me graze in peace in the meadows." The editors loved it. They ran it on page one with a head shot of the horse. The horse show people were not amused.

Then came July of 1967 and the infamous Detroit riot, or the 12th Street Riot. Police raided a blind pig, an after-hours drinking establishment occupied by blacks. The confrontation spilled into the streets and spread rapidly. Fires erupted. I spent the next three days on the roof of the *Free Press* building watching National Guard tanks rumbling through the streets as a large portion of the city burned. I couldn't get home.

A few days later I received a call from Si Burick, legendary sports editor of the *Dayton Daily News*. He asked me, "Would you like to come back to Dayton?"

"I'll be there tomorrow," I said.

My old boss, Ritter Collett, at the *Dayton Journal Herald*, thought it was a conspiracy, thought my return to Dayton with the rival *Daily News* was pre-planned. Although both Dayton papers were owned by Cox Newspapers and the editorial offices were in the same building, there was a great rivalry—starting with Ritter Collett and Si Burick, who barely spoke. (Ritter loved to call Burick "Saint Si," because Burick was the chosen one in the building.) If you worked for the *Journal Herald*, you referred to the writers with the *Daily News* as, "the people on the third floor." And the *Daily News* referred to the *Journal Herald* writers as "the people on the fifth floor."

There was a rule that even though the papers were owned by the same publisher, writers were forbidden to jump from one paper to the other. You have to leave and work for another paper before you could return.

Ritter Collett left this world believing that Si Burick and I conspired to have me leave the 100,000-circulation morning *Journal Herald*, work in Detroit for year, then return to Dayton to work for the 200,000-circulation afternoon *Daily News*.

It wasn't true. Collett once asked me, "Why didn't you call me if you wanted to return to Dayton?" My answer? "Because you didn't ask and Si Burick did."

Ritter Collett and Si Burick both are legends, both are in the Baseball Hall of Fame, and both were my mentors. And they couldn't have been more opposite in personality. Collett, an Ohio University graduate, loved opera music and it filled the inside of his company-provided Buick. And he was a culinary aficionado. If there was an excellent restaurant in the Tri-State area, he not only knew about it but he had eaten there. And many times he took me with him, mostly after we covered games together. He actually taught me which fork to use first. As a sports editor, he was mostly concerned about his daily column and dashed it off quickly. He wrote his own headlines and subheads for his column. He pretty much let the sports department run itself, designating authority.

He took me to the woodshed only once. In those days, every writer had to serve time on the copy desk, editing copy and writing subheads. Vanderbilt University's nickname is the Commodores, and I had to write a headline about them winning a game. Commodores didn't fit in the headline, so I shortened it and wrote "Commies beat Auburn." I thought it was kind of cute, but in those days of Communism and the cold war, Mr. Collett failed to grasp the humor.

Burick was more nationally-known than Collett and seemingly could pick up the telephone and call any sports figure in the country and get his calls returned. Immediately. He was a renowned punster, tossing them out every day, trying them out on his sports staff before unleashing them on the public. One of his favorites was a twist on the car commercial slogan, "Wouldn't you rather have a Buick." He changed it to, "Wouldn't you rather have a Burick." When the famous racehorse Secretariat retired to stud, Burick wrote, "He is everything that I am not. He is young; he is beautiful; he has lots of hair; he is fast; he is durable; he has a large bank account; and his sex life is all in front of him."

As was Collett, Burick was all about his daily column, which he wrote six days a week, but "Never on Saturday." His public persona was as a mild-mannered, fun-loving, happy-go-lucky guy. As a boss, he was a tyrant and a taskmaster. He edited his own column, but after it was sent to the composing room he retrieved a printout for one of his writers to proofread. When he came into the office carrying his column, we all acted extremely busy, or we tried to slip out the back door. Whoever read the proof had better catch every typographical error, every misspelling, every misplaced comma or quotation mark. If an error slipped into the newspaper, there was hell to pay. But after venting his wrath, fifteen minutes later he would pat the offender on the back of the head and try out a new pun.

I learned much from both. From Collett, I learned to write quickly and descriptively. From Burick, I learned the value of cultivating contacts and to be accurate. If people consider me an amalgam of both, I'm deeply humbled.

When I told the *Detroit Free Press* sports editor George Puscas I was going back to Dayton, he said, "What can I do to keep you? More money? What do you want to do?" When I told him I eventually wanted to be a baseball writer, he stunned me by saying, "We'll make *you* our baseball writer."

I had covered a few Detroit Tigers games on the beat writer's days off and spent a lot of time at the old stadium. The *Free Press* office was within walking distance of the stadium, and some days a couple of us would leave the sports department to have dinner in the media dining room and watch a few innings before going back to work at the office.

It was tempting. It was what I wanted to do, and the offer to return to Dayton was to cover the University of Dayton Flyers and auto racing— which I knew nothing about. The only auto race I ever attended was the 1964 Indianapolis 500. I attended the race with *Dayton Journal Herald* auto racing writer Bucky Albers when I worked there. It was the year Eddie Sachs and Dave McDonald died in a fiery crash early in the race. McDonald T-boned Sachs and flames shot high into the Indiana skies, a chilling experience to witness. Later, my favorite sportswriter, Jim Murray of the *Los Angeles Times*, wrote, "Indianapolis is where they pick up crash victims with an ash tray."

Nevertheless, I had told Si Burick I would pack my bags, empty my closet, and be back in Dayton as fast as I could.

The University of Dayton played Division I football at the time, and while the Flyers were having little success in the won-loss column, the coaching staff was nearly legendary. The head coach was John McVay, who later coached the San Francisco 49ers and was also the team's general manager. The coaching staff included Wayne Fontes, who later coached the Detroit Lions; Tom Moore, who was offensive coordinator for the Pittsburgh Steelers and Indianapolis Colts; and Jim Gruden, father of Tampa Bay Buccaneers coach and TV commentator John Gruden.

Xavier University also played Division I football at the time, and the Musketeers were Dayton's big rivalry. There was a game in the late 1960s where Xavier scored the winning touchdown late in the game with an extra man on the field. It wasn't called but a photo appeared in the *Dayton Daily News* the next day, an overview of the touchdown play that showed every player on the field—twelve Xavier players and eleven Dayton players.

Xavier coach Ed Biles, who went on to coach the Houston Oilers in the early 1980s, always denied that it was a planned play. But thirty-five years later, after I was inducted into baseball's Hall of Fame, I received a congratulatory note from Biles and he signed it, "Ed Biles, 12th Man Theme."

Lee Corso, the college football broadcaster whose shtick is to put a team mascot's head on his own head when he picks that team to win the game, was head coach at the University of Louisville when I covered the Flyers. Before one UD-UL game, I foolishly made fun of the Kentucky heritage, saying that most Louisville fans sit on their front porches in wicker rocking chairs smoking corncob pipes. It wasn't humorous to Corso and after Louisville beat Dayton, 24–17, he penned me a letter expressing his dissatisfaction. He probably would have liked to put an alligator head on my shoulders—a live alligator.

College basketball was (and is) king at the University of Dayton, and the Flyers advanced to the NCAA final game in 1967, losing to UCLA. I was re-united with Don May of Dayton Belmont High School fame for the 1967–1968 season and many good things were expected from that team. But they started poorly and were 7–9 after sixteen games. They lost their ninth game at Eastern Kentucky.

I always traveled with the Flyers, riding the buses and planes on trips. On this trip to Richmond, Kentucky, we were on a chartered Greyhound bus. After the loss, Coach Don Donoher boarded the bus and said, "Everybody to the back of the bus. Double up in the seats. I want the stink to rub off on each other." And that's the way the Flyers rode from Richmond to Dayton.

Donoher benched two players after that game, Glinder Torain and Rudy Waterman. It worked. The team won its last fourteen games, including its last four in the prestigious NIT. They beat West Virginia, 87–68, Fordham, 61–60, Notre Dame, 76–74 and Kansas in the finals, 61–48. May was named the tournament's Most Valuable Player.

It was also the only time in my career that I nearly engaged in a fist fight. Working space in the Madison Square Garden was tight, so I arrived early the first night to grab a spot. I placed my typewriter on the table and my coat on a chair and went to my courtside seat. When I returned, a New York writer was at my seat, and my typewriter and coat occupied a space on the floor.

I challenged the writer and he jumped from his chair and invaded my facial space. I shoved him. Hard. He fell over the table and leaped to his feet, fist clenched. Fortunately, other writers intervened and no punches were thrown. Muhammad Ali had nothing to worry about.

Somebody had to cover auto racing, and because I covered University of Dayton football in the fall and University of Dayton basketball in the winter, I had nothing to cover in the summer. That's how I became the auto racing writer. I read, time after time, that cars in the Indianapolis 500 left the race with broken magnetos. I had no clue what a magneto was, or is, and still don't to this day, even though I covered auto racing from 1967 to 1972.

The assignment was to cover the local tracks like Dayton Speedway, Eldora Speedway, New Bremen Speedway, and Tri-County Speedway near Cincinnati. The reward was to spend a month each year at Indianapolis to cover the 500, plus a week at Daytona Beach for the Daytona 500. It was an easy assignment because race car drivers were among the easiest athletes in the world to cover. In those days, they received little publicity and appreciated every word one wrote about them.

Well, almost. Famed USAC (United States Auto Club) stock car driver Jack Bowsher didn't appreciate a phrase I used about a race at Tri-County. I wrote, "Jack Bowsher would run over his mother to win a race." To put it mildly, he didn't grasp the humor, intended as a compliment. Before the race, another writer told me, "Jack Bowsher is looking for you and he is carrying a wrench." Fortunately, they wouldn't let him in the press box, and that day I never left my seat.

Tim Bleck and Hal McCoy for the *Dayton Journal Herald* with Miss Hurst Shifter at the Indianapolis 500, 1965.

There was a famous family in Dayton and its patriarch was George Walther, founder of the Dayton Steel Foundry, the world's largest manufacturer of truck wheels. The family loved auto racing and dabbled in the Indianapolis 500, trying to compete on a shoestring budget and seldom making the race. It was a family endeavor and the Walthers turned every nut and bolt themselves in an effort to find more speed. Race promoter Blair Ratliff said one day, "As long as there is one moving part on a race car, the Walthers will screw it up." But they worked hard at trying to be competitive. And it was a big deal each year as to what driver would try to qualify a Walther car.

The USAC sprint car champion at the time was Larry Dickson of Marietta, Ohio. Since sprint cars were big in the Miami Valley, running races at Dayton, Eldora, New Bremen, and Tri-County, I wrote often about Dickson and developed a relationship with him. Just on a hunch one year, when the Walthers were looking for a driver, I called Dickson and said,

"Congratulations on getting the Walther ride this year," even though no-body had told me a thing.

"Thanks a lot," he said. "I'm looking forward to it." And that's how scoops are obtained.

One of Walther's sons, David "Salt" Walther, loved to drive race cars and unlimited hydroplane boats, another Walther family hobby. Salt oper-ated Walther Marine, a boat dealership, in West Carrollton, a couple of miles from my house. He built a Ford T-bucket roadster and offered to give me a ride, something I could write about. I climbed into the T-bucket's passenger seat, expected a nice quiet demonstration drive down a short strip of gravel road in front of the dealership. By the end of the quarter mile, Salt had the light little machine roaring at 125 miles an hour. After I changed my pants, I wrote a piece about escaping death. Barely.

Undaunted, I permitted Salt to talk me into riding with him on a test run of U-77, the Walther hydroplane, on Caesar Creek Lake. Salt's brother, Skipp Walther, died in 1974 in a crash while trying to qualify for a hydroplane race. After that harrowing ride I never set foot in an-other boat, not even a rowboat, until my wife, Nadine, and I were in-vited on a Hall of Fame cruise in the Caribbean with Cincinnati Reds fans in 2003.

Salt Walther not only marched to the beat of a different drummer, he *was* the drummer. He was over the top in everything he did. I was invited to his wedding at the Walther mansion, high atop a hill in Centerville. When it came time to cut the cake, the bride did what nearly every bride does. She shoved a piece of cake into Salt's face. That's all he needed. Soon the cake was flying. Everybody grabbed hunks of the wedding cake and a cake fight erupted. When it ended, everybody was covered in cake and icing drenched the Walther mansion walls.

The first year after I left the auto racing beat, Salt Walther was involved in one of the most spectacular crashes in Indianapolis history, the 1973 race. Walther started seventeenth in the field of thirty-three. When the green flag dropped to start the race, Steve Krisiloff's engine blew. His car slowed, creating a jam-up on the front straight. Walther, trying evasive ma-neuvers, ran over the rear wheel of Jerry Grant's car, then vaulted the wall and into a wire fence. The impact snapped off the nose cone of Walther's car, exposing his legs. The fuel tanks were punctured and flames burst into the stands, injuring several fans.

Walther's car bounced back onto the track, trailing a huge fireball, which made visibility impossible, and several other cars crashed into Walther. His car spun to a stop at turn one, his legs showing out the front of the decimated car. He suffered burns over half his body, especially to his hands. The fingers on his left hand were amputated and the fingers on his right hand healed at grotesque angles. He was in the Michigan Burn Center for two and a half months and lost fifty pounds off his body-builder frame. Nevertheless, he returned to racing cars. That's why I always loved race car drivers. They risk their lives every time they slip behind the wheel but do it for the love of the sport and usually for a very small return.

After his accident, Salt Walther was forced to live on painkillers and he became addicted. His life spiraled downward quickly. Many years later, for some reason Walther's wallet was found in a trash can at Our Lady of the Rosary School, where my wife teaches. They called him and he showed up to pick it up. My wife was stunned by his disheveled appearance. They struck up a conversation and he discovered who she was and said, "Ah, Hal McCoy. We had some great times together." Salt, though, had few good times the rest of his life, and he died in 2012.

05 | LEARNING THE ROPES
DRAFTED INTO THE MAJORS

Dayton Daily News executive sports editor Ralph Morrow summoned me to his desk in late 1972 and made me a double offer, one I could refuse and one I couldn't refuse. "We have two beats open and I want to know which one you want," he said. "You can have the Cincinnati Reds beat or the Cincinnati Bengals beat. Which is it?" Because baseball is my passion, it was no decision at all and I quickly said, without a first thought, "I'll take the Reds."

All through my years in Dayton, I wanted desperately to be a baseball writer and went to Reds games as often as possible with whoever was covering games. *Dayton Journal Herald* sports editor Ritter Collett covered home games, and when he asked me to accompany him I never said no. It was a pleasure to sit in the media dining room at a table with broadcaster Waite Hoyt and listen to his stories. One of my favorites was when he told of his days as a pitcher for the New York Yankees and someone asked Ping Bodie, Babe Ruth's roommate, what it was like to room with the Babe—who was as active off the field as on it. Said Bodie, "I don't room with The Babe. I room with his suitcase."

When I came back to Dayton from Detroit the baseball writer was Jim Ferguson, a young guy who loved baseball as much as I did, and I thought he would be the beat writer forever. But I did get to cover a few games on his days off and made a road trip to St. Louis when his wife, JoAnne, was having a baby.

The first time I filled in for Ferguson, he had some specific instructions. Star pitcher Gary Nolan was on the disabled list and scheduled to test his recuperating arm in the bullpen before that night's game. "Be sure to ask manager Dave Bristol how Nolan did," Ferguson instructed me. The Reds won a tight game that night, winning 2–1. After the game, wanting to be the dutiful and bold reporter, before any other writer could ask a question, I asked Bristol, "How did Gary Nolan do during his bullpen session?"

Bristol dropped a sandwich he was eating onto the top of his desk and glared at me. "We just won a great damn ballgame and you want to know how a sore-armed pitcher did in the bullpen?"

Bristol intimidated me so much that I didn't ask him another question for four or five games. Later during his career, when he was a third base coach for the Reds, I told him that story and he smiled gleefully and said, "Yeah, I loved to intimidate young writers."

During one west coast road trip when Bristol was manager, the Reds lost five straight games. After the fifth loss he addressed the clubhouse with this message: "Before tomorrow's game there will be two buses from the hotel to the ballpark. The first bus, at 2:30, will be for all the players who need extra practice, extra hitting, extra fielding practice. The empty bus will leave at 4:30."

On the morning of June 23, 1971, executive sports editor Ralph Morrow called me at home to tell me Ferguson needed the day off and I was to cover the Reds-Philadelphia Phillies game that night in Riverfront Stadium. And that's how I got to cover one of the most memorable games in baseball history. Not only did Rick Wise pitch a no-hitter that night, he also hit two home runs off Reds starter Ross Grimsley. It was the first time in baseball history that a pitcher threw a no-hitter and hit two home runs. And it has not been repeated.

Pitching a no-hitter against the Reds that season was no easy task because the Cincinnati lineup was populated by Pete Rose, George Foster, Lee May, Johnny Bench, Tony Perez, and Hal McRae.

My dream came true before the 1973 season when Jim Ferguson left the paper to become the publicity director of the Reds. I was excited but apprehensive about covering a major-league team. On my first day, veteran Hall of Fame writer Earl Lawson of the *Cincinnati Post* took me aside and said, "Listen, kid. Your boss, Si Burick, was always good to me, always helped me when I first started. I never forgot that. So I'm going to take you under my wing. Just follow me around, keep quiet, and learn."

And I did just that. Earl knew everybody in baseball and introduced me to everybody we encountered. We went into all the visiting clubhouses and he introduced me, and then I kept quiet and listened to the conversations. He was my mentor and I couldn't have asked for a better one. And I was able to write stories about many, many conversations of superstars—all coming from interviews conducted by Lawson while I listened and took notes. And I learned the baseball writing craft because of him and his willingness to teach a young guy how to do the job. It is why that when I became a veteran I tried to treat every young writer the same way Earl Lawson treated me. I tried to help each and every one and answered any questions they had.

Lawson and I were inseparable on the road. He took me to all his favorite night spots and restaurants. We shared cabs. Since we both worked for afternoon papers, we went back to our hotel rooms after games to write our stories and then we hit the streets. One night in New York we went to the Carnegie Delicatessen, where he introduced me to a salami omelette that was as big around as a truck tire. The restaurant was stuffed with celebrity photos, all of whom had eaten at the Carnegie and endorsed it with their signatures. I was admiring a photo of Helen Hunt, one of my favorite actresses, when somebody brushed my shoulder on the way to the table next to us. It was Helen Hunt, in the flesh. My salami omelette went uneaten as I stared holes through her.

Lawson never softened a punch in his stories, which led to fights with Vada Pinson and Johnny Temple (twice). Mike LaCoss was a pitcher with the Reds in the early 1980s and was struggling. Lawson wrote, "What Mike LaCoss needs is for somebody to turn him over their knee and spank him."

The next night the team flew to Montreal, and as we were retrieving our luggage at the carousel LaCoss verbally accosted Lawson. Lawson never backed down to anybody, and he whipped off his glasses and thrust his jaw close to the pitcher's face. I stepped between the two as a peacemaker, something I did often when accompanying Lawson.

But Lawson was good-hearted, too. He was single at the time we were in a late night establishment in San Francisco. The Reds had given the beat writers World Series rings after the 1975 and 1976 seasons—writers were permitted to accept such gifts in those days. Lawson met a pretty young women after he had imbibed a bit too much, and he whipped off his ring and gave it to her.

"Are you crazy?" I asked. "That's your World Series ring." Lawson flicked his wrist and said, "Ah, that's okay, I have another one."

But I decided it best to retrieve it. When I asked the woman to return the ring, her boyfriend approached me with a pool stick and told me to get lost. But I did some of my best diplomatic work and explained what the ring represented. She returned the ring, but the boyfriend stood menacingly with the pool stick. I grabbed Lawson and we vacated the premises.

When I was presented my 1975 World Series ring, I weighed 225 pounds. I then lost forty pounds and the ring hung loosely on my finger. One night in Dodger Stadium I stood up and made a quick, sharp gesture with my hand. The ring flew off my hand, out the press box, and clanked to the concrete floor in the lower deck. A fan picked it up, looked at it, and began passing it down the row for his friends to see. I sprinted out of the press box, down two flights of escalators, and to the section where my ring landed. It took only a $20 bill to get my ring back.

The 1973 season was one of disappointment for the Reds. They had appeared in the 1970 World Series, losing to Baltimore in five games, then the revamped Reds won ninety-five games in 1972 and the National League championship, only to lose the World Series to Oakland and Catfish Hunter, 3–2, with a save by Rollie Fingers, in Game Seven. The 1973 season was to be the year they finally won a World Series.

On November 29, 1971, club president/general manager Bob Howsam made The Deal of the Century. He traded first baseman Lee May, second baseman Tommy Helms, and infielder Jimmy Stewart to the Houston Astros. In return, he received second baseman Joe Morgan, pitcher Jack Billingham, center fielder Cesar Geronimo, outfielder Ed Armbrister, and infielder Denis Menke. Morgan became a superstar, Billingham became one of the team's best pitchers, and Geronimo became the National League's best center fielder. None of the players the Reds traded did much to help the Astros.

So optimism was high for 1973 and the Reds won ninety-nine games to win the division, but it wasn't that easy. On July 1, they were all but dead, just waiting for dirt to be shoveled onto the corpse. They were in fourth place, ten games behind the division-leading Los Angeles Dodgers. They were playing a doubleheader that day and trailed the Dodgers, 3–1, with two outs in the bottom of the ninth—one out away from falling eleven games behind. With two runners on base, manager Sparky Anderson sent a pudgy third-string catcher named Hal King up to pinch-hit. He drilled a three-run walk-off home run to win the game, 4–3. And the Reds won the second game, too.

Unbeknownst to anybody at the time, it was the start of an incredible stretch during which the Reds went 60–28 to win the division by three-and-a-half games over the Dodgers. I cannot remember a single word King said after the game, but what he was doing during the interview left an indelible mark. He was stark naked during the interview and nervously twirled his manhood with his right hand as he talked.

The New York Mets won the National League East, winning only eighty-two games, so the Reds were huge favorites to win. But it didn't happen. The Mets won the five-game series, three games to two. It was a memorable series, though, because of a play at second base involving Cincinnati's Pete Rose and New York shortstop Bud Harrelson.

During Game Two in Shea Stadium, left hander Jon Matlack shut out the Reds, 5–0, and after the game the light-hitting Harrelson (.238 average) said, "Jon Matlack made the Reds look like me at the plate."

Joe Morgan, after reading the quote in the morning papers, confronted Harrelson during batting practice the next day, telling him the comment was unprofessional. Then during the game, New York pitcher Jerry Koosman threw a pitch high and tight on Rose and Pete took umbrage.

"I don't know if he was throwing at me, but he had had great control the whole game," said Rose. The Mets led, 9–2, in the fifth inning with one out when Rose singled. Morgan grounded to first baseman John Milner. He threw to second to start a double play. The brushback pitch, coupled with Harrelson's comment and the 9–2 deficit, had Rose in a foul mood, and he slid high and hard into Harrelson. Then one of the 200-pound Rose's elbows connected with the 140-pound Harrelson's face. Rose, who always played the game like an NFL linebacker, said he slid into second base the way he always slid into second base.

"He called me a name and I grabbed him," said Rose. "He came after me, so I grabbed him and we went down. I play hard and I don't play dirty."

Both benches emptied and a free-for-all broke out, with one of baseball's most humorous events unfolding after the fight. Relief pitcher Pedro Borbon sprinted from the bullpen with all the relief pitchers. He, as did many players, lost their caps during the skirmish. When it was over, Borbon picked up a hat and slapped it on his head. It was a blue hat, not the red ones the Reds wore, and it belonged to Mets outfielder Cleon Jones. When Borbon discovered his mistake, he whipped off the hat and bit a hunk out of the bill.

Pedro Borbon aka "The Dominican Dracula," made his last Major League Baseball appearance in 1980.

To those who knew the eccentric Borbon, it was not unusual for him to use his teeth. When clubhouse manager Bernie Stowe re-strung glove webbings with rawhide, he would take the glove to Borbon and have him bite off the end of the rawhide. In 1974 the Reds became embroiled in a fight with the Pittsburgh Pirates and Borbon bit pitcher Daryl Patterson on the neck, earning him the nickname "The Dominican Dracula." And

Patterson was given a tetanus shot. During a cicada invasion of Riverfront Stadium one year, Borbon made a bundle of cash when teammates bet him he wouldn't bite off the heads of the insects. He did, of course.

Borbon was, uh, different. In the off-season he returned to the Dominican Republic to participate in cockfighting. Once, before a six-day road trip, he obtained a German Shepherd dog. But he had nobody to watch it. So he filled the bathtub full of water for the dog to drink and left a couple of open twenty-pound bags of dry dog food for the dog to eat. When he returned from the trip, he was stunned to see most of the apartment's furniture in chewed tatters and the place smelling like a zoo, only worse.

But the man could pitch—and pitch often, every day, if the team would let him. His arm was never sore. He was never in the training room, never used ice on his arm, never was on the disabled list. He gave his all to the Reds and then, as a believer in voodoo, put a curse on the Reds. He was angry when the Reds traded him in mid-season 1979 to the San Francisco Giants for outfielder Hector Cruz. Borbon said he was putting a hex and a curse on the Reds, "They'll never win another World Series," he said.

And for a decade they didn't. They didn't even make the World Series. It ended in 1990 when the Reds made it back. Somebody located Borbon and he said, "I am lifting the curse. The hex is over." And the Reds, heavy underdogs, swept the Oakland Athletics in four straight games.

Rose, of course, became Public Enemy No. 1, 2 and 3 in New York after the Harrelson incident, and he further enraged the fans in game four when he hit a game-winning home run in the 12th inning and ran the bases pumping his fists.

The Reds, though, lost game five, 7–2, and the Reds traveling party, consisting of front office personnel and their families, were escorted late in the game from their seats behind the Reds dugout to safety under the stands.

My first year as a Reds beat writer was over, and by that time I was even bold enough to ask my own questions.

06 | BIG RED MACHINE

HOW SUPERSTARS WERE MADE

It is amazing what sticks in the mind about an iconic baseball team such as The Big Red Machine, especially the 1975 and 1976 World Series champions. Even though this was, by far, the best baseball team I ever saw (and contrary to what some might think, I never saw the 1927 New York Yankees), what I remember isn't much about runs, hits, errors, and earned run averages.

This was a team of stars and superstars, a team that no current franchise could afford, not even that Evil Empire in New York. Under today's going rate, each member of the starting eight would command $20 million a year and more. And that isn't even considering the pitching staff, as unheralded as it was because of the magnificence of the starting eight: Johnny Bench, Tony Perez, Joe Morgan, Dave Concepcion, Pete Rose, George Foster, Cesar Geronimo, and Ken Griffey Sr.

But these weren't just robotic baseball players, although it seemed that way because of the manner in which they totally dominated the opposition and made winning seem easy. They were led by their prematurely gray manager, George "Sparky" Anderson. He was such a no-name when club president Bob Howsam hired him that one Cincinnati newspaper's headline read, "Sparky Who?" Anderson, though, was the perfect pick. He was a people person, a manager who knew how to handle a clubhouse full of massive egos. He knew how to handle each individual personality, how long a rope to give one player, and how short a rope to give another.

"I've heard that a manager needs to handle a team by treating each player the same way," he once said. "I don't agree. Some players have earned special treatment, and others have to earn it." And he gave his superstars a long, long chain while keeping close tabs on the fringe players. They knew it and the extra players called themselves "The Turds." They even had tee shirts made up with "The Turds" on the front.

In mid-May, the Reds were in Philadelphia for a four-game series and lost all four games. And I did nothing to help the immediate future, and, in fact, worried that I might have helped ruin it.

The Reds were staying at a hotel in close proximity to Veterans Stadium, a short walk. After the first game of the series, a 4–0 loss, I was leaving the stadium and headed for the sidewalk. A security guard asked me if I was walking back to the hotel and I said I was. "There's a shortcut that will take you half the time," he said. "Walk to the back of the parking lot and there's a gate real close to the hotel." I took his advice and, indeed, it was half the distance.

The next night as I was leaving, the Reds two best pitchers, Don Gullett and Gary Nolan, were also leaving. As they turned toward the sidewalk, I said, "Hey, guys, follow me. I know a short-cut."

They followed. But when we arrived at the back gate it was closed and locked. It was about ten feet high with barbed wire strung across the top. We studied it. We didn't want to retreat and make it a long, long walk. So we mutually decided we could climb over it. I went first. It was in my younger days, and after shoving my typewriter under the gate I quickly scrambled over.

Nolan was next. When he reached the top and jumped over, the tail of his new suit—the first time he had worn it—snagged on the barbed wire and ripped it up the back. Gullett was next. When he reached the top and jumped to the ground, he rolled his ankle and twisted it. He ended up on the disabled list and missed a couple of starts.

He never told on me, never revealed how he twisted his ankle, and I prayed nightly for a quick recovery. He was back quickly, and Sparky Anderson went to his grave not knowing how I nearly destroyed his season by jeopardizing his two best pitchers.

Sparky had said earlier, "Over 162 games, if my best guys are hitting and we even get halfway decent pitching, we'll beat our opponents' brains out." Gullett and Nolan were more than halfway decent. Gullett was 15–9 with a 2.42 earned run average and Nolan was 15–9 with a 3.16

earned run average. Both were instrumental in the Reds recovering from that four-game sweep in Philadelphia and went from 18–18 to winning ninety of their next 126 games to finish 108–54 to win the National League West pennant.

Gullett was a special athlete, a shy farm kid from Lynn, Kentucky, who lived up to the adage that you don't speak until spoken to, and even then he still didn't have much to say. But could he ever throw a baseball. As Pete Rose said, "He could throw a baseball through a car wash and not get the ball wet."

Gene Bennett, the legendary scout who worked more than fifty years for the Reds and had signed Gullett, witnessed an incredible feat when Gullett pitched for McKell (Kentucky) High School. "He pitched a perfect seven-inning game. He struck out twenty of the twenty-one batters he faced, and the other guy bunted the ball back to the mound. Only three other hitters touched the ball and they fouled it back to the screen. He was the best high school pitcher I ever saw."

Excellence in baseball wasn't Gullett's only sports acumen. He once scored seventy-two points in a McKell High School football game—eleven rushing touchdowns and six extra points. "The McKell coach was upset with the other team's coach, so he turned Gullett loose on him," said Bennett. Gullett also scored fifty-two points in one high school basketball game. In his senior year, he was All-State in football, basketball, *and* baseball.

It seemed certain that Gullett was headed for the Hall of Fame. Anderson thought so, but Gullett's career was cut short with an arm injury when he was only twenty-seven. His record was 108–50 for his nine years and because it was before Tommy John surgery was perfected, Gullett's arm was never repaired. Gullett later became a pitching coach for the Reds and one of his managers, Jack McKeon said, "Gullett was the best in the business, the best pitching coach I ever saw."

Amazingly, Nolan, too, was victimized by arm troubles and pitched only ten years, compiling a 110–70 record with a 3.08 earned run average. His career ended at age twenty-nine and he fled to Las Vegas where he became a blackjack dealer, a pit boss, and a croupier. He and Gullett were inseparable, even after they retired. In 1980 they were together in the MGM Grand when it caught fire. They escaped down a smoke-filled staircase, but eighty-five people were killed.

Before the Reds put on their amazing run to the 1975 title, Anderson was not pleased with his team's performance and after one bad game he imposed a midnight curfew. And he enforced it in a unique manner. He took a baseball to the late night bellman at the front door of the hotel and told him, "I want you to get the autograph of every one of my players that comes through that door after midnight." The bellman complied, the culprits signed their own evidence, and Anderson collected the fines. Only one of them got away. Someone signed the ball, "Abraham Lincoln," and Anderson never did discover who it was.

Hal shares a laugh with Sparky Anderson.

Anderson was a man of habits and he rarely missed the team bus from the hotel to the ball park. One day, Sparky decided to go to Shea Stadium early, and he jumped into a cab. "Take me to the stadium," he told the cabbie. Then he concentrated on his newspaper. When they arrived, the cabbie said, "Here we are. The Stadium." It was Yankee Stadium, not Shea Stadium, and that's when Anderson learned that there is only one stadium in New York, and that's Yankee Stadium.

After winning the National League West by twenty games, the Reds destroyed the Pittsburgh Pirates in the National League Championship Series, sweeping three games behind the hitting of roommates Dave Concepcion and Tony Perez. And Don Gullett helped, pitching a complete game in game one and hitting a home run. The Reds won 8–3, 6–1, and 5–3 in ten innings.

Concepcion hit .444 and Perez hit .417. It was Perez who brought the once-shy and reserved Concepcion out of his shell and turned him into the same kind of player he was—a guy who could be counted upon in the clutch. Anderson once said, "In a clutch situation, I'd like to have Dave Concepcion up there as much as anybody else."

Before the 1975 World Series, I had never been to Fenway Park in Boston. When I got off the team bus I didn't head directly to the press box. I walked up the ramps and out a portal into the stands. When I emerged behind first base, the view took my breath away. There in front of me was the famous thirty-seven-foot-high Green Monster left-field wall. To me, it looked like The Great Wall of China.

The World Series did not begin suitably for the Reds because Boston's Luis Tiant, when he wasn't pitching, always had a ten-inch cigar in his mouth. He was so relaxed on the mound in Game One that he looked as if he was pitching in a smoking jacket. He shut out the Reds, 6–0. And it looked dismal in Game Two when the Reds trailed, 2–1, with two outs in the ninth. But Concepcion struck again. His single tied the game, then he stole second and scored the game-winner on Ken Griffey's single to even the World Series at one game each.

The Series moved to Cincinnati for Game Three, and it ended in swirling controversy. The Reds blew a 5–1 lead and it was 5–5 in the bottom of the 10th with Cesar Geronimo on first base. Pinch-hitter Ed Armbrister was sent up to put down a sacrifice bunt. And he did it. Not only did he do it, he stood in front of home plate admiring his work. Boston catcher Carlton Fisk ran into Armbrister, picking up the bunt and throwing off balance toward second to get Geronimo. The ball whizzed into center field and Geronimo ended up at third and Armbrister at second. The Red Sox were red-faced, particularly Fisk. He thought he had been interfered with and appealed heatedly to umpire Larry Barnett that Armbrister should be called out and Geronimo sent back to first. Barnett disagreed and Joe Morgan drove in Geronimo for the 6–5 victory.

Tiant beat the Reds again in Game Four, 5–4, but the Reds took a three-games-to-two lead in Game Five when Tony Perez emerged from a 0-for-15 skid to hit two home runs off Reggie Cleveland for a 6–2 Reds win behind Don Gullett.

Now it was back to Boston, the Reds needing one win in two chances to win their first World Series in thirty-five years. But Mother Nature had other ideas. Game Five was postponed for three straight days due to non-stop rain. As the team sat in the hotel waiting to play, manager Sparky Anderson decided the team needed to practice. But where? And how? He discovered that Tufts University in nearby Medford, Massachusetts, had a huge dirt-floored indoor arena, large enough to permit practice. Traveling secretary Paul Campbell made arrangements for the Reds to work out there and the team, fully dressed in game uniforms, boarded a bus.

The driver, unfamiliar with the location of Tufts, wandered the streets of Medford, unable to locate it. Even though there were no women on the bus, the driver was convinced to stop for directions. He stopped at a gas station and Sparky Anderson, wearing Cincinnati Reds uniform number 10, disembarked to ask the attendant for directions. Not only did the attendant know how to get there, he had a lifetime tale to tell about how Cincinnati Reds manager Sparky Anderson, in his baseball uniform, stopped at his service station to ask directions.

Finally, after more than seventy-two hours of waiting, the Reds boarded the bus for the trip to Fenway Park and Game Six. A group of fans, some of them minority owners, stood outside the Sheraton-Boston hotel serenading the bus occupants with a goofy song: "The whole town's batty about Cincinnati, what a team, what a team, what a team."

Game Six became baseball lore. It looked as if it was all over when the Reds led, 6–3, heading into the bottom of the eighth. But with two outs and two on, pinch-hitter Bernie Carbo blasted a three-run, game-tying home run. Ironically, Carbo was the Reds' No. 1 draft pick in 1965. And who was the Reds' No. 2 pick? Johnny Bench.

In the press box, I was seated nearly behind a pillar that limited both my vision and my work space, and as the game progressed I developed a crick in my neck. And like most writers watching the drama unfold, I wrote revise after revise of my game story. With the game at 6–6, it continued long into the night—the ninth, the 10th, the 11th. At one point when he was batting, Pete Rose turned to catcher Carlton Fisk and said, "Isn't this great? Isn't this a great game?" Rose didn't realize how ironic his question was.

As the bottom of the 12th began, Cincinnati relief pitcher Pat Darcy began his third inning—the eighth pitcher in the game. Fisk stepped into the box and drove a towering fly ball down the left-field line, directly at the left-field foul pole atop The Green Monster. After taking a few stutter steps toward first, Fisk began gesturing with his arms for the ball to stay fair. It kissed off the foul pole, a game-winning home run that sent the series into a deciding Game Seven.

About twenty years later, the History Channel produced a documentary on baseball writers and graciously included me. They asked me to recall a favorite story that I had written. I quickly remember Game Six, but I didn't remember what I wrote. They said they were going to the archives to find my story and they would have me read the first few paragraphs while they showed Fisk hitting the historic home run. I broke into a sweat. I was barely more than a rookie baseball writer when I wrote that story. But when I saw the documentary and heard myself read the first few paragraphs of my story as I watched the footage, I knew I had nailed it. Everything I described happened on the screen. It was a proud moment.

And how about the baseball. Whatever happened to that baseball that banged against the foul pole and sent Red Sox Nation into ecstasy? All of Fenway watched Fisk leaping and pleading with the baseball to stay fair. When it did, they all watched him dash around the bases. The game was over. But what happened to the baseball? Nobody knew that Reds left fielder George Foster picked up the baseball and tucked into his pocket. He told nobody. He kept it for twenty years. Then he put it up for auction and it was reported the baseball sold for $113,000.

When the 1975 World Series is replayed on television, the Fisk home run is always the centerpiece, as if that home run ended the World Series and the Red Sox won it. Not so. There was a Game Seven to be played and while it wasn't nearly as dramatic, it was still exciting. Boston grabbed an early 3–0 lead by the third inning. Tony Perez whacked a two-run home run off Bill "Spaceman" Lee in the sixth and Perez struck again with a single to score Pete Rose and tie it, 3–3. It stayed tied until the ninth when Ken Griffey singled to lead off the ninth. He reached third on a sacrifice and a ground ball. Pitcher Jim Burton intentionally walked Pete Rose, which infuriated the proud Joe Morgan, the next hitter.

Morgan singled to center to score Griffey for a 4–3 lead, and the Reds were three outs away from the championship. Relief pitcher Will McEnaney, a short stocky left hander, pitched a 1-2-3 ninth and "The Carlton Fisk World Series" belonged to the Reds.

The post-game clubhouse was a zoo, only smellier because of the spraying champagne mixed with beer, both of which were aimed at anybody in the room. I was doused with the stuff and later as I wrote in the press box, behind the pillar, the keys on my typewriter kept sticking.

Oh, the woes of a baseball writer.

THAT '76 MACHINE

CHRISTMAS IN CINCINNATI—AGAIN

With apologies to Bill Dickey, Yogi Berra, Yadier Molina, Thurman Munson, and all the catchers who ever strapped on the shin guards and chest protectors, Cincinnati Reds manager Sparky Anderson was dead solid perfect. After the Reds swept the New York Yankees in four straight games to win the 1976 World Series, Anderson was standing at the podium in the bowels of old Yankee Stadium during a press conference. I was near the back of the room and as Sparky talked, Yankees catcher Thurman Munson slipped into the room near me, awaiting his turn to be interviewed.

During the stunning four losses, Munson was a Broadway klieg light for the Yankees. He had nine hits in seventeen at-bats for a .529 average. Meanwhile, on the other side, Reds catcher Johnny Bench was even better. He had eight hits in fifteen at-bats for a .533 average. While Munson didn't hit a home run and drove in only two runs, Bench had two homers and drove in six runs.

And Bench was at his best in the final game when he hit both of his home runs and drove in five runs as the Reds ripped the Yankees, 7–2. So Bench's performance was fresh in Anderson's mind when a New York writer asked him if Munson could be considered in Bench's class. Without pause, without hesitation, without a second thought, Sparky said, "I don't want to embarrass any other catcher by comparing him to Johnny Bench."

It was not only Anderson's honest answer, it was his final answer. It was how he felt about his Hall of Fame catcher—the best ever. Anderson always gave writers honest answers and let them deal with it. To the New York writers, it was as if Anderson had slapped Babe Ruth in the face and kicked dirt in Lou Gehrig's face. I looked at Munson when Anderson said it and a grimace crossed Munson's face and his head dropped. I thought I even saw his bushy mustache twitch.

It was not a fair question. Munson was good, very good, but he was not Johnny Bench. Anderson had it right: "Don't ever embarrass another catcher by comparing him to Johnny Bench." The man asked a question and Anderson gave his opinion. But it became a major controversy. With nothing positive to write about their team getting swept, the New York media jumped on Anderson with big, black, bold type, claiming Anderson had been disrespectful to Munson.

But maybe it *was* a fair question. Bench did not have a good year in 1976. He hit only .234 with sixteen home runs and seventy-four RBI, definitely subpar for him. And Munson won the American League Most Valuable Player award. But Bench was the World Series MVP.

The day before the 1976 World Series began in Cincinnati, I was sitting in Anderson's Riverfront Stadium office when a wave of writers walked in. Several questions were asked, one writer asked a specific question, and Anderson gave one of his long, complex answers that satisfied the writers. They left the room. I stayed. Another group of writers entered the office and another question-and-answer session began. A different writer asked the same question as the writer from the first group had asked. Anderson launched into a long, complex answer, but he gave just the opposite answer to what he had given the first writer.

When the second group left, I said, "Sparky, two writers asked you the same question and you gave a totally opposite answer to each one." Anderson gave me an impish grin and said, "Well, you can't give the same story to everybody." Maybe when he was asked about Munson he should have given one answer to the New York writers in support of Munson, then dismissed them and given the opposite answer in support of Bench to the other writers.

Not only was Bench the best to squat behind the plate, he was intelligent and incisive in his interviews. And you always knew where you stood with him. If I wrote something he didn't like, he let me know about it the next day and then he forgot about it, didn't hold a grudge.

The demands on a catcher's body eventually caught up with Bench. By the time he was thirty he owned a pair of old man's creaky knees, and before the 1983 season, his last, he decided he wanted to play third base to eliminate squatting behind home plate. They gave him the opportunity during spring training in Tampa at Al Lopez Field. It was an unmitigated disaster. Ball after ball went through his legs at third base. In fairness, the infield of Al Lopez Field was as lumpy as an old mattress, and fielding ground balls was not easy for the best of defensive players. But at one point that spring I wrote, "Johnny Bench is doing a great imitation of a croquet wicket playing third base." He didn't much like that and let me know about it. Then he never mentioned it again.

When Johnny Bench was six, he and his brother used an empty can of evaporated milk for a ball and a cracked bat for batting practice.

In 1978, the Reds spent most of the season chasing the Los Angeles Dodgers and eventually finished second. On the road many Reds, Bench and Anderson included, spent a lot of their late mornings and early afternoons sunning themselves next to the hotel swimming pools. That gave me an idea for a column and I wrote one that said, "It appears the Cincinnati Reds are more interested in working on their suntans than they are about winning baseball games."

When we returned from the road, I walked into the clubhouse in Riverfront Stadium for the first home game and Bench was standing at the bulletin board reading something. I checked what he was reading and it was my column. Bench saw me and turned on me. He said loud enough for the entire clubhouse to hear, "Tell me, Hal, what do suntans have to do with winning baseball games?"

Outfielder George Foster had a man-mountain physique, a guy with broad shoulders, a twenty-eight-inch waist, and biceps bigger than my thighs. But he also had a high, squeaky voice, almost feminine. Before I could try to make up some reply to Bench's question, Foster's high-pitched voice came from a far corner: "If the shoe fits, wear it." George Foster, by his comment *and* his voice, saved me that day—and Bench never again mentioned it.

But a few days later I was standing by the elevator to the press box when general manager Dick Wagner approached. Wagner and I were not on great terms. He didn't like a lot of the stuff I wrote and pretty much ignored my presence. On this day, though, he turned to me and said, "That was a very interesting column you wrote this week." I thanked him and thought nothing about it until after the season.

There was another story involving Bench that year that was startling and out of character. The controversy quickly faded and hardly anybody remembers the day Bench aimed some heavy criticism at Sparky Anderson. It was in August and the Reds had lost fourteen of twenty games, giving up a lead in the National League West and falling five games behind the Los Angeles Dodgers. I walked into the clubhouse before a game after the Reds had lost six straight. Bench's locker in old Riverfront Stadium was the first one a visitor encountered when walking into the clubhouse, a cage and a bench just to the right of the door. Bench was pulling on a pair of white sanitary hose to wear under his Reds baseball socks when I walked up and said casually, "What's wrong with this team?"

Bench was ready for the question. He said Anderson was intimidated by the superstars in the clubhouse and was not providing the necessary leadership. "Our manager is too low key. This is just one man's opinion, mine, but Sparky has withdrawn from it all," Bench said. "Intimidated isn't exactly the word, but it is close. Anderson is too nice, perhaps in awe of us. This team won the World Series for him twice, actually did it for him. It is awfully difficult to manage a team that has been as successful as ours. It is difficult to reprimand people who have been so good to you, though we keep making the same absurd fundamental mistakes every day, all year, day after day."

Anderson, sitting in his small office behind a metal desk with a picture of Bench hanging on the wall, reacted by saying, "The only people who can turn it around are the people playing the game. Every man has his own opinion. I know one thing, we've won a whole bunch of ball games here. I don't think I've changed one bit since I've been here."

Wagner didn't rise to Anderson's defense and said, in fact, "A manager can't play for his players. But John brings out some objective points. I'm not going to comment on his remarks about Sparky because they are good friends. But John has played here for eleven years and he has seen us go from a growing club at Crosley Field to a pennant club to this situation now. His message tells quite a story."

That was when Wagner fired Sparky Anderson. The Reds made a goodwill trip to Japan after the 1978 season and when they returned Anderson was fired—after finishing no lower than second in seven of his eight years. Fired after finishing first five times. Fired after winning four National League pennants. Fired after winning two World Series.

And then it hit me. Wagner was looking for an excuse to get rid of Anderson and that column made Anderson look bad. As it turned out, Anderson was fired for being loyal to his coaches. When the Reds returned from Japan, Wagner wanted Anderson to fire pitching coach Larry Shepard and bench coach Alex Grammas. Anderson said no and added, "If you fire them you might as well fire me, too." So Wagner fired him.

Of course, I wrote disparagingly about Anderson's unjustified firing, the absurdity of it all, and my relationship with Wagner deteriorated even more. Wagner once was an executive for the Ice Capades and I wrote, "With decisions like this Wagner is skating on thin ice." The animosity reached its depths in 1982. Prior to the 1982 season Wagner traded third baseman Ray Knight to Houston for center fielder Cesar Cedeno. I called Wagner to get his comments and the conversation went like this:

Wagner picked up the phone and said, "Hello."

"Hey, Dick, this is Hal McCoy and I…"

"Why in the hell are you calling me? All you want to do is rip me," said Wagner.

I slammed down the phone, and we never spoke again. I didn't have to deal with him for long because when Marge Schott bought the team in 1983 she fired him. Amazingly, when I was voted into the Hall of Fame in 2002, Wagner sent me an extremely cordial congratulatory note.

The cast of characters of the 1976 Cincinnati Reds, The Big Red Machine, is familiar to most everybody—Bench, Tony Perez, Joe Morgan, Dave Concepcion, Pete Rose, George Foster, Cesar Geronimo, and Ken Griffey Sr. as the position players and Don Gullett, Jack Billingham, Gary Nolan, and Fred Norman on the mound. But how many remember the supporting cast?

How many remember the fifth starter on that team? His name was Pat Zachry and he won fourteen games and lost only seven that year, good enough for him to be National League Rookie of the Year. Zachry, though, is best remembered among teammates for a stunt he pulled in Wrigley Field that season.

Although Dave Concepcion hit .281 that year, he was in a slump in early May and was ready to try anything to snap out of it. On the route from the hotel to the ball park there is a huge statue of Civil War General Philip Sheridan. He is astride his horse, Winchester, and the horse is rearing on its hind legs, exposing the anatomically correct genitals. When teams came to town, the rookies were forced to make late night forays to the statue with buckets of Sherwin-Williams paint to cover the horse's genitals in team colors. You could always tell what team was in town by the color of the horse's genitals.

On this day Concepcion had the driver stop the team bus so he could dash to the horse and plant a kiss on the horse's genitals, freshly painted bright Cincinnati red. When he got to the ball park, he climbed into his uniform and took a shower with his uniform on, "To wash away the slump." Then he took his uniform off and headed for his locker. He spotted a large industrial dryer with a round glass window. So he climbed in. Zachry saw him in the dryer, pushed the door shut, and turned it on. There was Concepcion's face in the window going around and around and around. It singed nearly all the hair off his body. And after all that work to shed his slump, Concepcion played that day against the Chicago Cubs and went 0-for-5.

How many remember Dominican pitcher Santo Alcala? He was 11-and-4 that year and was fond of saying, "My fastball, she is fantastic." When the Reds played in Chicago, they stayed at a Sheraton hotel on Michigan Avenue. And there were two Sheraton hotels on Michigan Avenue. When the Reds arrived in Chicago and checked in at the Sheraton, Alcala grabbed his room key but didn't go directly to his room. He bolted for a meal. After eating, he grabbed a cab and said, "Take me to the Sheraton." When he arrived he checked his key for the room number and headed for his room. The key didn't work. He returned to the desk and showed his key and said, "My key doesn't work." The clerk, barely looking up from shuffling papers, told him. "You not only have the wrong room, you have the wrong hotel. You are at the wrong Sheraton."

While the hitters and sluggers on the 1976 team received the attention and the glory, the Reds had six pitchers win more than ten games (Gary Nolan, 15–9; Pat Zachry, 14–7; Jack Billingham, 13–11; Don Gullett, 11–3; Santo Alcala 11–4; and relief pitcher Rawlins Jackson Eastwick III, 11–5, twenty-nine saves). Eastwick, the team's closer, studied under famous realist artist Andrew Wyeth and sold some of his pieces to teammates. He was a deep thinker and said that when he pitched he felt like he was floating above the stadium, looking down at the field, but that it was probably his superego, his id.

The bullpen also contained a quiet young Dominican right-hander named Manny Sarmiento. He appeared in twenty-two games and was 5–1 with a 2.06 earned run average, but Anderson never could pronounce his name. Anderson had a gift for mispronunciations. Manny's last name was pronounced *Sar-mee-en-toe*, but Sparky pronounced it *Sar-men-tee-no*.

Is it any wonder the Reds finished 102–60 and finished ten games ahead of the second place Los Angeles Dodgers? They didn't lose a game in the post-season, winning three straight from the Philadelphia Phillies in the National

League playoffs and four straight from the Yankees in the World Series. Joe Morgan was the National League MVP for the second straight year when he hit .320 with twenty-seven homers and 111 RBI. Many thought there was a better player on his own team deserving of the MVP award: George Foster hit .306 with twenty-nine homers and 111 RBI.

Pete Rose played all 162 games and hit .323. Tony Perez hit .260 with nineteen homers and ninety-one RBI. Cesar Geronimo, who had never hit .300—and never would again—hit .307. He only hit two home runs and because many of his hits were bloops and seeing-eye grounders, his teammates began calling his bat "The Magic Wand."

An incident on the last day of the season turned Ken Griffey Sr. sour on manager Sparky Anderson. Griffey was leading the league in hitting at .337 and Sparky kept him out of the lineup against the Atlanta Braves to protect his average. As he sat in the dugout, Pittsburgh's Bill Madlock was collecting four hits to pass Griffey. Anderson quickly put Griffey into the lineup but he went 0-for-2 and lost the title. While Griffey still speaks highly of Sparky, it is best not to bring up the last day of the 1976 season.

The National League playoffs were over in the blink of a swing or two, and the stage was perfectly set in game one in Philadelphia. Pete Rose had two doubles and a triple, George Foster hit a home run, and Don Gullett held a strong-hitting Phillies team—led by Mike Schmidt, Greg Luzinski, Dick Allen, and Dave Cash—to two hits over eight innings and the Reds won, 6–3.

Game two was almost as easy, a 6–2 Reds victory in Philadelphia. Pete Rose had two more hits, Ken Griffey had two hits and, after starter Pat Zachry struggled, Pedro Borbon pitched four scoreless innings. Game three in Cincinnati was not so easy, a 7–6 Reds win. The Reds were behind, 6–4, in the bottom of the ninth, but The Big Red Machine showed why it was called The Big Red Machine. The Reds scored three runs on back-to-back home runs by Johnny Bench and George Foster to send the Reds against the Yankees in the World Series.

The two best defensive shortstops in the league at that time were Concepcion and Philadelphia's Larry Bowa, a bantam rooster with a Type-A personality. Before one game, while Concepcion was taking ground balls at shortstop, Bowa began yelling from the Phillies dugout, "Hey, Elmer. Elmer. Hey, Elmer." Concepcion came over to the dugout and asked, "Why you call me Elmer?" Bowa laughed and said, "Because every time I check the box score I see, 'E-Concepcion, so I thought maybe your first name was Elmer." (An 'E' in the box score designates errors.)

The World Series began on a positive note, too, when Joe Morgan homered in the first inning of Game One in Cincinnati and Tony Perez had three hits. Don Gullett, manager Sparky Anderson's choice to start nearly every first game of the postseason, held the Yankees to one run and five hits over seven-and-a-third innings during the 5–1 victory. Game Two was a major turning point and once again was emblematic of what The Big Red Machine was all about. The game was tied, 3–3, in the bottom of the ninth with two outs and nobody on. New York shortstop Fred Stanley threw Ken Griffey's potential inning-ending ground ball into the dugout, and Griffey ended up on second. Then it was Mr. Clutch, Tony Perez, who singled Griffey home to end the game. When Dave Bristol managed the Reds in the late 1960s, he often said, "If there is a way to win a ballgame, Tony Perez will find it."

The Series moved to New York for Game Three and the Yankees rued the day the American League began using the designated hitter. It was the first year of the DH, and when the Series moved to New York the Reds had to use it. Dan Driessen became the National League's first designated hitter and he banged three hits, including a home run, and the Reds won, 6–2. It was more of the same in Game Four, an easy 7–2 Reds win. Bench did his thing—two homers, five RBI—and the Munson-Bench controversy came out of Sparky Anderson's mouth. The Yankees and Munson had their feelings hurt, but Sparky Anderson and The Big Red Machine took their second straight World Series trophy back to Cincinnati.

08 | BIG DEAD MACHINE
NEXT STOP, THE BASEMENT

The demise of The Big Red Machine began shortly after the celebration of two straight World Series championships subsided in the fall of 1976. The first to go was pitcher Don Gullett, of whom manager Sparky Anderson said, "He is headed for the Hall of Fame." Gullett was one of the first players in baseball to declare free agency after a seven-year career with the Reds during which he was 91–44.

Reds executives Bob Howsam and Dick Wagner were anti-free agency and decided to fight it to the bitter end, refusing to play the bidding game with other teams, and refusing to sign free agents. And the end for the Reds was bitter as star after star left. Gullett signed with the New York Yankees but pitched only two more years before arm problems derailed not only his trip to the Hall of Fame but any further advancement of his career. After Gullett's departure, Pete Rose and Joe Morgan followed the free agent route out of Cincinnati.

Not only did Howsam permit Gullett to leave of his own volition, but he made a trade a month after Gullett's departure that haunted him until the day he died. The Reds had a young first baseman named Dan Driessen, a kid who carried a big bat. But with Perez at first base, there was no place for Driessen. They tried him at third base, but he could not cover the position nor stop ground balls nor make consistent throws to first base. His position was first base. Period. Paragraph.

Howsam decided it was time for Driessen to play every day and time for Perez to go. So on December 16, 1976, a month after Gullett signed with the Yankees, Howsam traded another important piece of the Big Red

Machine tapestry to the Montreal Expos. It was not only a public relations nightmare, it was disastrous on the field and in the clubhouse.

For Perez—and tossing relief pitcher Will McEnaney into the deal—the Reds obtained pitchers Woodie Fryman and Dale Murray. Fryman, who owned a farm across the Ohio River in Northern Kentucky, did not want to pitch in Cincinnati and his performance showed it. He was 5–5 with a 5.38 ERA in seventeen appearances in 1977, and after the season the Reds traded him to the Chicago Cubs for pitcher Bill Bonham. Murray pitched out of the bullpen in 1977 and until May of 1978 and was 8–3 over seventy-six games before the Reds traded him to the New York Mets for outfielder Ken Henderson.

Henderson spent most of 1978 nursing injuries and spent so much time in the whirlpool tub that Pete Rose designated the tub "The SS Henderson." Meanwhile, Perez spent another ten productive years in the major leagues, returned to Cincinnati for the final three years of his career, then became the team's batting coach and for a brief time as manager.

"Trading Tony Perez was the biggest mistake of my career," Howsam said. "I didn't realize how important he was to the team, especially in the clubhouse." Perez was the unofficial leader of the club, a master with his droll sense of humor at bursting the huge ego bubbles that permeated the clubhouse. He was adept at keeping the superstars planted on earth. If he heard one of them bragging about his exploits, Perez would point out some foible or a bad game or a bad play and remind him, "You ain't as good as you talk."

It was Howsam who made the trade that fit together the final pieces of The Big Red Machine when, in one trade with Houston, he brought in Joe Morgan, Cesar Geronimo, Jack Billingham, and Ed Armbrister. But he admitted his Perez deal goes down as one of the worst in franchise history.

Fans argue incessantly about the worst trades in club history and most agree that it was when Bill DeWitt traded outfielder Frank Robinson to the Baltimore Orioles on December 9, 1965, for pitchers Jack Baldschun and Milt Pappas, plus outfielder Dick Simpson. All three were gone from the Reds by 1970 when Robinson helped beat the Reds in the World Series. Robinson remains the only player to win Most Valuable Player in both leagues. He was MVP in the National League for the Reds in 1961, then was not only MVP for the Orioles in 1966 but won the Triple Crown (leading the league in batting average, home runs, and RBIs) and was MVP of the 1966 World Series.

I wasn't covering the Reds at the time of the trade in 1965, but all I have to do is mention two words—worst trade—to any Reds fan and Frank Robinson's name sputters out of their mouth. The Tony Perez trade is next. And then there is the trade of outfielder Paul O'Neill to the New York Yankees on November 3, 1992, for outfielder Roberto Kelly. O'Neill went on to collect a dresser drawer full of World Series rings while Kelly played parts of two seasons with the Reds—.319 in seventy-nine games in 1993 and .302 in forty-seven games in 1994 before he was traded midway through the 1994 season to Atlanta for outfielder Neon Deion Sanders.

Pete Rose was the next to go after Perez, and the Reds barely made him an offer to stay. So Rose went on a whirlwind recruiting trip. The St. Louis Cardinals were owned by Gussie Busch of the Budweiser family, and Rose said he was offered a Budweiser distributorship to sign with the Cardinals, which was humorous in a way because Rose never touched alcohol. The Pittsburgh Pirates were owned by horse racing magnate John Galbreath, and Rose was offered a thoroughbred racehorse to sign with the Pirates. That offer made sense. Rose's love for racehorses is well-documented.

The media, me included, followed this soap opera every day for a month until on December 5, 1978, Rose made the big announcement: He was signing with the Philadelphia Phillies, and now three Big Red Machine icons were gone.

Next to go was second baseman Joe Morgan, who became a free agent after the 1979 season. Late in the 1979 season, when Morgan talked about going elsewhere because the Reds weren't actively pursuing him, I wrote a column saying that it was time for Morgan to go, that the Big Red Machine was being systematically dismantled. I didn't say that Morgan was finished or over the hill, I just said he no longer fit in the future plans of the Cincinnati Reds. The next day when I walked into the clubhouse he stuck a finger in my face and said, "Don't ever try to talk to me again." That was in September of 1979.

Joe Morgan flapped his back arm like a chicken when he was at bat in order to help him hold the bat properly.

Morgan signed with the Houston Astros on January 30, 1980, and for the rest of his playing career, I never had a reason to talk with him. But after he retired, he came back to Cincinnati and started his TV broadcasting career. A couple of times we played doubles tennis against each other. We didn't speak. We've stood next to each other as the only occupants of an elevator. We didn't speak. We've stood next to each other at a urinal. We didn't speak.

Childish? Very childish. And it was on both sides. When I was to be inducted into the Hall of Fame in 2003 I knew Morgan would be there and thought it would be a good time to quit acting like kindergarteners. I mentioned Morgan in my acceptance speech. After the speech I was standing on the steps of the Otesage Hotel, where the Hall of Famers stay during induction weekend. I was with my wife, Nadine, my father, my sisters, my brother, and several friends when a white limousine pulled up and Joe Morgan stepped out of the back seat.

Now would be a good time to end this, a good time to stick out my hand and say, 'Hey, Joe, how are you?' I thought. Morgan started up the steps and said hello to my wife, said hello to my dad, said hello to my sisters, said hello to my brother. As he reached the top of the steps I started to stick out my hand but he brushed by me quickly and disappeared inside the front door. It was still on. Morgan became a special assistant to general manager Walt Jocketty and was often in the clubhouse, on the field, and in the elevator after games. But we didn't speak. When a friend once asked him about it, Morgan told him, "I don't really know Hal McCoy. I always dealt with Ritter Collett (*Dayton Journal Herald* sports editor)."

If he didn't know me, he wasn't paying much attention, because I covered nearly every game he played for the Reds and was in the clubhouse every day and interviewed him time after time after time. An ESPN radio station asked me to be on, and they said they were going to try to get Joe Morgan on with me. Morgan said he was busy. *Maybe sometime soon*, I thought, *I'll get the courage to approach him and ask, "Do you even remember what I wrote in 1979 that was so bad that we haven't talked in thirty-five years?"*

But it had a happy ending, just thirty-five years later. On April 16, 2014, I was standing nonchalantly in the spacious Reds clubhouse watching a baseball show on one of the six huge flat screen televisions hanging from the ceiling. Morgan was seated by himself in a far corner. He had been Jocketty's special assistant for four years and was often in the clubhouse. We never spoke, never acknowledged each other's presence.

I glanced his way and saw him motioning toward me. I looked over my shoulder behind me to see to whom he was gesturing, because I knew it wasn't me. When I looked back, he was heading my way. He stopped in front of me, stuck out his hand, and said, "I want to apologize." At that moment, Morgan and I buried the hatchet and it wasn't in each other's foreheads. That proved one thing. He is a bigger man than I. After thirty-five years, the feud—if you can call it that—one that lasted longer than the McCoy-Hatfield feud, was over.

After saying, "I apologize," Morgan added, "I was a lot younger and we do things when we're younger that we sometimes regret." I had to fight back some tears as I put my arm on his shoulder and said something like, "Joe, you don't know how much this means to me. I always respected you so much as a player and for the way you played the game, even after our falling out."

"I know that," he said. "And thanks for accepting my apology. Come down early some day and I'll buy you lunch." What he didn't do was tell me to stop at his Honda dealership on I-75 on my way home and pick out an Acura, darn it. But I had seldom felt better. As broadcaster Al Michaels asked, "Do you believe in miracles?" Yes.

The next to go was outfielder Ken Griffey Sr., traded on November 14, 1981, to the New York Yankees for pitchers Brian Ryder and Freddie Toliver, neither of whom made an impact in Cincinnati. Then on February 7, 1982, the Reds traded Griffey's best friend, left fielder George Foster, to the New York Mets for pitchers Greg Harris and Jim Kern, two more non-impact players, and catcher Alex Trevino.

To this day, George Foster remains the most underrated and unappreciated member of the Big Red Machine and in 1976, 1977 and 1978 was the most feared power hitter in the game. But he never received the accolades. He was the first to use a black bat, a bat he called "Black Beauty," and said he used it "to integrate the bat rack."

He led the National League in home runs in 1977 and 1978 and he led in RBI in 1976, 1977, and 1978. His 1977 season was incredible, one of the best all-around offensive seasons ever put together by a member of the Reds. He hit fifty-two home runs and no player had hit fifty home runs in the major leagues since Willie Mays in 1955. No other player did it until Detroit's Cecil Fielder hit fifty-one in 1990. "Yahtzee," as his teammates called him, almost won the Triple Crown that year and did win the Most Valuable Player award. His fifty-two homers and 149 RBI led the league and his .320 batting average was fourth best. He also led the league in runs scored with 124, in slugging percentage with .631, and in total bases with 388.

Foster was a tough interview. Prying quotes out of him was like getting the first olive out of a bottle. You had to learn how to handle him. He liked to joke and dodge questions at first, but if you stuck around long enough you could get what you wanted. But many writers, working on tight deadlines, couldn't stick around long enough to play his game, and they considered him a bad interview. He wasn't. He was a good interview. Whenever he hit a home run at home, writer Joe Minster of the *Hamilton Journal-News* always asked him, "What did you hit?" He wanted to know if he hit a fastball or a curveball or a change. Foster would put an index finger to his ample chin, as if in deep thought, then he would say, "A

Rawlings. I hit a Rawlings." And he usually knocked them lopsided and unstitched the covers.

Foster hit some mammoth home runs in Riverfront Stadium. Not many balls landed in the upper deck red seats, but Foster banged those seats six times. The hardest ball I ever saw hit in Riverfront was hit by Foster. And it didn't make the seats. He hit one on a rising, straight plane to left center field and it banged against the concrete upper deck façade in front of the red seats. Then it ricocheted all the way to shortstop.

In the press box I turned to the writer next to me and said, "Did I just see a ball bounce off the façade all the way back to shortstop?" I'd never seen anything like that. A human being can't hit a ball that hard. But then sometimes I think Foster wasn't human.

Foster remembers that home run vividly, as if it happened two days ago. "It was against the Cubs and left-handed pitcher Willie Hernandez," said Foster. "I was really hot at that time and I couldn't believe they pitched to me. But I hit that ball so hard that Willie Fernandez moved to the American League and changed his name (to Guillermo Villanueva)."

Even outfielder Cesar Geronimo was sent packing for what amounted to an old resin bag and a broken bat. On January 21, 1981, "The Chief," as his teammates called him, was traded to the Kansas City Royals for infielder German Barranca. His career with the Reds lasted for fifty-seven at-bats, and it was over.

So before the 1982 season began, the foundation and support beams of The Big Red Machine were gone—Don Gullett, Tony Perez, Pete Rose, Joe Morgan, Ken Griffey Sr., and George Foster. The only starters remaining were catcher Johnny Bench and shortstop Dave Concepcion. And reconstruction did not go well. The 1982 team lost 101 games, the only team in Reds franchise history to lose more than a hundred games. And it was during that long 1982 season when I realized that I didn't appreciate what I was seeing when The Big Red Machine was functioning. As a young baseball writer, I thought what I was seeing was what was going to happen forever. I didn't take time to sniff the roses. Only when I endured the drudgery of covering a team on its way to losing 101 games did it hit me. I had seen one of the best teams in baseball history and I was there when it was taken apart, piece by piece.

09 | HIS IRISH TEMPER

MAC AND THE LITTLE RED WAGON

After the Reds fired manager Sparky Anderson they hired John McNamara, a red-faced Irishman with a big hooked nose and an abrasive personality. He treated his beat writers well, but outsiders were subject to his disdain. If a writer with whom he was unfamiliar asked a question he didn't like, McNamara would rub his nose and say sarcastically, "Who are you with?"

For some reason never explained, in football, basketball, hockey—and almost any sport—the head man or woman is called coach. Not in baseball. The head man is called manager, and historically baseball managers hate to be called coach. They have coaches working under them, but they, themselves, are managers.

The mistake by media people is made often and usually ignored. But not by McNamara. Seg Dennison, one of the hardest working radio sports guys I've ever known and an extremely likable guy, always popular with the players, made the mistake in 1979, McNamara's first year. He began a question with, "Coach…" That's as far as he got. McNamara interrupted him and said, "I am not a coach. I am the manager. If you want to talk to the coaches, they dress down the hall."

Dennison was fairly new at the job and went back to his WLW radio station and told talk show host Bob Trumpy what happened. "Trumpy told me that I had to go to McNamara's office the next day and apologize to him for calling him coach," said Dennison. "It was one of the most embarrassing moments in my life."

McNamara was a career baseball man and managed five teams—Oakland (1969–1970), San Diego (1974–1977), Cincinnati (1979–1982), California (1983–1984) and Boston (1985–1986). He had a losing record of 1,167–1,242 and made it to the post-season only twice. His 1979 Reds won the division but lost to the Pittsburgh Pirates in the playoffs. And his 1986 Red Sox lost the World Series to the New York Mets, a World Series most remembered for the ball that squirted through first baseman Bill Buckner's leg in game six when the Red Sox led the game and could have won the series. After Buckner's error, however, the Mets rescued the game, then won Game Seven.

But it was the 1981 season that I remember most about McNamara because it truly represented his Irish temper. A player strike interrupted the season. When the strike hit, the Reds were 31–21, one-and-a-half games behind the Houston Astros in the National League West. When the strike was settled, baseball had to determine how the season would play out. Would they pick up where the season left off or do something different? They did something different and McNamara's dander flew all over Ann Arbor, Michigan.

After the strike ended, teams were given a week to get ready to resume the season and the Reds went to Ann Arbor to conduct workouts at the University of Michigan, and they stayed at a Ramada Inn. During that week, baseball made its decision. The season would be divided into two halves, and the winner of each half would meet after the season in a playoff. That meant Houston was in the playoff as the first-half winner. And it meant that the Reds would have to win the second half to make the playoffs.

McNamara was in the Ramada lobby when he received word of the format. His face turned crimson. There was a rack filled with brochures behind him. McNamara picked up the rack and hurled it across the lobby, brochures telling hotel guests to visit Boyne Mountain or the Ford Museum or a Detroit brewery fluttering all over the floor. Then he turned to a potted tree and ripped it out of its stand and tossed it across the floor, dirt pods flying.

And he was right. The Reds again finished second, and their overall record of 66–42 was not only the best in the National League West, it was the best in baseball. But the Reds stayed home. The Los Angeles Dodgers finished fourth in the first half with a 27–26 record, but they won the second half with a 35–21 record and made the playoffs. To push it into base-ball's face, the Reds flew a banner over Riverfront Stadium the next year that read, "66–42, The Best Record in Baseball." They could have added a footnote: "But we had to stay home during the playoffs."

While the mid-1970s Reds were known as The Big Red Machine, by 1979, McNamara's first year, the team was called The Little Red Wagon. Despite a feeble offensive output, the '79 team won the National League West with a 90–71 record, nudging the Houston Astros by one and a half games. Other than George Foster, who hit thirty home runs, drove in ninety-eight and batted .302, the rest of the lineup produced little. John-ny Bench was underpar for him—twenty-two homers, eighty RBI, .276 average. Joe Morgan suffered his worst year with the Reds, batting only .250 with nine homers, thirty-two RBI and only twenty-eight stolen bases. Shortstop Dave Concepcion had one of his best years, hitting .281 with sixteen homers and eighty-four RBI. Ray Knight hit .318 as the team's third baseman with ten homers and seventy-nine RBI. Ken Griffey Sr. hit a solid .316, but hit only eight homers and drove in only thirty-two runs.

Early in the season, seldom-used outfielder Champ Summers hit an inside-the- park home run, collapsing head first into the dirt at home plate. And he stayed down. He didn't get up for several moments. Was he hurt? Was he unconscious from lack of oxygen after the long run? When the trainer reached home plate, Summers' face was green and he was gagging. After finally catching his breath, Summers said, "I'm okay. I just swallowed my tobacco." It was his only home run of the year, and he was traded in late May.

The Little Red Wagon was carried by its pitching staff. Not a single starter had an earned run average higher than 3.89 and the staff was led by legendary right-hander Tom Seaver. Seaver was an icon with the New York Mets but became embroiled in a nasty confrontation with ownership and asked to be traded. The Mets accommodated him in mid-1977 by send-ing him to the Reds for four players—infielder Doug Flynn, pitcher Pat Zachry, outfielder Steve Henderson, and outfielder Dan Norman.

Seaver was 16–6 with a 3.14 earned run average in thirty-two starts in 1977 and, of course, was looked up to by every pitcher on the staff. He and relief pitcher Tom Hume became inseparable friends, and Hume flourished under Seaver's guidance. Early in his career Hume was a starter but didn't do well, and after one bad game a *Cincinnati Enquirer* writer called him Tom "Boom Boom" Hume. But Hume found himself in the bullpen, and pitching in middle and late relief he compiled a 10–9 record with a 2.76 earned run average and seventeen saves over 163 innings and fifty-seven games. If Hume did well in the middle of games, then McNamara permitted him to finish. If not, he called on Doug Bair, who was 11–7 with a 4.29 average and sixteen saves in sixty-five games.

Hal with Tom Seaver (L) and Tony Perez (R) at Cooperstown, 2003.

Frank Pastore began the season in the starting rotation and was a mirror-image on the mound of Seaver, copying and mimicking Seaver's every piece of mechanics. But it didn't work for him. During the first inning of one game Pastore walked the first three batters and went 2-and-0 on the next. McNamara trudged to the mound and asked, "What are you doing?"

"I'm working on my mechanics," Pastore said.

"Fuck the mechanics," the red-faced McNamara promptly said. "Throw strikes."

Pastore was removed from the rotation and placed in the bullpen and writers dubbed him "Mr. Goodwrench" because he always talked about working on his mechanics. After his baseball career ended, Pastore turned to religion and was the host of America's most popular Christian radio show on KKLA-FM (99.5) in Los Angeles. Pastore rode back and forth to the studio on a motorcycle, on the 210 highway. On the night of November 19, 2012, Pastore told his listeners, "Look, you guys know I ride a motorcycle, right? So at any moment, especially with the idiot people who cross the diamond lane into my lane without blinkers —not that I'm angry about it—at any minute I could be spread all over the 210." Three hours later, after the show, while riding home on his motorcycle, a car crashed into him and Pastore died. He was fifty-five.

Not only was Seaver a master at his craft, he was highly intelligent, well-read, humorous, and a prankster. After one game, several writers were gathered around him, including *Hamilton Journal-News* writer Joe Minster. Minster always wore a suit and tie to every game and the ties were godawful and often spotted with gravy. Midway through the interview that day, Seaver took a pair of scissors and cut off Minster's tie just below the knot. The next day Seaver presented Minster with a new—and very expensive—silk tie, which Minster promptly splashed with meat loaf sauce the first time he wore it.

Outfielder Dave Collins loved to torture Minster. His glasses were always smudged so much it was a wonder he could see out of them. Every time Collins saw Minster, he grabbed Minster's glasses and ran to the bathroom to clean them up, but when he returned them they always were more smudged and dirtier than when Collins took them. Minster never noticed. Nor did he usually notice that when Collins replaced Minster's glasses on his nose with one hand, he had a coat hanger in the other hand. He would slip the coat hanger onto Minster's belt loop then hang a roll of toilet paper on the hanger, and Poor Ol' Joe, as Minster liked to call himself, would walk around the clubhouse streaming toilet paper behind him.

Minster was a Runyanesque character in the press box, a foil of jokes and pranks and while he sometimes acted as if he hated it, he loved the attention. Every writer in the league pulled the same prank on him. They all obtained the number of the telephone at his seat in the press box. They would dial the number and hang up. Minster always picked it up, even if it rang ten straight times, and he could never figure out who was doing it.

Minster conducted a daily attendance pool. Anybody in the press box who wanted to participate would give Minster a dollar and a guess on the night's paid attendance. Whoever was closest won the entire pool. Well, they *thought* they won the entire pool. One night when the Los Angeles Dodgers were in town, there were twenty-one entries. That figure was confirmed by *Columbus Dispatch* columnist Bob Hunter. Minster wrote the guesses down on his reporter's notebook and one night Hunter counted the entries. Twenty-one.

When the attendance was announced and the winner was paid, Hunter asked the winner, "How much did you win?"

"I won $17," the winner said.

We checked a few more times and sure enough, Minster was skimming the pool. He knew we knew and we didn't care. It was humorous and he deserved a cut for running the pool every day. Gordon Verrell of the *Long Beach Press Telegram*, one of Minster's chief tormentors, asked him one day, "How was your trip to Hawaii with all that money you made off of us?"

One day, Jeff Horrigan of the *Cincinnati Post* made out a name card, "Ralph, CNN," and placed it next to Minster's seat. There was no Ralph from CNN but the writers would call Minster and ask for Ralph from CNN. Minster would tell them he wasn't there and hadn't seen him. And he would ask the writers, "Who is this Ralph?" We'd tell him that we saw him on the field or in the clubhouse, but he doesn't come to the press box.

Minster loved potato chips and would rescue three or four bags from the media dining room and bring them to his seat. One time he left his press credentials on his seat and Horrigan picked them up. He slit the bottom of one of the potato chip bags, inserted Minster's credential and re-sealed the bag. As Minster ate from the bag he found his credential and was mystified at first, then angry, knowing he had been had. "Hey, it's a prize," Horrigan told him, "Just like in the Cracker Jack box."

And you thought all we did in the press box was watch baseball games?

After Seaver, the 1979 rotation was Mike LaCoss (14–8, 3.50), thirty-six-year-old left hander Fred Norman (11–13, 3.64), Bill Bonham (9–7, 3.78) and Paul Moskau took Pastore's place and was 5–4 with a 3.89 ERA. The Reds lack of efficiency on offense caught up with them in the National League Championship Series against the Pirates. They were swept in three games, but with a few key hits, the first two were easily attainable by the Reds. Both games went extra innings. The Reds lost the first one in eleven innings, 5–2, when Tom Hume gave up three runs. They lost the second game, 3–2, in ten innings. The series shifted to Pittsburgh, and the Pirates completed the series with a 7–1 romp over Mike LaCoss. It was no consolation to the Reds, but the Pirates went on to win the World Series.

10 | 101 IN '82

FANS GET JOLT OF REALITY

Never in the history of the Cincinnati Reds, which began in 1869, had they lost a hundred games in a season. In 1982 they lost 101, the first and last time they lost more than a hundred. It was a dreadful period in the press box and in the clubhouse. And the 1982 season showed how spring training can be a mirage. The team had one of the best spring training records of all the teams, but once the regular season began the team sunk to its level. They finished last for the first time since 1937, they had a losing record for the first time since 1971, and they finished twenty-eight games behind first place Atlanta in the National League West.

It should have been clear from the second pitch on Opening Day. Bump Wills of the Chicago Cubs—and a son of base-stealing magician Maury Wills—hit Mario Soto's second pitch of the season over the right field wall. In the press box, one writer said, "Well, there goes the season." How right he was. The Reds lost that game, 3–2, and lost seven of their first nine to drop comfortably and permanently into last place.

John McNamara was fired at mid-season with a 34–58 record and was replaced by Russ Nixon, who finished the season at 27–43. No matter who the manager was, most of the players just wanted the season to end or to get out of Dodge. Club President/General Manager Dick Wagner still enforced the no facial hair rule. And he continued his dismantlement of The Big Red Machine, nearly completing it on February 10, 1982, when he traded outfielder George Foster to the New York Mets for pitcher Jim Kern, catcher Alex Trevino, and pitcher Greg Harris. Kern was extremely unhappy and wanted out. He figured out how to do it. He grew a long, scraggly beard, refused to shave it, and said, "If it was good enough for Jesus and good enough for Abraham Lincoln, it is good enough for me."

It worked. Wagner traded him to the Chicago White Sox on August 23, 1982, for infielder Wade Rowdon. In three years with the Reds, Rowdon played only forty-seven games and had ninety-six at-bats. But he had a surreal day on July 9, 1986, in Shea Stadium when he went five-for-five against the New York Mets, five of the twenty hits he had that year. On February 17, 1987, he was traded to the Chicago Cubs for pitcher Guy Hoffman.

Wagner was active in the trade market that year, but nothing he did worked. Before the season, he traded third baseman Ray Knight to Houston for outfielder Cesar Cedeno, a superstar with the Astros but a bust with the Reds, and he traded pitcher Scott Brown to the Kansas City Royals for Clint Hurdle, thereby trading one distinctive character for another.

Brown was a fourth-round draft pick by the Reds in 1975 out of De-Quincy, Louisiana, a lumber town in Calcasieu County. He didn't make it to the majors until 1981, and his total major-league career consisted of ten games in '81 when he gave up four runs and sixteen hits in thirteen innings. He was a fun-loving big ol' country boy and not well-schooled in baseball. During his first spring training with the Reds, he saw other pitchers throwing curveballs. He asked clubhouse manager Bernie Stowe, "How do I get those curveballs?" Stowe told him to go to a sporting goods store and ask for a box of them. Stowe says Brown did it, but the clerk told him, "We're all out."

Hurdle was Kansas City's No. 1 draft pick in 1975 and, with his rugged good looks and flamboyant style, a *Sports Illustrated* cover boy. He didn't achieve expectations in Kansas City and was shipped to Cincinnati, where I dubbed him "The Marlboro Man." He started in left field on Opening Day and when he threw a runner out at home plate, he blew on the fingers of his right hand and shoved them into an invisible holster, telling the fans, "I just shot that guy down." But a back injury had slowed him down after 1981 in Kansas City when he hit .329. He hit only .206 in nineteen games with the Reds and was demoted to Class AAA Indianapolis, then released.

Hurdle became a manager, one of the best, a man respected for his knowledge of the game and his pithy and humorous by-play with the media. He was named National League Manager of the Year in 2007 with the Colorado Rockies and was twice National League Manager of the Year with the Pittsburgh Pirates, 2011 and 2013. He quotes Shakespeare and he quotes the Beatles. And he enters "Thought of the Day" nearly every day with a make-a-difference theme into his smartphone and sends it to a thousand people—his players, his coaches, their wives, his wife, and friends all over the world. But he couldn't make a difference with the 1982 Reds. Nobody could.

If nothing else, the 1982 Reds had one of the most unusual players of the era—pitcher Brad "The Animal" Lesley. The Reds drafted him No. 1 in 1978 and for that they received a 0-and-3 record for forty-nine appearances in three seasons. Lesley made a name for himself, though. When he struck out a batter, he would charge down the mound with his arms spread wide and he'd growl like a gorilla. He did it every time. The Reds played the Houston Astros and faced Nolan Ryan, normally a staid guy who showed no emotion and performed no antics on the mound. He struck you out, grabbed the baseball, then struck out the next guy. But on this day, when he struck out the first Reds batter, he stomped down the front of the mound, spread his arms wide, and growled loud enough for fans in the upper deck to hear. It was humorous, but more shocking, because Ryan never did anything like that.

The Reds sold Lesley to the Milwaukee Brewers in 1985 and he was quickly released. Instead of pursuing baseball, Lesley took his acting talents to Japan and became a mammoth star in B-grade Godzilla-type movies. It was so fitting because he acted like Godzilla on the mound, with nothing to back up his macho image.

The 1982 Reds also had well-traveled pitcher Bob Shirley, who pitched in San Diego, St. Louis, Cincinnati, New York, and Kansas City. The team bus in San Diego always had the team names on its marquee. If the Reds were in town the marquee read, "Cincinnati Reds." One day as the team was boarding the bus, somebody noticed that the marquee said "San Francisco Giants." It was pointed out to the driver and he began spinning the names to find the Cincinnati Reds. As the different team names spun through the marquee, Shirley watched it and said, "That looks like my career spinning past."

Left handed pitcher Bill Scherrer, now a scout for the Chicago White Sox and one of the most amiable and humorous guys around, pitched both as a starter and relief for the Reds. Scherrer loved bowling and why not? He was from Buffalo, New York, a bowling hub. One night he went bowling before a scheduled start but couldn't make the start because his pitching thumb was swollen. He had a lot of strikes the night before on the lanes, but didn't throw any on the baseball field the next night.

Pitcher Mario Soto put together an incredible season—and finished 14–13, outstanding for a team that lost 101 games. But he should have won twenty. His ERA was 2.79 and he struck out 274 batters in 257.2 innings. And most unbelievable, Soto went through his entire career with only two pitches, a fastball and one of most baffling change-ups any hitter ever saw. A hitter knew, "I'm going to get a fastball or I'm going to get a change-up." But he still couldn't hit it. Soto had the misfortune of playing for bad and mediocre teams most of his career in Cincinnati and the bad karma rubbed off.

On May 12, 1985, Soto took a no-hitter into the ninth inning against the St. Louis Cardinals in Riverfront Stadium. He retired the first two batters—one out from a no-hitter. Then George Hendrick hit a home run to ruin the no-hitter and the shutout. Fortunately for Soto, the Reds scored a run in the top of the ninth so he had a 2–0 lead when Hendrick homered and Soto still received a win on one hit with five walks and twelve strikeouts.

Soto remembers that day in vivid color, as if it happened yesterday. "I never threw him anything but change-ups," he said. "On that last at-bat I threw him a couple in the dirt, bounced them, and he still swung at them and fouled them off. So I had two strikes, one strike away from the no-hitter. But as soon as I let go of the next pitch, I knew it was a mistake. It was another change-up, but I threw it belt-high. I knew I was in trouble. I saw his eyes get as big as dinner plates and he ripped it out of the park."

And of that 1982 season when Soto was oh-so-good and the team was oh-so-bad, Soto said, "It was tough. If you gave up one or two runs in the first two innings, you were going to lose. That's the way it was. We couldn't buy a run. But it was a good year for me. I tried to find a way that wouldn't take me to the ball park. It was so tough. People would ask me, 'Are they ever going to score you some runs?' And I'd tell them, 'Don't ask me. I just pitch. I can't hit, either.' All I did was get ready to pitch every fifth day and pray for a couple of runs."

The other starters in 1982? Bruce Berenyi was 9–18, Frank Pastore was 8–13, Tom Seaver had his worst season with a 5–13 record and a 5.50 ERA, Bob Shirley was 8–13. The offense was inoffensive on that 1982 team. The team batted .251, hit only eighty-two homers and scored only 545 runs, 3.4 runs a game. Nobody hit .300 and Dan Driessen led the team with seventeen homers and fifty-seven RBI. Johnny Bench had only thirteen homers and thirty-eight RBI, but maybe he was distracted. It was the first year of his TV show, *The Baseball Bunch*, which he co-hosted with—are you ready?—The San Diego Chicken.

Second baseman Ron Oester, a Cincinnati native, was the toughest player, pound-for-pound I ever saw. He took guff and grief from nobody, even though he was as skinny as the foul pole. Center fielder Cesar Cedeno, a heavily muscled tough guy (well, everybody thought he was tough), missed several games and was sitting out another game when the lineup card went up. Oester, who played injured and who played hurt and who played no matter what, couldn't play that night against Houston pitcher Mike Scott. Cedeno, sitting out the game, said to Oester, "You ain't hurt. You've just got Scott-it is." The words were barely out of Cedeno's mouth when Oester was on top of him, pounding him with rights and lefts. Cedeno never landed a blow and teammates had to pull Oester off Cedeno, who was pinned on the floor.

Oester doesn't want to remember that incident or anything about the 1982 season when he hit .260 with seven homers and forty-seven RBI. "I try to forget everything I can about that year," he said. "That was the longest year of my baseball career."

But everybody should have known that Cedeno wasn't Mr. Macho. During a spring training game that year on a grubby field in Cocoa Beach, Florida, spring home of the Houston Astros at the time, Cedeno was playing center field. Suddenly, in the middle of the inning, Cedeno sprinted off the field and into the dugout. Everybody assumed he had to go to the bathroom, an emergency that couldn't wait. That wasn't the case. What happened was that Cedeno spotted a snake slithering in the grass in front of him. He was deathly frightened of snakes and he never returned to the field.

Oester wasn't alone in the sentiment that 1982 was a year to obliterate from the memory bank. The 1982 team was not very good. It was, in fact, awful. But it was entertaining in a non-baseball way, and I learned my lesson about not taking good teams for granted for the rest of my career.

11 | TURN OF FORTUNE

THE PRODIGAL SON COMES HOME

The wreckage of the 1982 season was carried over for two more seasons. The team finished last in 1983 and next-to-last in 1984. It was no fun to be a Cincinnati Reds fan—or a writer—covering the daily dalliances of the team. There was no better indicator of what was going on than the case of Jeffrey Raymond Jones.

Jones, a redheaded, 6-foot-2, 200-pound mass of muscle from the University of Iowa was drafted by the Reds in 1979 in the twentieth round. But four years after he was signed, he was still playing in the lowly Class A Midwest League. In his fourth year, playing mostly against younger kids right out of high school, Jones hit forty-two home runs and drove in 101. He caught the attention of Reds President/General Manager Dick Wagner, and he was invited to work out with the major-league team in spring training of 1983.

He was impressive. He hit and he hit and he hit. Wagner decided he had earned a spot in the majors, despite the fact he had never advanced beyond Class A, the lowest rung on the minor-league ladder. Manager Russ Nixon, a life-long baseball guy who had seen it all, was against it. But his boss prevailed and not only did Wagner want him on the roster, he wanted him to play. So on Opening Day, 1983, Jones was in right field, batting seventh.

He survived for sixteen games, thirteen as a starter in right field, left field, and first base. He batted .221, struck out thirteen times in forty-four at-bats, and quickly found himself back in the minors where he spent the rest of his baseball career. He hit 125 minor-league home runs but struck out 749 times in 694 games, and he was never again seen in a major-league uniform.

The most significant thing about the 1983 Cincinnati Reds was that it was the last year for Hall of Fame catcher Johnny Bench. By 1983 his knees were so bad that he experienced excruciating pain squatting behind home plate, so he caught only five games that year and played in 110. Mostly he played third base, with some appearances at first base and several as a pinch-hitter.

On September 17, Johnny Bench Night, he made his final appearance behind home plate, against the Houston Astros, in front of 53,790 fans in Riverfront Stadium. And there was a dramatic moment that most everybody in the stadium saw and will savor the rest of their lives. Almost everybody. I was not in the press box. I was on a ramp under the stands visiting a friend. Bench was batting in the bottom of the third against right hander Mike Madden. The count was 0-and-2 with Paul Householder on first base when I heard the roar.

I sprinted up the ramp in time to see Bench rounding first base. He had hit a home run, the 389th and last of his career, a line drive deep into the left-field seats—and I missed it. But I watched it several times on replay and was able to describe the moment the next day in the *Dayton Daily News*. Bench never played on the field after that home run. He made five pinch-hitting appearances, and his career was over. And I foolishly missed the big moment and learned a lesson—never leave the press box during a possible momentous occasion.

Other than Johnny Bench Day, the 1983 season was an improvement over 1982's 101 losses, but not much. The team finished last, five games behind fifth-place San Diego and seventeen games behind the Los Angeles Dodgers, winners of the National League West. It took three catchers to replace Bench—Dann Bilardello, Alex Trevino, and Alan Knicely. In twenty-nine years of combined major-league service, those three hit fifty-three homers and drove in 395 runs. In seventeen seasons, Bench hit 389 homers and drove in 1,376.

The most mysterious player on the 1983 team was a pitcher named Greg Harris. Was he left handed? Was he right-handed? No, he was both. He was able to pitch with either hand and owned a special six-fingered glove so that he could stick both hands into the glove before he threw a pitch—with either hand.

He only did it once in a major-league game, and it wasn't with the Reds. But with the season they were having, they might have drawn a huge crowd had they permitted him to start a game, advertising that he would throw with both hands. Ironically, he did it *against* the Cincinnati Reds, pitching for the Montreal Expos, who had picked him up off waivers from the Reds after the 1983 season. He had been wanting to display his ambidextrous arm for ten years, but no manager would permit it.

Then on September 28, 1995, the next-to-last game of his career, the Expos permitted him to pitch—with both hands—in the ninth inning. He pitched right-handed against right-handed batters and left-handed against left-handed batters. He faced four batters and the Reds didn't get a hit. Pitching right-handed, he retired Reggie Sanders. He switched to his left hand for the next two left-handed batters. He walked Hal Morris and Eddie Taubensee grounded out. He switched back to right-handed to end the inning by retiring Bret Boone in a game the Reds won, 9–7.

Instead of trekking to the Reds clubhouse for quotes and comments, as I usually did, I trudged to the Expos clubhouse to hear what Harris had to say after becoming the first and last pitcher in the majors to pitch with both hands in one game. He was talking about his former manager in Texas, Bobby Valentine, a guy with the guts and personality to let Harris do his thing. But Valentine never did.

"I never understood why Valentine never let me do it," said Harris. "Bobby said he would let me if I could master three things. I had to be able to throw twenty-five strikes in thirty pitches with both hands, which I could do. I had to have a curveball with both hands, which I did. And I had to throw more than eighty miles an hour with both hands, which I could do. But he never let me do it."

In 1978, the Reds drafted outfielder Gary Redus in the 15th round and sent him to Billings, Montana. There, in the Pioneer Rookie League, he hit an astounding .462 with forty-two steals in sixty-eight games. He arrived in the big leagues for his first full season in 1983 and played left field. And he had his best season with the Reds, if you can call .242 with twelve homers, fifty-one RBI, and thirty-eight steals a best. In 1986 he was traded, along with pitcher Tom Hume, to the Philadelphia Phillies for pitchers John Denny and Jeff Gray, neither of whom wore a Reds uniform for very long.

John Denny may have been the only player I ever feared, because he had piercing steely gray eyes and was surly. When the team was in Philadelphia, *Cincinnati Post* beat writer Bruce Schoenfeld made a wrong turn in the tunnel under Veterans Stadium and encountered Denny doing some exercises. Denny asked Schoenfeld why he was spying on him, words were exchanged, and Denny eventually punched the writer, giving him a black eye. I always steered clear of him and when I later learned he became a minister after retiring from baseball I asked, "What church, the Church of the Latter Day Contradictions?"

The Reds went into immediate action a month after the 1983 season, trying to reverse their misfortunes. In less than thirty days they signed free agent catcher Brad Gulden, whose nickname was "Rockpile" because he always looked as if he spent three hours playing with dirt and rocks. They purchased pitcher Bob Owchinko from the Pittsburgh Pirates. They signed free agent infielder Wayne Krenchicki, forcing some quick artwork. The Reds still had their no facial hair policy and Krenchicki wore a full mustache. The media guide was set to go to press and there was no time to take a new picture. So they used Krenchicki's photo from Detroit, with his mustache, although they airbrushed his mustache and his picture in the 1984 Reds media guide has a white slash on his upper lip.

Most significantly, they brought back one of the franchise's most popular players ever, Tony Perez, by purchasing him from the Philadelphia Phillies. A day later, they signed free agent superstar Dave Parker, who had grown up in Cincinnati and hung around old Crosley Field when he was a kid. In addition to being an outstanding hitter, both for power and for average, as well as the owner of a scoped rifle for an arm, Parker was a writer's delight with his witticisms and sense of humor. After one game in which pitcher Ted Power excelled and Parker contributed little, a gaggle of writers gathered around Parker after the game. Power was sitting by himself directly across the clubhouse from Parker and said, "Hey, Parkway. Why are they talking to you? You didn't do a thing." Said Parker with a broad smile, "Because I'm a humorous motherfucker."

On the field, the Reds were almost as humorous as Parker. They finished next-to-last, but their record of 70–92 was worse than the previous season when they finished last. They finished ahead of the San Francisco Giants, but they were twenty-two games behind the division-winning San Diego Padres.

There were two memorable incidents involving frustrated pitcher Mario Soto, who was 18–7 with a 3.53 earned run average. The rest of the pitching staff won only fifty-two games. And Soto won those eighteen games despite serving two separate sentences on the suspended list.

On May 27, the Reds were in Chicago playing the Cubs when third baseman Ron Cey hit a deep fly ball to left, near the foul pole. Third base umpire Steve Rippley called it fair, a home run. Soto charged Rippley, and in the argument he bumped the umpire. While the argument unfolded, fans in the left field stands took Old Style beer cups and inserted them into the wire fence above the wall, forming a large "X," indicating where the ball hit. In foul territory. The umpires huddled and reversed the call, ruling it a foul ball. But Soto was ejected because he'd bumped Rippley. When Soto heard that, he charged the field and knocked down Cubs coach Don Zimmer, a guy who grew up in Cincinnati. (When Zimmer was a coach in Boston, pitcher Bill Lee called him a gerbil. When he apologized, Lee's apology was, "I apologize to all gerbils.") And so Soto was suspended five games.

Less than a month later, the Reds were in Atlanta and Soto buzzed Braves batter Claudell Washington with three straight under-the-chin pitches. After the third chin-scraper, Washington flung his bat in Soto's direction. As he walked to pick up his bat, Soto shouted at him and Washington started for the mound. Umpire Lanny Harris tackled Washington, and Soto punched Washington. Then he fired another message pitch, this one into a pile of Atlanta players, striking coach Joe Pignatano. Soto obviously had something against coaches. For that indiscretion, he was suspended three days. But Washington got five days for wrestling with the umpire.

The Reds, though, made a trade of historical significance on August 15, 1984, although most people don't remember it *was* a trade. They sent second baseman Tom Lawless to the Montreal Expos. In exchange, the Expos sent Peter Edward Rose back to Cincinnati. He was immediately named player-manager, although Rose spent most of his playing career saying he didn't ever want to be a major-league manager. "I'd like to be a coach, just to stay in baseball, and help young kids. But I don't want the problems of being a manager," he once told me.

But Reds President Bob Howsam and owner Marge Schott wanted the prodigal son back home in Cincinnati, asking him to take over a team that at the time was the worst-hitting team in the National League—and a pitching staff that was second worst in the National League. And although the 43-year-old Rose said at his introductory press conference, "Nick Es-asky is still our first baseman and I'll just fill in," he put himself in the lineup for August 17, batting second and playing first base. Said Rose, "Fans don't come to the game to watch me change pitchers."

People will say Riverfront Stadium was full that night, but it wasn't. There were 36,038 there that night to watch the Reds play the Chicago Cubs. Nobody remembers that the Reds won, 6–5, or that Soto won his thirteenth game, a complete game five-hitter. What they *do* remember is this: with a runner on second early in the game, Rose, batting left-handed against right-hander Dick Ruthven, drilled a base hit to center field, scoring a run. When the ball skipped past center fielder Bob Dernier and rolled to the wall, Rose fled for second and never stopped. He dove head first into third base, diving back into the hearts and souls of Reds fans everywhere. Charlie Hustle was back and things were going to be different.

Oh, were they.

12 | THE HIT KING

BIG NIGHT ON THE RIVERFRONT

Pete Rose wears his title, "The Hit King," like the badge of honor that it is, 4,256 hits, most ever by a major league baseball player. "Hit King" is stitched on the collar of many of his shirts, and it is on many of the baseball caps he wears everywhere. While it is a monumental accomplishment, his signature accomplishment—to me, anyway—isn't the most noteworthy.

Accumulating all those hits was, of course, a product of his proficiency with a baseball bat, a bat he waved like a magic wand to spray hits all over every major league baseball park in America and Canada. But it is also a product of playing twenty-four years and playing every game as if it were his last, or as he called it, "Playing balls-out every second I'm on the field."

But he didn't have to get a hit every day. Even when he came close to catching Ty Cobb's record of 4,191 hits, he didn't have to get a hit every day. It was an inevitable march that every baseball fan in America knew he was going to reach.

To me, Rose's more astonishing accomplishment was the forty-four-game hitting streak he put together in 1978, twelve short of Joe DiMaggio's record fifty-six-game streak, a record many baseball purists believe won't be broken. Rose came close. And what made it so mesmerizing as I chronicled it every day was that he had to get a hit every day, every game. As the streak mounted, the pressure had to be mind-boggling. But Rose displayed no outward negativity. He enjoyed the moment. When Roger Maris was chasing Babe Ruth's home run record of sixty in 1961, his hair fell out, and he tried to hide from the media. Rose made it a baseball spectacular, enjoying every second, cracking jokes along the way and engaging in entertaining post-game press conferences.

The streak began on June 14, 1978, with two hits off Chicago's Dave Roberts and Rose had two hits in each of the next two games—six hits in three games, vintage Pete Rose. More than a month previously, on May 5, Rose lined a single to left field off Montreal's Steve Rogers, his 3,000th hit, and everyone thought that would be the signifying moment of Rose's 1978 season. How wrong we all were.

After the six hits in three games in mid-June, Rose kept on hitting in game after game after game. When his streak reached thirty, the baseball world took notice. After every game, Rose trudged to an interview room to talk about the streak. It reached a crescendo in New York—of course, it always reached a crescendo in New York—when he hit in his thirty-eighth straight game to pass Tommy Holmes's thirty-seven straight, which he hit for the Boston Braves in 1945, the last year of the war. In the interview room Rose said, "Pitchers are good people. They give me a hell of a living."

On July 31 in Atlanta, Rose singled off a knuckleball thrown by future Hall of Fame pitcher Phil Niekro, extending the streak to forty-four games and tying Wee Willie Keeler for the National League record, set in 1897 when Baltimore was in the National League. It was to be his last hit of the streak. Along the way he batted .379 with sixty-six hits in the forty-four games. He had fifty-three singles and thirteen doubles. No home runs. He had six three-hit games and ten two-hit games. He walked eleven times and struck out only six times.

His closest call was a game in Philadelphia on July 19 when he came to bat in the ninth inning without a hit. He walked, and it seemed the streak was over, ended at thirty-one. But his teammates saved him. They batted around and Rose came to bat again, and this time he put down a bunt single toward third base to keep the streak breathing.

It all came to an end on August 1 against the Atlanta Braves, and it ended in controversy. The Braves weren't very good and averaged only eleven thousand fans in cavernous Atlanta-Fulton County Stadium. And the Braves had just come off a road trip during which they lost a game in Montreal, 19–0. But with Rose's streak as the lure, 31,159 showed up—not to see the Braves but to see Rose continue his assault on Joltin' Joe

DiMaggio. As Atlanta's twenty-four-year-old rookie pitcher Larry McWilliams said, "Everybody but the pitcher wanted to see Rose get a hit. It was a magnificent thing going on."

McWilliams, as nervous as he would ever be, walked Rose in the first inning. Making certain he didn't do it again, McWilliams misplaced a fastball on Rose's second at-bat. Rose crushed one up the middle. A hit? Nope. McWilliams, acting in self-defense, reached down around his socks and speared the line drive. The third time Rose faced McWilliams, he hit a hard ground ball to shortstop Jerry Royster.

Meanwhile, the Braves were pounding the Reds en route to a 16–4 victory. The fans didn't care. They wanted Rose to get a hit. Rookie manager Bobby Cox, now in the Hall of Fame, put in change-up specialist Gene Garber in the seventh inning. Charlie Hustle lined into a double play and was 0-for-4. Cox wanted to take Garber out, but Garber stubbornly convinced his manager to leave him in. "Because I want to end his streak," he said. "I told my wife before the game I was going to stop his streak."

So Garber, who had 141 career saves for the Braves, was still in there when Rose came to bat in the top of the ninth with two outs, the streak on the precipice. Flashbulbs popped all over the stadium and the full press box—most writers there to chronicle Rose—stopped typing and paid attention. It was as a quiet as a mausoleum on a cold winter's night. Garber fell behind 2-and-1, and he said he thought to himself, *I can't walk him or I'll be a horse's ass everywhere for ending his streak on a walk.*

So Garber went to his best pitch, the change-up. He said he threw one of the best he's ever thrown and Rose fouled it off to go 2-and-2. Rose was expecting Garber to challenge him with a he-man fastball, *mano y mano.* Instead, Garber threw another change-up. A bad one. "It's a feel pitch and I could always tell when I released it if it was a good one," Garber said after the game. "When I released the last one I could feel it wasn't a good one. It was right down the middle and I said, 'Oh, no.' But when he swung through it, I changed it to, 'Oh, yeah.' But it was not a good pitch." It was eighty miles an hour, the speed of a batting practice pitch. But it was Rose's sixth strikeout of the forty-four-game streak. And it was over.

I hurried from the press box to get to the interview room but the small, creaky, slow-moving elevator was full. By the time I reached the room,

Rose was at the microphone, wearing a tee shirt that said, "Hustle Made it Happen." As I walked in the door, a writer asked Rose how it felt now that the streak was over. Unaware that his interview was on live television, and in typical Rose fashion, he smiled and said, "At least I don't have to deal with you bastards any more."

Then came the controversy from the frustrated Rose. He said, "Garber pitched me like it was the seventh game of the World Series. He must have thought I was Joe DiMaggio. Why wouldn't he challenge me, especially with his team ahead, 16–4." To the baseball world, it sounded as if Rose was a sore loser. As for Garber, he said he *did* challenge him, "With the best pitch I had. It is what made me what I was." Garber pitched nineteen seasons and retired to raise 110,000 chickens on three farms with his two sons and to this day says, "if I had it to do over I'd do it the same way. That's the way I pitched the nine hundred some odd games I pitched. For him to say I pitched him like the seventh game of the World Series, well, that was a compliment, because that's the way I pitched every time out."

By 1985, Rose was player/manager of the Reds and while the team improved, he couldn't quite push them to the top. They finished second in 1985, 1986, 1987, and 1988. In late 1985, Rose was approaching Ty Cobb's record and evoked another media frenzy. The Reds were in Chicago on Sunday, September 8. Rose was two hits away from tying Cobb and three away from breaking the record. The Cubs were scheduled to pitch left-hander Steve Trout that day and Rose usually didn't put himself in the lineup against left-handers, using Tony Perez instead. So Rose wasn't scheduled to play.

That suited the national press corps just fine. The smallish Wrigley Field press box was cramped and overpopulated. Some had to cover the game on television in the Pink Poodle media dining room. So with Rose not playing, most of the writers decided to go to Soldier Field to cover a Chicago Bears NFL game. And they all nearly missed what they were assigned to cover.

When Cubs pitcher Trout arrived at Wrigley Field Sunday morning, he reported that he had fallen off a bicycle Saturday night, probably fleeing the culinary and imbibing establishments that made Rush Street famous, and hurt his elbow and shoulder. He couldn't pitch. While National writers were seating themselves comfortably in Soldier Field to watch the Bears beat the Tampa Bay Buccaneers, 38–28, Rose discovered the rookie right-hander Reggie Patterson would pitch for the Cubs. He made out a new lineup card, erasing Perez and putting himself in the lineup.

In the fifth inning, Rose lined his second hit and tied Cobb— 4,190 hits. The record was one swing of the bat away as the regular Reds and Cubs beat writers readied themselves to write history. I was squirming in my seat, not ready for this. We all hoped it would happen at home, in Riverfront Stadium.

Pete Rose and Hal. Pete was a running back for his high school freshman football team which may have helped him learn how to hustle.

After his second hit, as Rose stood on first base as first baseman and Cincinnati native Leon Durham told him, "Just stand here for a while. I want to get some TV face time." Then he called time and ran to the mound and told Patterson, "Pete Rose just told me that he is going to buy you a steak dinner."

Rose had two chances to break the record, but he grounded out to shortstop Shawon Dunston in the seventh, and relief pitcher Lee Smith struck him out in the ninth. But the game wasn't over. It was tied, 5–5, when rain swooped in off Lake Michigan. Mother Nature must have wanted Rose to break the record in Cincinnati. They waited more than two hours before umpire crew chief Bob Engel called it off at 6:10 because it was too dark and Wrigley Field, at the time, had no lights. And a pack of baseball writers bowed deeply to Mother Nature for saving them the problem of explaining why they were at a mean-nothing Bears-Buccaneers football game when Pete Rose passed Ty Cobb.

The Reds were off on Monday, and on Tuesday, August 10, the national baseball writers—their faces and their jobs safe—were seated in the Riverfront Stadium press box along with 51,000 fans. It was a disappointing night to all but San Diego Padres pitcher LaMarr Hoyt, who pinned an 0-for-4 on Rose, four straight pop-ups. The national writers grumbled. They wanted this chase over. They wanted to go home. They were out of fresh underwear. And I, too, just wanted this to end, wanted to see baseball history and to write it and get on with things.

Even though he was hitting only .267, manager Rose put himself in the lineup, batting second, to face San Diego pitcher Eric Show, known as one of baseball's more intelligent players and a bit of an eccentric, a proponent of the highly controversial right wing John Birch Society. Rose came to bat in the bottom of the first after leadoff hitter Eddie Milner popped out. On Show's fourth pitch, an inside fastball, Rose lobbed one over the shortstop's head and it one-bounced into left fielder Carmelo Martinez's glove—a single to break Ty Cobb's record.

It was bedlam and pandemonium for seven and a half minutes. Standing at first base, San Diego first baseman Steve Garvey applauded into his glove. Tony Perez rushed to the field and lifted Rose to his shoulders. First base coach Tommy Helms, a former Reds second baseman who roomed with Rose on the road in the early days, gave him a hug. Pete Rose Jr., the batboy, rushed to his dad's side. And everybody saw a side of Peter Edward Rose they had never seen. He bowed his head and cried. Later he would say he held it in until "I looked in the sky and saw my dad and Ty Cobb looking down."

Owner Marge Schott rushed to the field, too, and a red Corvette was driven to the field with the license plate that read: PR4192. "This is for you, this is yours," she said. Meanwhile, a distraught and unhappy Show sat on the mound like a kid in a sandbox and watched with a scowl on his face. And up in the press box I observed something I had never seen before and haven't seen since. There is a code in the press box. No cheering. Famous baseball writer Jerome Holtzman wrote a book entitled, *No Cheering in the Press Box*. But on this night, at that historic moment, even though the press box was full, every seat was empty. The writers didn't cheer, but they were standing and applauding, including me.

And who was the Reds pitcher that night? It was rookie Tom Browning, who won twenty games that year and only three years later would make history of his own by pitching a perfect game against the Los Angeles Dodgers. It was September 16, 1988, and it rained all day. And it rained into the night. The start of the game was delayed three hours and didn't start until 10 p.m. They sold only 16,591 tickets because the first place Dodgers were comfortably ahead of the second-place Reds and would win the National League West by five-and-a-half games. Because of the rain and possible postponement, no more than five thousand fans remained, if that many, when the first pitch was thrown. With a midnight deadline I almost left, thinking I could listen on the radio and write a few quick paragraphs from home on this meaningless game. But I stayed. Fortunately. As Browning would later say, "If everybody who told me they were at that game were really at that game we would have had three hundred thousand in the stands."

In Browning's perfect game, his opponent was Tim Belcher, who later pitched for the Reds and he took a no-hitter into the fifth. And he pitched a complete game three-hitter, but lost, 1–0. It was 11:51 when umpire Jim Quick jerked his thumb to call strike three on pinch-hitter Tracy Woodson to complete the perfect game. I had nine minutes until deadline. The *Daily News* graciously gave me five extra minutes to compose a story on the first perfect game in Cincinnati Reds history. I somehow did it. I've never missed a deadline, and I certainly wasn't going to miss this one.

Browning, whose best pitch was a rarely used screwball, a pitch that takes its toll on arms, needed only 102 pitches, seventy-two of them strikes, to do the deed. Said Browning, "I remember Ron Oester tackling me and after that I honestly felt like an out-of-body experience. It was like I was fifteen or twenty feet above the pile and looking down on it." Browning, a great guy who loved beer as much as baseball, was not an effusive quotable guy and rarely said anything memorable after he pitched. After one game, *Dayton Journal Herald* beat writer Paul Meyer approached him and said, "Are you going to say anything interesting or just the same old shit?"

While recalling his perfect game several years later, Browning told me, "I thought it was over when first baseman Mike Marshall drilled one to right field, hit really hard. But Paul O'Neill caught it on the run. And Marshall hit another one that third baseman Chris Sabo backhanded and threw him out. The other hard-hit ball was by catcher Rick Dempsey, and O'Neill ran that one down at the right field line." Opposing pitcher Tim Belcher said, "If I had known Browning was going to pitch a perfect game, I would have pitched one, too. And we would have had a tie."

While Rose received a Corvette from owner Marge Schott for passing Ty Cobb, Browning received nothing. But Schott did purchase a fur coat for his wife. And the baseball, the ball with which he struck out Woodson to end the game? "It sat on my mantel for a while. But I think the kids took it and played with it and it is somewhere in the woods. That's okay. I never did write anything on it."

Remember the screwball? It put tremendous torque on Browning's left arm because the pitch is thrown with an outward twist of the arm. It led to one of the most frightening things I ever witnessed on a baseball field and created a sound I'll never forget.

It was a balmy Monday night in San Diego, where the nights are always balmy. On May 9, 1994. Browning was pitching in the sixth inning and had a 0-and-1 count on Archi Cianfrocco. When he made his next pitch, the sound could be heard where I was sitting in the front row of the Jack Murphy/San Diego Stadium pressbox. It sounded like a rooftop sniper pulling the trigger on a rifle. It was Browning's arm snapping. He broke the humerus bone about three inches below his left shoulder. The ball rolled toward home plate and Browning collapsed on the mound, eyes closed and mouth open, for five minutes.

Browning said his arm was killing him the series before when he pitched in Chicago and took some blood thinner, "Which probably didn't help matters." When he went down he said, "I thought I heard a rifle shot. I thought somebody shot me in the arm. Shortstop Barry Larkin rushed over and I said, 'My arm, Barry. Is my arm still there?' And Larkin said, 'Yeah, it's there, buddy.'"

Browning tried to come back and signed with the Kansas City Royals for the 1995 season. But he made only two starts and was 0-and-2 with an 8.05 earned run average and gave it up. But he remains in the Reds family as a highly respected and productive pitching coach.

13 FALL OF THE IDOL
THE CIRCUS COMES TO TOWN

The year 1989 was the worst year of Pete Rose's life. And because of the investigation into Rose's gambling on baseball, it was also the worst year of mine, professionally, at least.

The dew was still on the Plant City Stadium grass the first week of spring training in 1989, the smell of cow deposits wafting from the pasture across the narrow two-lane road adjacent the facility. *Cincinnati Enquirer* beat writer Mike Paolercio and I drove the forty minutes from Tampa to Plant City from our Sailport Inn condominiums on the Courtney Campbell Causeway. Plant City was a wasteland in central Florida, and we preferred the scent of the Tampa Bay breezes. As we climbed out of my rental car in the stadium parking lot we spotted Rose, the team manager, standing by himself on the infield of one of the practice fields beyond the clubhouse.

We decided to go talk to him, and when we arrived he casually dropped into the conversation a time bomb, one that was ticking, but we didn't hear it. It was just a strange remark. "I won't be here for the next couple of days," Rose said. When we asked why, he said, "The commissioner (Pete Ueberroth) wants to ask my opinion on some things."

What? Why would the commissioner ask a major-league manager to drop everything and travel to New York to ask his opinion on "some things?" Couldn't he do it by telephone? What we didn't know at the time was that Ueberroth was summoning Rose to New York to ask him about his gambling habits and reports that Rose was betting on baseball.

When I returned from spring training, executive sports editor Ralph Morrow called me into his office and asked, "How close are you to Pete

Rose?" I told him, "Very close. I consider him a good friend. After all, I've covered him for sixteen years as a player and as a manager."

Morrow dropped his head and said, "Well, *Sports Illustrated* is coming out with a story that Rose is being investigated for possibly betting on baseball. Can you cover this objectively and do stories on it, or should we put somebody else on it?"

I was a bit miffed. Yes, Rose was a friend. But I considered myself a professional and if I had a job to do, I'd do it. I told him, "Of course I'll do it. It's my beat. My story." Morrow agreed to let me pursue the story, but it was clear that I would be watched closely.

What a story it was, what a circus mess it became, and I was embroiled in it over the next five months, along with every media outlet in the country. When the season began, all three major networks of that time had crews at nearly every game—ABC, NBC, CBS. In addition to covering the games, I had to do daily stories on the investigation as Rose denied, denied, and denied. After games, the clubhouse was a media menagerie. There were so many media stuffing the clubhouse that they not only stepped all over each other, they stepped on the players' equipment and asked them more questions about their manager's gambling habits than they did about games.

Eventually, publicity director Jim Ferguson stepped in. After every game, Rose was taken to an interview room with stipulations that he would answer only questions about the game and nothing about the gambling investigation. We were instructed by Ferguson, "Only questions about the game. The first time anybody asks a question about the investigation will end the interview." And after every game two or three questions would be asked about the game and then one of the network reporters would ask a question about the investigation and that ended the press conference.

Everybody was digging, digging, and digging for any morsel of information about Rose's gambling. Since I was breaking stories nearly every day, the network people followed me everywhere I went, called me at home, surrounded me in the press box. One network offered me $500 a week if I would feed them some of my information. I declined, although I could have used the $500.

I was actually the front guy for the paper. We had three or four investigative reporters working on the story from the inside. They would dig up information, feed it to me, and it was my job to ask Rose about it—and some of the rumors were outlandish, but I had to ask the questions. My friendship with Rose evaporated and he took a "Kill the Messenger" attitude toward me. I was the one asking the questions and writing the stories.

After Rose was banished in August, he appeared in front of Hamilton County Common Pleas Judge Norbert Nadel, seeking an injunction to stop baseball from disqualifying him from the game. Nadel granted a temporary injunction, a decision I called "The ultimate home court decision," in my story.

As I sat in the courtroom, I was joined by *Dayton Daily News* reporter Wes Hills, a talented and hard-digging investigative reporter. He had done considerable work on the Rose case. He wrote stories on the Rose investigation from Dayton and fed me questions to ask Rose. Hill was not a baseball fan and as he sat next to me he looked around the room and asked, "Which one is Pete Rose?"

Rose, of course, had his supporters because they believed him when he said, day after day, that he never bet on baseball. One was radio sports talk show host Bob Trumpy, a former Cincinnati Bengals star who worked for WLW, the team's flagship station that broadcast all the games. Trumpy, a genuinely nice guy and a talented man with a deep, resonant voice, believed Rose and shot down many of my stories on his show. During one show, he said, "If Pete Rose bet on baseball, I'll jump from the top of the Carew Tower (then Cincinnati's tallest building—forty-nine stories)." Trumpy either used a parachute or never jumped because he is still standing tall.

Anybody who knew Rose knew he loved to gamble. He often frequented horse racing and dog racing emporiums. It began when his dad, Harry "Big Pete" Rose took him to River Downs in Cincinnati on the banks of the Ohio River. Horse racing and dog racing, of course, are legal and more than once I attended greyhound races with Rose at Derby Lane in St. Petersburg, Florida, during spring training.

But bet on baseball? Nobody thought Rose would be that reckless. As he walked into the clubhouse every day he couldn't help but see the large placard hanging on the door that listed baseball's rules. Rule 21 states that betting on baseball earns the violator a lifetime ban. But there were hints, and I personally observed one. Baseball hired Washington, D.C., attorney John C. Dowd to investigate Rose. Dowd issued a 225-page document, *The Dowd Report*, on his findings. He mentioned a red, hard cover notebook in which Rose made betting notations. I had seen that notebook in Rose's possession in his office but never asked what it was for.

And there was the day I sat in Rose's office and he made a telephone call to Sparky Anderson, former Reds manager then managing the Detroit Tigers. It was before the advent of interleague play and I heard Rose ask Anderson, "How is your pitcher tonight?" When Rose replaced the telephone into its cradle I asked him why he was interested in the Detroit pitcher that night when the Reds never play the Tigers.

"Ah, you know me, Hal," said Rose. "I'm just interested in everything about baseball."

After mid-August, following Dowd's report, when Rose was banished from baseball for life, I became persona non grata in Rose's eyes. We didn't speak for seventeen years, although he often spoke of me in disparaging ways on a radio show he did from his restaurant, The Pete Rose Ballpark Café, in Boynton Beach, Florida.

After Rose admitted in March of 2007 that he *did* bet on baseball, he began appearing at a sports memorabilia shop in The Forum at Caesars Palace in Las Vegas. During the All-Star break a couple of years later my wife, Nadine, and our friends, Jeff and Nancy Gordon (no, not the NASCAR driver), were in Las Vegas, shopping in the Forum. We walked past the memorabilia shop and Rose was seated inside the door, signing autographs. Nadine spotted him and said, "Why don't you go in and say hello." I looked at her as if marbles were rolling out of her mouth and said, "Are you kidding? Do you want to start a riot? He hates my guts."

She insisted and nearly pushed me in the front door. Rose had his head down, signing a baseball, when I walked in and awkwardly said, "What do you say, old-timer?"

He looked up and his face flushed. But he jumped to his feet, shook my hand, and invited me to sit next to him at the table. He called to an associate and said, "Take our picture." While we talked, the associate developed the picture, put it in a leather case, and he signed it, "To a great Hall of Famer from the Hit King, Pete Rose." And he gave me one of his Reds' game jerseys and signed that, too.

Hal and Pete. Friends again at last.

The season began the next day in New York. When I walked into the Reds clubhouse, team medical director Dr. Tim Kremchek, a close friend to Rose, walked up to me and said, "I hear you saw Pete Rose yesterday."

I was startled. I said, "How in the hell do you know that? I haven't told anybody." He smiled and said, "Pete called me today and said, 'Guess who stopped in to see me in Las Vegas? Hal McCoy. I thought he hated my guts.'"

And that's how Rose and I began speaking again. A few weeks later, Rose showed up at Great American Ball Park, which he often does. He isn't permitted free access. He can't go into the clubhouse and he can't go into the press box. He has to pay his way in and often does, sitting behind home plate in the expensive Diamond Seats. And when they show him on the giant screen on the Great American Ball Park scoreboard, he always draws huge applause and the chant, "Pete, Pete, Pete."

One day after our meeting in Las Vegas, he stepped off the elevator outside the press box in Great American, which is as far as he is permitted to go. I heard he was out there and went to see him. Hall of Fame broad-caster Marty Brennman joined us and we chatted. A fan with a camera spotted us and asked if we would pose for a photograph. We agreed and the man said, "Look at this. Three Hall of Famers." And Rose quickly said, "Well, two-and-a-half."

Rose, of course, is not in the Hall of Fame but should be. Should he be permitted back in the game as a coach or manager? Probably not. Does he belong in the Hall of Fame? Absolutely. Think about it. He has 4,256 hits. For another player to come close to that number he would have to collect two hundred hits for twenty straight years, and he would still be 256 hits short. Who plays twenty years? Who gets two hundred hits every year? Only Peter Edward Rose. Rose not only has the most hits in the history of the game, he has more at-bats and more plate appear-ances. And as he likes to laughingly say, "I also made the most outs in the history of the game."

There is a catch-22 to Rose getting into the Hall of Fame. To be eligible he has to be reinstated to the game and that probably won't hap-pen. Shoeless Joe Jackson was banned as one of the Eight Men Out in the 1919 World Series when several players on the Chicago White Sox conspired to throw the World Series to the Cincinnati Reds. Jackson was part of the original conspiracy, allegedly knew about it, but said nothing. He didn't accept the $5,000 bribe, which would have doubled his salary, and he hit .375 with three doubles, a home run, and six RBI during the World Series.

But Commissioner Kennesaw Mountain Landis banished him and sev-en other members of the team that became known as the Chicago Black Sox. Jackson supporters have tried to clear his name, tried to get him re-instated so he can go into the Hall of Fame, but they've been unsuccessful. So what chance does Rose have?

My contention is that if Rose had admitted his indiscretions imme-diately, shown remorse and apologized to the baseball world right when Ueberroth summoned him to New York, he might have been given a year's suspension. This is a forgiving society. We forgive and forget. But Rose continued his denials for fifteen years, and that is something society can't and won't forget.

Ueberroth resigned as commissioner shortly after the investigation began and it was picked up by new commissioner Bart Giamatti, the man
who banned Rose. There have been fourteen players banned for life under Rule 21. None was ever reinstated. Rose signed a lifetime banishment
agreement, but when he signed it he believed he would get a hearing for
reinstatement after a year or two.

He is still waiting.

14 DOG YEARS

A SCHOTT IN THE DARK

Marge Schott would not utter my name out loud, even though she knew it, and it was obvious she read my stories. The controversial woman owned the Reds from 1984 through 1999, but in 1996 she was banned by Major League Baseball from running the team for a string of racial slurs against African Americans, Japanese, Jews, and a comment about Adolf Hitler of whom she said, "He was good in the beginning." At a party at her Indian Hill mansion, an employee found a swastika armband in a drawer, although I never did find out why the employee was snooping in her belongings.

She maintained ownership until after the 1998 season, although she was not permitted to operate the team or make any decisions after her banishment/suspension in 1996. But she maintained her office in Riverfront Stadium, and everybody surrounding the Reds knew she *was* making decisions.

She called me "that guy from Dayton." Schott had difficulty remembering names and resorted to calling most people "honey" and "babe." When she passed out 1990 World Series rings during a 1991 on the field ceremony, she came to relief pitcher Rob Dibble and paused for a long time before saying, "And here's a good player. (Long pause.) Dibble." She called *Cincinnati Post* beat writer Jeff Horrigan "That red-faced Irish-Catholic guy," and she called *Cincinnati Enquirer* beat writer Chris Haft "That cute little Indian guy," because of Haft's dark complexion and Filipino heritage.

Before MLB banned her, Schott delighted in banning me from the media dining room. At the time, dinner in the dining room was free and writers were given a card to gain entrance. Now all major league teams charge for the meals. Schott banned me four times when I wrote stories about things she didn't want printed.

The first time I was banned was after I wrote a story about her becoming a donut salesman. She hosted a breakfast for season ticket holders and served donuts. Several were left over, so she boxed them up and spent the next few days selling them to office employees. One of her employees told me, I wrote it, and I was banned.

The second time was after Opening Day, 1996, when umpire John McSherry died of a heart attack during the game. Reds employees told me that Schott had removed a card from a bouquet of flowers she received, wishing her good luck for the upcoming season. She wrote another card and placed it on the used flowers and sent them to the umpires' room. I was banned from my seat in the media dining room.

The third time was after the announcement that the Cincinnati Bengals would get a new stadium before the Reds would, and Schott lit into Hamilton County, the City of Cincinnati, and the Bengals, using disparaging remarks about each of them during a spring-training conversation. The season hadn't even started, but Media Relations Director Jon Braude walked up to me the day the story appeared, stuck out his hand, and said, "You know what I want." I handed over my just-issued media dining room pass.

The fourth time was after I wrote a story quoting Barry Larkin, representing the team, complaining about Schott parading her St. Bernard, Schottzie 02, on the AstroTurf playing field before games. Schottzie 02 often did what dogs do, leaving before one game a deposit at Larkin's shortstop position. The mess was cleaned up, but it left a large brown stain on the playing carpet. Larkin told me before the game, laughingly, "If they think I'm going to dive for a ball today, they're crazy." Early in the game, Larkin *did* dive for a ball, right on Schottzie 02's spot, and came up with a brown stain across the wishbone-C on his uniform top. I wrote it. Again, I was banned from crossing the threshold of the media dining room.

But I didn't starve. Outfielder Eric Davis sent me pizzas. And the other writers conducted a canned goods collection and left them at my seat in a large cardboard Campbell's Soup carton. Mostly, though, I brought Subway sandwiches to the ball park.

I was not the only writer banned from the dining room, but I was the only one banned more than once. Writers Rob Parker, Jerry Crasnick, Big Bill Staubitz, and sports cartoonist Jerry Dowling were also banned. We had white baseball caps made up with the words "Barred By Marge" inscribed in red. We wore them proudly, and even Mrs. Schott smiled when she walked past us and saw the caps.

Exiled from the Cincinnati Reds' press lounge, the late Bill Staubitz, Rob Parker, and Hal McCoy sport "Barred by Marge" hats in 1991.

As difficult as Schott was to work for, she loved the fans and was proud of the $1 hot dog she sold at concession stands. And lines to her front row seat behind the Reds dugout formed up the aisle the entire length of the lower deck. She signed autographs and chatted amiably with the fans. But it was no secret that she loved cigarettes and vodka. One day before a game, she boarded the press box elevator on the fourth floor to ride down to the field to her seat. Associated Press writer Joe Kay and I spotted a full bottle of cheap vodka tucked under her arm.

When the game began, it dragged and dragged, a slow-moving affair. Kay said, "They've been playing for an hour and-and-half, and it's only the bottom of the third. And I quickly said, "But Mrs. Schott is at the bottom of the fifth."

Fortunately she never heard *that* remark, and I wasn't banished from the dining room. Nor was I banished when the subject of team marketing surfaced. The team had no marketing strategy and advertised very little. I once asked director of marketing Chip Baker what the team's marketing strategy was, and he said, "It's traditional." I asked what traditional meant and he smiled and said, "We open the ticket windows, sell tickets, and let 'em in." When the team's marketing came up in the press box, I said, "The only marketing Mrs. Schott does is to shop at Kroger for vodka." It was a cruel comment but it received a load of laughs, which is what we were always looking for in the press box during games.

Schott, an animal-lover and huge benefactor to the Cincinnati Zoo, loved to bring animals from the zoo for pre-game parades on Opening Day. In 1998, the last year she owned the team, she brought elephants onto the field for the parade, complete with roustabouts walking behind the pachyderms to catch the droppings.

Pokey Reese, known for his defense, made his debut at shortstop, and it was a memorable day. He made four errors, three in one inning, as the Reds lost to the San Diego Padres, 10–2. The elephants were the high point of the day. After the game, Reese said glumly, "Instead of playing short-stop, I should have been walking behind the elephants with a trash bag. But I probably would have missed."

Schott had a party at her palatial estate in Indian Hill every year for employees and team members. Tuxedos were required and Schott always had an elephant from the Cincinnati Zoo in the backyard. Certain players were required to climb aboard and take a ride. One was Terry Francona, current manager of the Cleveland Indians. He was an extra player for the Reds in 1987 and, yes, he rode the elephant. "You had to ride the elephant if you weren't good enough to say no. I wasn't good enough to say no." Neither was Lloyd McClendon. McClendon, another extra player on that 1987 team and currently manager of the Seattle Mariners, also climbed aboard Dumbo to satisfy Marge.

In the early 1990s, the Reds had a swift-running outfielder named Billy Bates. He made one appearance in the 1990 World Series and had a hit. But his bigger hit was when Schott came up with another promotion involving the Cincinnati Zoo. She decided to stage a match race between Bates and a cheetah from the center-field wall to home plate. And Bates won because the cheetah was cheated. As the race began, Bates' flipped his hat off and the cheetah, obviously a Reds fan, stopped to pick up the hat.

And how do I know Mrs. Schott knew my name? One day Dayton TV sportscaster Mike Hartsock approached me at my press box seat and was laughing heartily.

"What's so funny?" I asked.

He said, "Well, you know Marge keeps Schottzie 02 in her office when she is in there, right? I was just in her office doing an interview and she has a copy of the *Dayton Daily News* on the floor, turned to the sports page with your column picture on it. And you know what Schottzie does on it?"

She famously fired a large portion of her scouting staff and said, "Why do we need scouts? All they do is watch ball games." One surviving scout purchased a straw hat during spring training to fend off the searing Florida sun. When he put it on his expense account, Schott refused to pay it. Knowing he was about to quit, the scout wrote a notation on the bottom of his final expense account: "See if you can find the fucking hat."

When a team hosts the World Series, it always has a huge party for the media and baseball officials. Expenses be damned. They put up huge circus-type tents. They hire bands. They stack tables with shrimp and oysters on the half shell and steak and exotic desserts. In Baltimore they served lobster, whole lobster. I was going through the line after one game and the lobster fell to the floor. As I bent to pick it up, a waiter ran to it, grabbed it, tossed it in the trash and put another whole lobster on my plate. In 1990, when the Reds were in the World Series, the post-game party was held behind home plate at a concession stand where hot dogs and soft drinks were served. They didn't even provide music over the public address system.

When Schottzie, her original St. Bernard died, Schott kept some of the dog's fur in glassine bags and carried them with her. She delighted in walking up to manager Lou Piniella and rubbing the fur on his chest, "For good luck." Lou took it like a trooper but didn't like it.

When Bob Quinn was general manager, she had him run demeaning errands. She took away his spacious office and put him in a smaller office. And she took away his private box in which he watched the games. She also went into a tirade about the team showing out-of-town scores on the scoreboard and said, "It costs money to put those up there, and why should our fans care about the scores of other teams?"

Schott was definitely fan-friendly, but she was a tyrant to work for and employees dove for cover when they saw her coming. She made life miserable for the media relations people. The media game notes, distributed before games, were always four or five pages of information, and Schott demanded that the notes be cut to one page and printed on both sides of that one sheet. The media director used the smallest type possible, almost impossible to read, cramming as much information as he could on that one page.

And Schott was adamant that Mike Ringering not put out too many sheets in a distribution box behind the press box. If she came by during the game and saw some left over, she went into a tirade. The media relations staff used to hide extra sheets in case they were needed and put them in the box after Schott went away. One game, after Ringering thought it was safe, he put the extra sheets in the box. Schott, though, came back for something and saw six or seven sheets sitting in the box. She verbally assaulted Ringering and said, "You know, paper doesn't grow on trees."

As they say, Schott was an equal opportunity bigot. She didn't miss many races or nationalities. Writer Jeff Horrigan and I were sitting in the media dining room at the Sarasota spring training complex, one from which I was never banned, probably because it was named after me, "The Hal McCoy Media Dining Room." Australian pitcher Mark Hutton was in the room with Horrigan and me and Marge heard his Australian accent. She later asked us where he was from and we told her he was a native Australian. She said, "Oh, I don't like Australians." Actually, we later discovered, it was Austrians that Schott, with her German background, didn't like. But she didn't know the difference between Australia and Austria.

When I was permitted in the dining room, I made certain, as did most of the writers, that I went through the buffet line before Marge came in, with her St. Bernard on a leash. She would head behind the counter, go through the food with her fingers, and feed it to the dog.

It all changed for me during Schott's last year as Reds owner when she attended a wedding at which both my wife, Nadine, and I attended. Schott was seated at a table by herself and Nadine felt sorry for her.

"I'm going to go talk to her," said Nadine. "Knock yourself out," I said.

Nadine was with Mrs. Schott for a long time, and after that I could do no wrong against Schott. I continued to write all the absurd things she did and said, but she always smiled at me and said, "Hi, honey."

Nadine told her that we had a blind cocker spaniel and, of course, Marge loved dogs. Nadine told her that I smoked cigars and Marge's husband, Charlie, smoked cigars. Nadine told her that she was a teacher in a parochial school and Marge loved Catholic schools.

That's all it took. I was no longer "that guy from Dayton." She knew my name. Called me by name. I wrote the same stuff I always wrote about her, but she took it with a smile, never again banished me from the dining room, and every time she saw me she asked, "How is that sweet wife of yours and how is that blind cocker spaniel?" I would take a puff on my cigar, blow the smoke up in the air, and smile as I headed for the media dining room and my free meal.

15 SWEET LOU

HEARING THAT DIFFERENT DRUMMER

One of the first times I had a personal chat with Lou Piniella after he was hired before the 1990 season to replace the banished Pete Rose as manager of the Reds, he was sitting at his desk, pondering his team's immediate future. In the previous five years under Rose, the Reds finished second the first four years and slithered to fifth in 1989 as the investigation of Rose's gambling habits infected the clubhouse.

Piniella thought he had the makings of a good team, and that day in his office he looked at me and said, "You've been around this team a long time. What does it need most?"

I was taken aback. No manager or general manager had ever asked my opinion about the inner workings of the team. Without hesitation, I said, "You need a legitimate prototype leadoff hitter." Out of necessity, Rose had used shortstop Barry Larkin to lead off the previous two seasons, and Larkin was out of order. He was a productive hitter, one who could drive in runners as a No. 3 hitter or move runners along as a No. 2 hitter. He wasn't a bad leadoff hitter, but his talents were used to better advantage when he batted second or third.

Piniella decided that third baseman Chris Sabo might be a good choice, but early in the season Piniella said to me, "You were absolutely right. We don't really have a leadoff hitter." And I got the feeling that Piniella trusted my baseball acumen and respected my opinions.

It didn't last long, though. No other manager or general manager ever asked for my opinion on lineups. In fact, it worked just the opposite early in 1993 when Tony Perez was hired to succeed Piniella. The Reds were

19–18 after beating the Colorado Rockies, 14–2, at home on May 16 and packed their gear for a seven-game trip to Los Angeles and San Francisco. It was an unmitigated disaster. They lost six of seven.

On May 22, the Reds were to face the Giants and pitcher Bud Black. Perez did not have regular catcher Joe Oliver in the lineup that day, and Oliver said to me, "Why am I not playing? I hit Black really well." I told Oliver I would check with the manager and I told Perez what Oliver said. Perez checked some statistics and changed the lineup card, inserting Oliver as catcher.

I wrote what I thought was a cute little note about the by-play in my Reds Notebook column and when general manager Jim Bowden read it, he asked one of his assistants, "Who's running this team, the media or the manager?" When the team returned home the next day, 20–24, Bowden picked up the telephone and called Perez. Instead of asking him to come to the stadium, Bowden told Perez on the telephone that he was fired.

The only other time was I remotely involved in the dismissal of a manager was in 1984, and it was also a man who didn't manage a complete season. Vern Rapp was hired to manage the 1984 Reds and things didn't go well. On May 1, the Reds completed a three-game sweep in Montreal and were 17–14. I was sitting next to Rapp in Montreal's Dorval Airport, waiting to board the Reds chartered airplane, when he turned to me and said, "I really think we are going to win this thing."

Not quite.

On August 14 in St. Louis, another of those hot, steamy days under The Gateway Arch, the Reds were on a seven-game losing streak. I was in the Busch Stadium press box when I heard a scout from another team say that he heard the Reds were making a change. So I called Bill Williams, one of the Reds' owners and asked if the team was making a change. He confirmed that Rapp was being fired.

The Reds were taking batting practice and Rapp was leaning against the batting cage as I hung up the phone. I immediately trudged down to the field and walked up to Rapp.

"What's up, Hal?" he asked.

"I'm sorry to hear that you've been fired," I said, assuming he knew.

He turned on his heels, called the team off the field, and gathered them in the clubhouse. "It doesn't look good for me," he told them. "But I'm still your manager until I'm told otherwise." He managed that night and the Reds won, 3–2, and he was informed of his dismissal after the game. He went out with a win, but I had the story in the paper that he was fired. What I *didn't* have was the story that his replacement was Peter Edward Rose, returning to Cincinnati as player-manager.

But in 1990, Piniella searched and searched, all during that glorious run to the National League championship and the World Series title, for that elusive leadoff hitter. He eventually returned Larkin to leadoff and dropped Sabo to the bottom of the order, where he hit .563 with two homers with five RBIs in the four-game sweep of the Oakland A's.

Sabo was a curious fellow, short of stature, slim of waist, and the owner of an out-dated flattop haircut. He wore thick goggles held on by an equally thick elastic band when he played. When Pete Rose managed he nicknamed Sabo "Spuds," after a famous dog on Budweiser commercials named Spuds McKenzie. Strangely, Sabo did resemble Spuds.

Sabo once walked into a barber shop in Atlanta and asked the proprietor if he knew how to cut a flat-top. When the owner said he did, Sabo climbed into the chair. Halfway through the haircut, Sabo looked into the mirror, didn't like what he saw, and bolted from the shop, fleeing down a mall hall with half a haircut. Another time he was in a cab in Pittsburgh, en route to the ballpark when the driver lit a cigarette. Sabo asked him to put it out and the driver refused, so Sabo fled the cab and walked the rest of the way to the ballpark.

It was 1990 and Sabo was driving a 1981 Ford Escort with three hundred thousand miles on it. When asked why he didn't purchase a new car, he said, "Why? The car I'm driving is a good car. Nothing wrong with it." His best friend, outfielder Paul O'Neill, was in the car with him one day and O'Neill asked if they could turn on the radio and listen to some music. "Yeah, okay," said Sabo. "The broken antenna is on the floor, but if you hold it out the window the radio plays just fine."

Sabo was sitting at his locker one day, a forlorn look on his face, his head down as he stared at the floor. I asked him what was the matter and he said, "Aw, they're trading all my best friends."

Since the Reds hadn't made a trade all year, I asked, "Who?" And he said, "Paulie." He meant Paul O'Neill, whom the Reds had traded to the

New York Yankees over the winter of 1992. Sabo was pining for O'Neill at mid-season, 1993.

Sabo liked to arrive early to the clubhouse so he could commandeer the stereo system and play either Frank Sinatra or the University of Michigan fight song, "Hail to the Victors!" It drove the rest of the team batty and most of them evacuated the clubhouse for early batting practice.

There was a time when Sabo didn't like something I wrote about him and began avoiding me. He didn't confront me, didn't tell me he was miffed with me, he just avoided me. On a trip to Philadelphia, I was walking down Broad Street from lunch back to the Hershey Hotel. I saw Sabo coming the other way. Suddenly he disappeared. He walked into the entrance of a parking garage. After I passed and walked half-a-block, I looked back and there was Sabo emerging from the garage and headed up Broad Street the other way.

He loved to experiment with bats, always searching for the right stick of wood. One day he was rummaging through a storage room under Riverfront Stadium and found a bat he really liked and decided to use it that night in the game. He swung at a pitch, fouled it off, and the bat cracked. Sabo knew it but continued using it. On the next pitch he swung and the bat shattered, spraying cork and super balls all over the infield. Everybody was laughing, including the umpires, but crew chief Ed Montague ejected Sabo for using a corked bat. Sabo swore it wasn't his bat and later investigation revealed it probably belonged to first baseman Hal Morris, who corked it as a gag to try in batting practice but not for use in a game.

Asked why he didn't toss aside the bat when he cracked it, Sabo said, "I was hoping to draw a walk." In the umpires' room after the game, Montague said, "We figured it wasn't his bat. It didn't have his name on it." Then pounding his fist like a gavel in a judge's hand, Montague said, "So, man guilty."

Sabo had an incident with umpire Charlie Williams one night when Williams, on a close play, called Sabo out at first base. Sabo protesteth too loudly and too longly and was ejected. Williams was working home plate the next night, so Sabo took a magic marker and wrote on the knob of his bat, "Bite me." If Williams saw it, he didn't acknowledge it, or Sabo probably would have taken an early shower two nights in a row.

Sabo not only marched to the beat of a different drummer, he *was* the drummer. But he was a fan favorite, a player who gave everything he had every second he was on the field. He was a great athlete, a scratch golfer. And he was National League Rookie of the Year in 1988 and a three-time All-Star. But his best attribute was his attitude that he didn't care what people thought about his goggles, his car, or his music. Like Frank Sinatra's "My Way," Sabo did it his way and he did it well.

Piniella marched to a different drummer, too. Of all the managers I covered, he hated losing more than any of them and never hid his feelings.

In 1990, the Reds won thirty of their first forty-two games and seemed on their way to an easy divisional championship. But it wasn't easy because after that 30–12 start they finished 61–59 and had to hold off a couple of late-season charges by the San Francisco Giants and Los Angeles Dodgers. They held on and beat the Dodgers by five games and led the division wire-to-wire, maintaining first place from game one to game 162.

Nevertheless, because of their barely over .500 finish in their last 120 games, the media began saying that the Reds backed into the championship. And that term, "backed-in," rankled manager Piniella no end. He was close to exasperation before the playoffs began when a gentleman carrying a large tape recorder walked into his office. There was a decal on the recorder identifying it as belonging to a Cincinnati Christian radio station. The man asked, "Can I ask you a few questions?" Piniella said yes and the man clicked on the recorder and stuck a microphone into Piniella's face.

"Do you think the team backed into the championship?" the man asked. Piniella was close to apoplexy. He started his answer with, "Listen, my friend." Oh, oh. When Piniella answered a question by starting it with, "Listen, my friend," the "friend" was in for an ear-blasting. And he said, "Have you ever screwed a woman from behind?" The man stood there stunned. And Piniella added, "Well, if you have, is it screwing or is it *screwing*?"

The man clicked off the recorder, thanked Piniella, and left the room. After he was out of earshot, I said, "Lou, did you know that guy is from a Christian radio station?" Said Piniella, "I don't care, he should know better than to ask that stupid question."

There was the day in Riverfront Stadium when Piniella disagreed with a call at first base. After flinging his hat and kicking dirt on Rennert's shoes, he removed first base from its moorings and flung it into right field. Unhappy with his distance, Piniella walked to where the base landed, picked it up, and hurled it deeper into right field.

He laughed about it later and said, "It was embarrassing. I'm sorry I did that. My wife (Juanita, a lovely lady) wouldn't speak to me for a week." Broadcaster Joe Nuxhall said, "I'll bet if you knew your wife wouldn't speak to you, you would have done it a long time ago." Piniella smiled and said, "No, no. And I won't ever do that again." He didn't, but he often said he wanted to fling some more bags because it was self-satisfying and released steam.

There was a game in San Diego when the Reds blew a big lead and lost. Pitcher Ted Power threw back-to-back wild pitches in the ninth inning, and the winning run scored on the second one. After games, the clubhouse attendant in San Diego always put a washtub filled with ice and bottled beer on the floor next to the manager's desk. When writers walked into the office after the tough loss, the washtub was upside down and ice covered the office floor, which looked as if a hockey game could break out. Said Piniella with a grin, "Watch the ice, guys."

For some reason, a sponsor put a large gumball machine in Piniella's Riverfront Stadium office. It had a plastic globe about the size of a beach ball, filled with gumballs. When writers entered his office one night after another bad defeat, the plastic globe was in hundreds of tiny pieces and the floor was covered with marble-sized, multi-colored gum balls. "Watch the gumballs," Piniella said with a smirky smile.

There was a night when Piniella didn't use Rob Dibble, out of the famed Nasty Boys bullpen, in a game in which he should have pitched. I asked Piniella after the game, "Why didn't Dibble pitch?" Piniella said, "He told me before the game that he had some tenderness in his elbow." So I went to Dibble and asked, "What's wrong with your elbow?" He said, "What do you mean?" I said, "Your manager said you have tenderness in your elbow." Said Dibble, "Well, the manager is a liar."

I went dutifully back to Piniella's office and said, "Your closer (Dibble) just called you a liar." Piniella bolted from his office, nearly flattening me against the door, ran into the clubhouse, and jumped on Dibble. The skirmish was quickly over, but I had a great story.

Piniella was on the last year of his contract in 1992 and wanted to re-up, wanted to discuss a new contract. But owner Marge Schott kept putting him off, wouldn't talk about a new contract. And it angered Piniella. The team was in San Diego in mid-September, near the end of the season, and Piniella's contract situation was not resolved. Piniella and I shared a love of horse racing, and on a Friday night after the game, Piniella said, "Hey, they're running at Del Mar. We have a night game on Saturday, so let's go take in a few races."

I agree and we drove to the track in my rental car. Piniella had the touch that day and cashed tickets in three of the first four races. But it was getting late, time to leave for the ballpark. I looked at my watch and said, "Lou, we better leave. Batting practice will be starting soon and you haven't made out a lineup card." He didn't look up from his program and said, "Just a couple more races."

He hit a couple of more winners and it was *really* getting late. Reluctantly, he arose from his chair and said, "Let's go." As we were rolling down the interstate toward the ballpark I said, "Man, it's late. It's time for batting practice." Lou shrugged and said, "Ah, hell. I don't care. I'm not coming back next year anyway." I stepped on the gas to speed to the ballpark because I had another great story.

Dibble wasn't the only periodic pain in Piniella's posterior. Dibble was part of the Nasty Boys bullpen triumvirate—Dibble, Randy Myers, and Norm Charlton, who graduated from Rice University with three degrees. Myers was an enigma, a great pitcher, but a man of many eccentricities. When he was on the mound, he ran around indiscriminately. If a ball was popped up near the other team's dugout, Myers sprinted to the spot, often beating the catcher or first baseman. But there was a game when a batter put down a sacrifice bunt. Myers charged it and flubbed it and it cost the Reds the game. Afterwards a fuming Piniella told the writers, "Myers runs from foul line to fucking foul line, but he can't field a fucking bunt."

Myers later thought he might be traded and told the press that it would be okay with him. Myers's locker was right around the corner from Piniella's office. When Piniella heard about Myers's trade talk, he waited until he knew Myers was at his locker and said in a loud voice in his office, "You know, to be traded, some other team has to want you. If Myers doesn't want to play here, just take off the uniform and go the hell home. How's that?"

Piniella, though, was a great manager and a great man. He knew the game, and he knew how to push the right buttons on his players. When it comes to naming my all-time favorite people, Lou Piniella is at the top of the list.

16 | DAVEY & MARGE

REDS' THEATRE OF THE ABSURD

After the New York Mets fired him early into the 1990 season, Davey Johnson was out of baseball for two years, sharpening his chipping and putting on various golf courses. His 1986 Mets had won the World Series that became forever known for the ball that rolled through the legs of Boston Red Sox first baseman Bill Buckner in game six.

The '86 Mets were a team loved in New York and despised and reviled everywhere else. Jeff Perlman, in his excellent book, *The Bad Guys Won*, described them as a brawling, boozing, bimbo-chasing championship team. They had nicknames like "Doc" (Dwight Gooden), "Nails" (Lenny Dykstra), "Straw" (Darryl Stawberry), "Mookie" (William Wilson), and "The Kid" (Gary Carter).

Of the 1986 World Series, Mets pitcher Bob Ojeda would say, "I would rather eat shit than lose to the Boston Red Sox. We were a throwback, man. We were like, 'Gimme a steak, gimme a beer, gimme a smoke, and get the fuck out of our way.'" Of the team's propensity for heavy drinking, pitcher Doug Sisk said, "You don't win a World Series drinking milk." One of the zaniest Mets was Roger McDowell, a prank-playing pitcher who is now a highly respected pitching coach. Of McDowell, Kevin Mitchell said, "What do I say about Roger McDowell? How about this? 'The man was insane.'"

That was the team that Davey Johnson managed to 108 wins during the regular season and the 1986 World Series title, a team that destroyed the inside of a chartered United Airlines DC-10 on its flight from Houston after winning an emotional National League Championship Series six-game playoff with the Houston Astros.

Cincinnati Reds general manager Jim Bowden fired his manager, Tony Perez, just forty-four games into the 1993 season when the team was 20–24 and hired Johnson, handing over a motley group of players that would finish the season in fifth place in the seven-team National League West with a 73–89 record, thirty-one games behind the Atlanta Braves. The Reds used twenty-five different pitchers that season but Jose Rijo was the only one who seemed to know the difference between a fastball and a slider. Rijo, an upbeat, always smiling, ever optimistic Dominican, never visited the training room, never placed an ice pack on his shoulder. He survived by rubbing snake oil on his shoulder, keeping a bottle of the stuff on his locker shelf, complete with the dead snake coiled in the bottom of the jar. On hot days he walked in front of the Riverfront Stadium stands and soaked fans with a giant squirt gun.

Over the winter, Bowden signed free agent left-handed pitcher John Smiley, a quiet, moody guy who sat in front of his locker for two days before every start wearing earphones and daring anybody to say a single word to destroy his concentration. After losses—and there were nine of them with only three wins in 1993—his post-game interviews were terse, one-word answers. Most writers avoided him. Captain Barry Larkin, the supreme professional, observed Smiley's act for as long as he could stand it. After another loss Smiley was being obstinate with the media and Larkin said in a loud voice, so everybody in the clubhouse could hear it, "That's not how we do things around here. We show respect to the beat writers. They are just doing their job." It was a pattern Larkin followed throughout his long tenure with the Reds. He policed the clubhouse, made certain every player, rookie or veteran, acted in a professional manner with the writers. It is why there were seldom issues between players and writers.

There was an incident before the start of the 1990 playoffs involving relief pitcher Rob Dibble and *Cincinnati Enquirer* beat writer Mike Paolercio. When Paolercio entered the clubhouse, Dibble walked up and dumped a bucket of ice water over Paolercio's head and said, "That's what I think of what you wrote today." A mystified Paolercio wondered what set off Dibble and found out only later it was a headline on one of his stories. Unbeknownst to Dibble and most every player and fan, writers don't put headlines on their stories. A copyreader/editor at the paper does that, and writers often encounter problems with players over headlines. Afer Dibble's showering of Paolercio, Rijo dug a new shirt out of his locker and gave to the writer. And Larkin took Dibble aside for some refresher counseling.

One of the few times I encountered difficulty with a player was over a headline that wasn't even in my newspaper. I walked into the Pittsburgh Pirates clubhouse one day and pitcher Bruce Kison called me over to dress me down. "You asked me to appear at a luncheon for nothing and I did it. Then you write a headline in your paper making fun of me." I said, "What headline? I didn't even write about you today." Kison scrunched up his face and said, "Aren't you Bob Hertzel?" He thought I was the beat writer for the *Cincinnati Enquirer* and, of course, Hertzel didn't even write the headline that infuriated Kison.

Not only was Larkin the captain, he was The Honorable Barry Larkin, judge of the team's Kangaroo Court. Larkin would grab a mop and stuff the handle down the back of a black robe and use the mop as a judge's wig. Players were called before Judge Larkin for a myriad of offenses—missed signs, bad base running, throwing to the wrong base, missing planes or buses, disrespecting teammates or the media, wearing tasteless K-Mart shirts, eating too many Hershey bars, dozing off in the clubhouse—whatever Larkin determined needed a fine. And his decisions were final, no Court of Appeals.

Major League Baseball made a major revision before the 1994 season, breaking up the two-division system in each league to three divisions, placing the Reds in the new National League Central with St. Louis, Houston, Pittsburgh, and Chicago. Bowden made an off-season deal, trading catcher Don Wilson, a No. 1 draft pick, and relief pitcher Bobby Ayala, to Seattle for second baseman Bret Boone and pitcher Erick Hanson. In the middle of spring training he signed free agent Tony Fernandez to play third base, and two months into the season he signed free agent Kevin Mitchell, who was sitting home in San Diego without a job.

Boone was an instant success, both at the plate and in the field, and was a clubhouse clown. Catcher Joe Oliver was another clubhouse cutup, and his wit and humor made him a popular locker stop for the writers. He had an extra large head and would say, "I need it for my extra-large brain." One day Boone stopped at Oliver's locker, where I was standing, as I often did to talk with Oliver, and said, "Which would you rather have, a million dollars or Oliver's head full of nickels?" Relief pitcher Jeff Brantley wore cowboy boots, hence his nickname, "Cowboy." One day Boone fetched a pair of Brantley's expensive boots and put them on and paraded around the clubhouse, stark naked except for Brantley's boots.

The season began under storm clouds, a threat of a players' strike. But under Davey Johnson, the Reds were transformed into winners. By August 12, the Reds led the National League Central by a half-game over the Houston Astros. The owners were fighting to implement a salary cap and the players were fighting against it. When no progress was made through negotiations, the players went on strike on August 12. And that was the end of the season. The season was canceled, including the playoffs and the World Series. And for leading the division at the time the Reds received nothing.

When the season ended, Boone was hitting .320 with twelve homers and sixty-eight RBI. Kevin Mitchell, the man nobody wanted, was hitting .326 with thirty homers and seventy-seven RBI and Johnson said, "Mitch could roll out of bed and hit .300 in his pajamas." Sometimes Mitchell showed up in the clubhouse in white pants and a white guayabera that resembled pajamas. Hal Morris hit .335 with ten homers and seventy-eight RBI. Morris was fifth in the National League in batting average, but far behind San Diego's Tony Gwynn, who was hitting .394 and deprived of a chance at .400.

The Reds' pitching wasn't much that season. Even Jose Rijo was a bit off, 9–6 with a 3.08 ERA when the strike hit. The surprise was a left-handed pitcher named Pete Schourek, a free agent signed by Bowden off the scrap heap just as the season began. Schourek had encountered arm problems and the New York Mets dumped him. Schourek resembled Kramer from the television show *Seinfeld*. He even wore a tee shirt with Kramer's picture on it under his uniform when he pitched. Johnson called him, "a riverboat gambler," because when Schourek pitched he never showed emotion and displayed the guts of a card player who bluffed with nothing in his hand. Schourek was 7–2 with a 4.09 ERA when the players walked away from their jobs.

The strike was not settled over the winter, and baseball came up with an ill-fated alternative. They were not going to cancel the 1995 season.

They were going to use replacement players—strikebreakers—to play the season. It reached comedic proportions. Anybody who walked off the street could try out for the Reds. The man who drove the team bus in spring training told Bowden he could pitch. They gave him a tryout and he couldn't throw the ball from the pitcher's mound to home plate without the ball bouncing twice.

The Reds brought in one of their long-time minor-league players with the most descriptive name imaginable. He was Motorboat Jones, an outfielder who mopped gyms in Gadsden, Alabama, during the off-season. He played ten years in the minors without advancing above Double-A, and hardly anybody knew his real name was Eugene. He said he earned his nickname as a kid when he made sounds like a motorboat putt-putting out of the dock. The Reds also signed third baseman Barbaro Garbey. He was thirty-nine and hadn't played since appearing in thirty games for the 1988 Texas Rangers. Before that he played 196 games for the 1987–'88 Detroit Tigers.

At mid-spring, general manager Jim Bowden showed his disdain for the replacement system. He made an announcement that the Reds had signed a mystery player and that he would show up in camp the next day. When I arrived at the Plant City, Florida, camp the next day and walked into the clubhouse I saw a vision from the past, the distant past. Stuffing his portly body into a Reds' uniform was forty-eight-year-old Pedro Borbon. And that age was questionable because it was suspected he was even older when he had last pitched in the majors in 1980—fifteen years before that day in the Reds' clubhouse.

Manager Davey Johnson completely ignored the replacement players. While the so-called team was working out, Johnson sat in his office talking to the writers, about fishing holes around Plant City and the golf courses he planned to play or had already played. When the exhibition game began, Johnson planted a folding chair outside the dugout, sometimes facing the stands, so he could talk to the fans or his wife, Susan.

The farce ended just before Opening Day. The replacement players were getting ready for Opening Day in the Riverfront Stadium clubhouse when the strike was settled. The clubhouse staff passed out trash bags for the players to stuff their belongings into and vacate the premises. One player survived, the one replacement player for the Reds who was legitimate. He was pitcher Rick Reed and he had pitched with limited success for eight years in the majors, with the Pittsburgh Pirates, Kansas City Royals, and the Texas Rangers, posting a 10–12 career record.

As a strikebreaker he was shunned and ignored in the clubhouse and told me, "The reason I signed to be a strikebreaker was because I needed the money for my family. My mother was living out of a car." He only appeared in four games for the Reds—seventeen innings—before he was released. But the New York Mets signed him as a free agent before the 1996 season and he won fifty-six games over the next five years.

Davey Johnson and Marge Schott were never compatible. Johnson was his own man and Schott was her own woman. And they never met in the middle. It reached the Theatre of the Absurd at the end of the 1994 season. Schott wanted to fire Johnson after the '94 season, even though he had the team in first place when the strike began. She gave him a one-year reprieve and no more. Johnson could manage the 1995 season, then he would be replaced by Ray Knight, who played for Johnson on the 1986 Mets. Knight was installed as Johnson's bench coach and Johnson was told that no matter how the team did—even if it won the World Series—he wouldn't be back. His offense? Schott was not pleased that Johnson was living with his girlfriend, Susan, a lovely woman deeply involved in charity work. Johnson and Susan married after the 1994 season, but it made no difference.

Johnson was a lame-duck manager in 1995, and he nearly took the team to the World Series. Bowden made no moves in the off-season, standing pat with the hand that led the division when the strike hit. But he tried something during spring training. He signed forty-year-old pitcher Jack Morris, winner of 254 major-league games and the reputation of a big-game pitcher for the Detroit Tigers and Minnesota Twins.

Late in camp, just before it was time to start the season, I arrived early in the morning. As I walked in the front door, Jack Morris was walking out of it, carrying a bag. It didn't look good. I turned on my heels and followed Morris as he scrambled into his Corvette. Before he could start the engine I asked, "What's up?" He told me he had been released and that his career probably was over. As he talked, tears began streaming down his face. I asked a couple more questions and decided enough was enough. The man was in severe emotional pain and it was time to let him go. I stood in the parking lot and watched the Corvette leave the parking lot and turn left on Plant Road, a man driving to unwanted retirement.

The season was shortened to 144 games because of the strike and the Reds ran away with the division, winning eighty-five of the 144 games and beating the second-place Houston Astros by nine games.

On July 25, Bowden made a meaningful trade when he acquired right-handed pitchers Dave Burba and Mark Portugal from the San Francisco Giants for five players, the most significant of which were outfielder Deion Sanders and relief pitcher Scott Service. Burba went 6–2 the rest of the way, pitching both as a starter and out of the bullpen. Portugal, too, won six games as a starter. Then on July 31 he added another pitcher, left-hander David Wells, trading No. 1 draft pick C.J. Nitkowski to the Detroit Tigers.

But I felt I made the best trade that season. I walked into the clubhouse one day wearing a black baseball cap with the MLB logo in gold on the front. I received it free from Major League Baseball. Left-handed relief pitcher Chuck McElroy spotted the hat and said, "Hey, I like that hat. Where can I get one?" I told him I didn't know and he said, "What will you take for it?" He thought a moment and said, "Do you like cowboy boots?" I had never worn a pair but thought I'd like to try them, so I said yes. "What size do you wear?" I told him I wore thirteens and he said, "Perfect. Bring me the hat tomorrow." I brought the hat and McElroy presented me with a pair of black Tony Lama ostrich boots—a $600 pair of boots for a free hat.

Larkin led the way offensively by hitting .319 with fifty-one stolen bases, fifteen homers, sixty-six RBI, and he was named National League Most Valuable Player. Manager Davey Johnson managed some great players during his years with the New York Mets and later the Los Angeles Dodgers and Baltimore Orioles. Asked who was the best player he ever managed, he said without a pause, "Barry Larkin. He did so much for a team, on the field and in the clubhouse. There wasn't anything he couldn't do and he was consistently the best player I ever managed."

Outfielder Reggie Sanders hit .306 and led the team in home runs with twenty-eight and in RBI with 99. Santiago hit .289 with eleven homers and 44 RBI. The riverboat gambler, Schourek, went 18–7 with a 3.27 ERA and John Smiley, who lived up to his name by smiling a lot that year, was 12–5 with a 3.46 ERA. Wells, an eccentric fellow who later pitched a perfect game for the New York Yankees—and said he did it with a hangover—had a tattoo of his son stenciled life-sized on his back. Wells, too, won six games down the stretch for the Reds.

The Reds played the Los Angeles Dodgers in the National League Division Series and won three straight games in the best-of-five series, placing them in the National League Championship Series against the Atlanta Braves. Since the Braves were overloaded with left-handed hitters, Bowden and Johnson decided to start all left-handed pitching against them. The Braves had Tom Glavine, John Smoltz, Greg Maddu, and Steve Avery lined up, and it didn't go well for the Reds.

The first two games could have gone either way. Pete Schourek faced Glavine in game one and the Braves won in eleven innings, 2–1. John Smiley faced Smoltz in game two and the Braves won in ten innings, 6–2. David Wells faced Maddux in game three and the Braves won, 5–2. Johnson brought back Schourek for game four to face Avery, and Avery shut out the Reds, 5–0.

It was a nightmare for Reginald Laverne Sanders, the Reds outfielder who had his best season. The post-season was disastrous. In twenty-nine postseason at-bats he struck out nineteen times and hit .138. Despite a good major-league career, he is just like Bill Buckner. Buckner is remembered for that ground ball trickling though his legs, and Sanders is remembered for postseason futility.

Sanders, though, became a good luck charm later in his career. He played for three teams in the early 2000s and all three teams made the World Series—the 2001 Arizona Diamondbacks, the 2002 San Francisco Giants, and the 2004 St. Louis Cardinals.

The Reds? Not so lucky. After the 1995 National League Championship Series the Reds would not return to the playoffs for fifteen years.

17 | McKEON IN TOWN

The first time I met Jack McKeon he became a friend for life. He had just been hired by Cincinnati Reds general manager Jim Bowden as a special assistant, and it was an early spring training day in Plant City, Florida, in 1996. McKeon was already a baseball icon and had been for nearly twenty years as a manager and general manager at several venues, most notably as general manager for the San Diego Padres.

I had never met him personally, but on that day he walked up to me on a back field, a cigar stuck firmly between his lips. Cigars were his trademark and he was seldom seen without one. He stopped and handed me a Padrón Aniversario, a $15 cigar and one of my favorites. That's when he became a friend for life. From that day on, McKeon and I smoked hundreds of cigars together, mostly ones he gave me.

In 2003, McKeon was a special assistant to Florida Marlins owner Jeffrey Loria. The team spent nearly $200 million in the off-season, expecting big things. They got little things and were 16–22 on May 11. Manager Jeff Torborg was fired and Loria asked the seventy-three-year-old McKeon to take over. McKeon not only righted the listing ship, he steered Florida to a World Series championship. The Marlins went 75–49 under McKeon the rest of the season, good enough for the National League wild card. They won the National League pennant, beating the Chicago Cubs, then beat the New York Yankees in the World Series, making McKeon the oldest manager in history to win a World Series. That World Series was an unexpected pleasure for me, a royal treat with a smoky environment.

Before Game Three of the World Series in Miami, McKeon spotted me on the field and we immediately retreated to a far corner of the Marlins dugout. McKeon lit up a cigar, handed me one, and I said, "We can smoke here?" McKeon drew a deep breath and exhaled. "I'm the special assistant to the owner and manager. I can do what I want to do," he said. He was right. Security people walked past and said nothing. Marlins players and coaches walked by and said nothing.

So we puffed and reminisced. And it became a daily ritual, a way for McKeon to escape all the pre-game hassles. The next day we retreated to a small room behind the dugout, just McKeon and me. And the Marlins, huge underdogs, beat the Yankees in six games. After the World Series, Loria presented McKeon with the keys to a new BMW and while McKeon was appreciative, he asked me, "What in the hell do I do with a BMW? It's too high-falutin' for me. I'm a Chevy-Ford kind of guy."

When McKeon managed the Reds from 1997 through 2000 we often smoked cigars behind the closed door of his closet-sized office, smoke hanging in the air like rain clouds. He'd often keep me in there until almost game time. One night I had work to do about an hour before game time and got up to leave. McKeon said, "No, no. Sit down." I asked why he liked to keep me in the office so close to game time and he said, "Jim Bowden hates cigar smoke and he won't come here bothering me before the game if we stay in here smoking." So we puffed and puffed and puffed and Bowden stayed away.

McKeon was a devout Catholic and never missed Mass, not even on the road. One day in Milwaukee, McKeon lit up one his expensive Padróns as we walked out of the hotel and headed for a nearby cathedral. He had only puffed it a few times when we reached the door and McKeon frantically searched for a place to put his cigar. He finally placed it carefully on a windowsill near the doors and we walked in.

After the Mass we stopped outside the doors and McKeon frantically searched for his cigar. No cigar. He checked the ground. He checked the steps. He checked the window again. No cigar. We headed across the street to cut through a public park between the church and the hotel. As we passed a bench a bedraggled street person stopped us. Holding up a barely smoked Padrón, the man asked McKeon, "Hey, Mac, you got a light?"

McKeon whipped out a lighter and torched the cigar. As we walked away he said, "I've done my good deed for the day."

Another time, also in Milwaukee, McKeon, his bench coach and constant companion, Harry Dunlop, and I were sitting in McKeon's suite. Although it was against the law, we, of course, were smoking cigars. McKeon would open all the windows and stuff towels around the smoke detectors. On this night it didn't work. The alarm went off, all over the hotel. People vacated their rooms and several pieces of Milwaukee Fire Department equipment screeched to a halt in front of the famous and rumored-to-be-haunted Pfister Hotel. We all knew what was happening, but McKeon, cigar still lit and in his hand, was walking around the hotel lobby asking everybody, "What happened? What's going on?" Oh, we knew what was going on.

When he managed the Reds, McKeon decided one year that the bulge over his belt didn't look good in those tight baseball uniforms so he decided to shed a few pounds. He began walking inside the stadium, the circumference of the field, several laps. He did it in shorts and a tee shirt, but the lit cigar was always there. As he chugged along, smoke from the cigar trailing over his head, he resembled an old-time steam locomotive.

In my humble opinion, and, yes, I'm prejudiced, Jack McKeon belongs in the Hall of Fame. He is the only manager in history to win a thousand games as a manager in the minor leagues and a thousand games as a major-league manager. Everywhere he went he turned teams from losers into winners—Kansas City, San Diego, Oakland, Cincinnati, and Florida. He remains trim and sharp and alert and says he wants to mange when he is ninety to eclipse the age record of owner-manager Connie Mack, who managed the Philadelphia Athletics until he was eighty-seven. When Florida manager Edwin Rodriguez quit in June of the 2011 season, Loria came calling again. McKeon, at age eighty, finished that season as the team's manager.

When McKeon managed all those years in the minors he definitely had fun. He managed the Class AAA Denver Bears and his team had trouble with Portland because Portland was full of speedy players. It seemed that they beat out every close play at first base—*bam, bam,* safe. So before an important late-season series against Portland in Denver, McKeon held a private meeting with the stadium's head groundskeeper. He had a special request. The groundskeeper said, "Sure, I can do that."

The three-game series was played and the Bears won all three. And on nearly every close play at first base, the Portland base runner was out. How could that be? Much later McKeon revealed his secret: "I asked the groundskeeper to move first base back from ninety feet to ninety-one feet. That one foot made the difference and nobody ever suspected. Baseball truly *is* a game of inches."

In the lower minors, where managers have to coach third base, McKeon had a young Latino who constantly ran through McKeon's stop sign at third base and got thrown out at home. After it happened for the fourth time in half a season, McKeon told the kid, "The next time you run through a stop sign I'm going to pull out a pistol and shoot you dead." Then McKeon went to a sporting goods store and purchased a starter's pistol.

McKeon tucked the pistol into his back pocket and waited. A few games went by and eventually, the kid was on second base, and a ball was hit to shallow center field. The kid headed for third and McKeon held up the stop sign. Without hesitating, the kid rounded third and headed for home. McKeon withdrew the starter's pistol and fired. The kid dropped to his belly halfway home, expecting blood to be spurting from his back. "He realized he wasn't shot, but he never again ran through one of my stop signs," said McKeon.

McKeon first made his name as a general manager for the San Diego Padres in the early 1980s and earned his nickname, "Trader Jack." He would listen to any trade proposal and if he thought it beneficial to the Padres, he would make the trade. During the winter meetings one year, nothing was happening. No trades, no deals. So McKeon set up a table in the hotel lobby that resembled some kid's lemonade stand. Sitting on the table was his handmade sign: "Open for Business."

McKeon's 1984 San Diego team made it to the World Series, wearing those hideous mustard yellow and dirt brown uniforms that resembled something a baby leaves in its diaper. They lost to the Detroit Tigers, a night I shall never forget. After the game, when my writing was done, I left the stadium and boarded a media bus. Fans were out of control. They pounded on the windows, broke out the headlights, and began rocking the bus. We evacuated the bus and, as a group for self-preservation, walked down the middle of Michigan Avenue the two miles to the hotel, passing a burning taxicab on our way. Our password to remain unharmed as we walked was to shout to everybody we saw, "Go Tigers."

McKeon, the special assistant, left the front office and slipped into the Reds manager's office in mid-1997 to replace fired Ray Knight. By 1999 he had a contender. Just before spring training of 1999 the Reds made a significant trade, sending outfielder Reggie Sanders to the San Diego Padres for outfielder Greg Vaughn. Vaughn only played one year for the Reds but he had a lasting influence. Before Vaughn's arrival, the Reds still adhered to an old, old club rule instituted in the early 1970s by former club president/general manager Bob Howsam—no beards, no mustaches, no long sideburns, no facial hair at all. But Vaughn had a mustache and a short beard and was determined not to shave either. And he didn't and he got away with it. He also insisted that he take a cappuccino machine on the road with him and that it occupy a seat next to him on the plane.

The hair and machine were worth it. Vaughn only hit .243, but he hit forty-five home runs and drove in 118 batting clean-up. More important, he was a team leader, a tough guy with a foreboding look, one that said, "Don't cross me and don't invade my space."

The Reds, picked by nobody to be a contender, were the surprise of baseball that year. They won ninety-six games, and finished one game behind Houston in the National League Central. But they still had a chance to be the wild card team. First, they needed to beat Milwaukee on the road in their final game of the season. That didn't figure to be a problem. The Reds were so good on the road that year—winning fifty-one of their eighty-one games—that I nicknamed them "The Big Road Machine," and the team adopted that name.

On the morning of the final day of the season it was raining heavily in Milwaukee. On a normal day the game would have been postponed, but this was a game that had to be played and had to be played on that final day of the season. So they waited and waited and waited. And it rained and it rained and it rained. What could a guy do in the Milwaukee press box? Well, he could eat some of those delicious sausages they cooked in the press room. I believe I set the record that day with eight.

The game took more than seven hours to complete and it was played in either a downpour or a drizzle, depending upon the inning. The outfield was under so much water they could have sailed the Delta Queen on it. Right fielder Dmitri Young, a rather large man, ran hard toward a pop fly in short right field. When he dove for it, he trailed a rooster tail that resembled something behind an unlimited hydroplane racing boat. The Reds finally prevailed, 7–1, a victory that tied them with the New York Mets for the wild card spot and necessitated a one-game playoff the next night in Cincinnati.

After that game, I learned a dirty little trick about getting seated quickly in a crowded restaurant. When The Longest Day in Milwaukee ended, eleven writers decided to have dinner together at a popular Italian restaurant. We didn't have reservations, and when we arrived we were told there was a two-hour wait. We decided to wait.

Ten of us were there. One wasn't. That was *Dayton Daily News* columnist Tom Archdeacon, the most talented writer I ever worked with and I worked with a lot. Archdeacon is a meticulous writer. Before he pushes the first key on his computer, he outlines his piece on a legal pad. Then he writes. And he re-writes. And he re-writes again. He takes a very long time and his work shows it. It is always perfection. In addition, if there is a different off-beat story involved in the event he is covering, something nobody else knows about, Archdeacon finds it and usually is the only writer with that story. Archdeacon reminds me of Ernest Hemingway, both his writing and his appearance. It is no accident. When he worked in Miami he spent a lot of time in Key West and a whole lot of time in Sloppy Joe's, so much time that he had a bar stool with his name etched into the wooden seat. Hemingway spent even more time there and he, too, has a seat with his name on it.

As for writing, I am just the opposite of Archdeacon. I might be the fastest writer in the business. I sit down, put my fingers on the keys, and let the stream of consciousness flow. I never re-write and I seldom change a thing. My philosophy always has been, "I give it my best effort the first time and if I try to re-write or re-work it, it doesn't get better. Just worse." But when it comes to picking up tricks of the trade, picking them up from Tom Archdeacon is top of the line.

Hal with Tom Archdeacon at Great American Ball Park.

On this night in Milwaukee, true to form, Archdeacon was the last to leave the press box, crafting his piece, which turned out to be, as usual, the best thing to come out of the game. We were forty-five minutes into our two-hour wait when Archdeacon arrived and we told him, "It was a two-hour wait and now it's still an hour and fifteen minutes." Archdeacon shook his head and said, "No, it isn't. Wait here." He disappeared inside the restaurant and was gone about fifteen minutes. Then he returned and said, "Come on, we're in."

We sat down and I asked him, "How did you do that?" He told me he stood close to the check-in stand. He waited until a name was called twice, "Brown, party of four. Brown, party of four." When the Brown party of four didn't show and the hostess said, "Last call, Brown, part of four," Archdeacon waited about two more minutes. Then he approached the hostess and said, "Have you called for Brown yet? We were outside and couldn't hear."

The hostess, "Yes, are you Brown?" Archdeacon said he, indeed, was Mr. Brown. When the hostess grabbed four menus, Archdeacon said, "My party is for twelve. I told them twelve when I checked in." The perplexed hostess, rather than argue, quickly said she would have the spots available immediately and we sat down. Ashamedly, I pulled the same trick later on in Chicago when four of us wanted to eat at Harry Caray's restaurant and were told there was more than an hour wait. I used the same tactic and it worked.

Many Reds players had career years or near-career years in 1999. First baseman Sean Casey, "The Mayor," hit .332 with twenty-five homers and ninety-nine RBI. And Casey invented a special celebration at home plate when the team won a walk-off game. The entire team would encircle home plate, arms around each other's shoulders, and jump up down while hooting. It survives to this day and is used by most teams.

Catcher Eddie Taubensee, whom they called "Special Ed," had his career year by far—.311, twenty-one homers, eighty-seven RBI. Dmitri Young hit .300 with fourteen homers and fifty-six RBI. Hall of Fame shortstop Barry Larkin hit .293 with twelve homers and seventy-five RBI. Third baseman Aaron Boone hit .280 with fourteen homers and seventy-two RBI. Second baseman Pokey Reese hit .285 and center fielder Mike Cameron hit twenty-one home runs and drove in eighty-six runs.

The team could hit. The 865 runs they scored remains a club record, as is the 2,549 extra base hits and the most players with ten or more home runs (ten). Pitching, though, was adequate at best. McKeon had to use eight different starting pitchers and Pete Harnisch (16–10) was the only pitcher to win more than eleven games. Steve Avery (6–7), Ron "The Big Rig" Villone (9–7) and Denny Neagle (9–5) were inhibited due to injuries. Juan Guzman, an August acquisition from Baltimore, started twelve games the last month and went 8–2. A reliable bullpen of closer Danny Graves, Scott Sullivan, Stan Belinda, and Dennys Reyes (McKeon called him "Big Sweat" because he was perspiration-soaked by the time he laced up his spikes) did most of the heavy-lifting on the mound.

So the Reds were pretty much pitched out when that playoff game began and Steve Parris was asked to save the season on only three days of rest. Unfortunately for the Reds, the bats that were so vocal all season suddenly became a silent movie. They had only two hits against Al Leiter, singles by Pokey Reese and Jeffrey Hammonds, and lost, 5–0.

McKeon knew what the team needed. Pitching, pitching, pitching. The hitting certainly was there. But instead of acquiring the necessary pitching, general manager Jim Bowden traded Mike Cameron, pitcher Brett Tomko, and a couple of trinkets to Seattle for Ken Griffey Jr. And Bowden immediately signed Griffey to a ten-year $116.5 million contract. That left no money to re-sign Vaughn, who took free agency and signed with Tampa Bay.

McKeon was one unhappy manager. "While Griffey was a great player, we didn't need him. We needed pitching," said McKeon. "With a couple of good starters we would be a formidable team."

McKeon, who left after the 2000 season, was dead-on. Through no fault of Griffey, beset his entire career in Cincinnati by injuries, the Reds went into deep freeze. They would not win more than ninety games again until 2010 when they won ninety-one. They won eighty-five games and finished second in 2000, then McKeon left. They didn't finish above .500 for the next nine years.

McKeon went on to bigger and better things in Florida but still says, "We could have had something really big in Cincinnati, but Bowden had to have Griffey." To this day, McKeon believes Bowden sabotaged him on the last day of the 2000 season. With nothing at stake and the Reds en route to a 6–2 loss, Griffey and Larkin left the game early, dressed, and departed. They said they had permission from Bowden to leave early and fly home to Florida. McKeon said Bowden never mentioned it to him, and he was left hanging after the game when the media asked about the early departure of Griffey and Larkin.

18 | JUNIOR

BROTHER FROM ANOTHER PLANET

He was the best baseball player on the planet in the 1990s and a Cincinnati icon, the son of one of the Big Red Machinists, but I had never seen Ken Griffey Jr. play baseball in person. While I covered entire Cincinnati Reds seasons during his reign in the 1990s and covered the World Series every year, the Reds never played Griffey's team, the American League's Seattle Mariners, and the Mariners never made the World Series. In fact, I had never seen him in person, in or out of uniform, at any locale or venue.

My first glimpse of Griffey was in mid-February of 2000 at a press conference in the Crosley Room at old Riverfront Stadium. The Reds traded pitcher Brett Tomko, outfielder Mike Cameron, and two minor-leaguers to bring Griffey home to Cincinnati where he grew up with his dad and attended Cincinnati Moeller High School. The Crosley Room was over-stuffed and the room hot and muggy. Media occupied about fifty chairs and Reds' employees stood against the walls two and three deep. Team owner Carl Lindner, a man who made few public appearances, not only was there but he made a short speech.

General manager Jim Bowden, the man who made the trade, was beaming, his face aglow with a permanent smile slashed across his face. When he stood to speak he said, "Baseball is back in Cincinnati." It was a curious statement. Many wondered, "Baseball is back in Cincinnati? Where had it gone? We didn't know it went anywhere." At the end of the 1999 season, the Reds missed the playoffs only after losing a wild card tiebreaker game with the New York Mets. They won ninety-six games, finished second, and manager Jack McKeon thought he had the team on the verge of something big. "All we need is some pitching," he said.

But Bowden gave up pitching in Brett Tomko and one of McKeon's favorite players, center fielder Mike Cameron. And through no fault of Griffey, Bowden's bold statement later became laughable. They won eighty-five games in Griffey's first year and finished second. But what followed was a forgettable segment of Reds' history. They went eight straight years without a winning season, never finishing higher than third. From 2001 through 2009, the Reds were 588–708 and went through four managers (Jack McKeon, Bob Boone, Dave Miley, Jerry Narron) and four general managers (Jim Bowden, Dan O'Brien, Wayne Krivsky, Walt Jocketty).

Griffey was thirty years old when he arrived in Cincinnati as Bowen's Chosen One to bring baseball back to Cincinnati. He was not the same player, mostly due to a litany of injuries that beset him nearly every year. It was his misfortune to encounter season-ending injuries three straight years—2002, 2003, 2004—and many fans couldn't understand it, only pointing to the fact that he missed 260 of the 466 games over those three seasons.

After he stood at the podium that cold February night after the trade, he met the media in a corner of the room for another barrage of questions. When I asked one, he pointed at me and said, "I've checked up on you. My dad said I could trust you, so you are all right with me." And a close relationship was born, one that transcended the baseball field, more like a friendship than a relationship.

I never had a baseball player call me on Christmas Eve to wish me and my family a happy holiday season. Griffey did that. I never had a baseball player call me, without being called first, to talk with me after his retirement. Griffey did that.

The Reds traded Griffey to the Chicago White Sox midway through the 2008 season, and I'll admit it brought tears to my eyes. Griffey returned to the Seattle Mariners a free agent for the 2009 season and suddenly in June of 2010 he left the game, announced his retirement, and walked away. I was sitting in my man cave in the garage a couple of days later when my cell phone rang. It was Griffey.

"Where are you? What are you doing?" I asked. "I'm driving home," he said. "Just driving home by myself to clear my head. I'm driving through

Rapid City (South Dakota) and I'm going to drive it straight through." That drive was from Seattle to his home near Orlando, Florida, 3,112 miles, forty-five hours by car. I told him he was out of his mind to attempt such a feat, but he did it and probably continued to call old friends along the way to keep him awake.

After my eyes went bad, my wife, Nadine, would call me every day during spring training in Sarasota at about 11:30, about the time the Reds were taking batting practice. Griffey saw me several days in a row on the phone and finally one day he asked, "Who do you talk to every day at 11:30?" I told him it was my wife. When my phone rang the next day Griffey grabbed it out of my hands and told Nadine, "Don't worry about the old coot. We're taking care of him. I won't let anything happen to him."

Really? Later that year during the season I was walking from a parking garage toward the stadium on a Sunday morning when I tripped over a curb and sprawled head-first on the sidewalk. Fortunately, I did no damage. But when I reached the clubhouse Griffey said, "I was driving by and saw you fall on your face. You have to watch where you're walking." I facetiously thanked him for stopping his car and getting out to make sure I didn't break both arms and crack open my skull.

Fans, of course, expected much more out of Griffey than they received, things he couldn't produce because of injuries. The natives were not only restless but in April of 2005, they were riotous. Heading into the last game in April, Griffey had no home runs—zip, zero, nada. He finally hit one on April 30, but fans were not appeased. Shortly after I wrote a bold column and said, "If Ken Griffey Jr. stays healthy and doesn't hit thirty home runs the rest of the year I will eat this column on Courthouse Square and I'll furnish the ketchup." And I forgot about it. Griffey never said a word, never said he had read that column.

The Reds were in Washington on August 25 and Griffey homered— number thirty for the season. I thought to myself, "He made it. I'll make a small note of my prediction in my notes column for anybody who might have remembered it." But nobody had mentioned that column written four months ago. I was standing outside the Reds' clubhouse after the game, waiting for admission to do interviews. Griffey walked by and said one word, "Hal." I looked his way and he flipped me the baseball he had hit for a home run that night and on it he had written: *To Hal: Thanks so much for the friendship. All my best, Ken Griffey Jr., Home run No. 30, career #531, 8-25-05.* I don't keep much baseball memorabilia, but that ball remains in my possession and shall remain in my possession forever.

One of the things I admired most about Griffey, among many, many things I admired, was his refusal to follow the crowd of steroids and performance enhancement drugs. And during his years in Cincinnati, with all the injuries, he could easily have sunk to that level to keep up with some of his peers. In 1998, when Mark McGwire hit seventy home runs and Sammy Sosa hit sixty-six, both under the cloudy shroud of steroids, Griffey led the American League with fifty-six, without a whisper of using performance-enhancing drugs. But he hardly rated a mention as the Baseball Nation went crazy over the McGwire-Sosa chase of home run legends Roger Maris and Babe Ruth. Amazingly, Griffey had hit fifty-six the year before (1997) to lead the American League.

If there was anything Griffey didn't like to do, it was talk about himself. If the media asked him questions about himself they were mostly likely to get mumbling three- or four-word answers as he sat on a large black steamer trunk always in front of his locker. If you wanted to talk to Griffey you walked up and said, "How's the family?" And then you listened for the next forty-five minutes to an hour as he talked about his wife, Melissa, and his kids.

He learned early not to talk boastfully about himself, learned it from his father, Ken Griffey Sr., who knew what the word "team" meant from his days with The Big Red Machine. "I came home one day after one of my sandlot games when I was a kid and told my dad that I had hit two home runs," Griffey told me. "He threatened to smack me up side of the head if I ever did that again. All he wanted to know was how my team did, not how I did personally."

He was a favorite of the clubhouse attendants, too. It was not uncommon during spring training for Griffey to buy his teammates breakfast. He would walk into the clubhouse and flip his Mercedes keys to a young clubhouse attendant, hand him a $100 bill, and send him to McDonald's for breakfast sandwiches. He would tell the kid to keep the change, even if the bill was no more than $50.

While he was battlefield-serious on the baseball field, Griffey loved clubhouse practical jokes and pranks. There was a time when Griffey owed Fogg $1,500, but paying by check just wasn't in Griffey's wheelhouse. When Fogg arrived at his clubhouse dressing stall one day he found his locker filled with 150,000 pennies—sixty boxes each weighing sixteen pounds and containing $25 worth of pennies. "Basically it's like having sixty bowling balls in your locker, only there are no holes to pick them up with," said Griffey.

Neither player revealed why Griffey owed Fogg $1,500, but Griffey consistently threatened to pay it off in pennies and Fogg didn't believe him. "I'm going to take them out to the bullpen and count them to make sure it's all there," said Fogg. "I have a lot of time on my hands out there."

Octogenarian owner Carl Lindner kept an extremely low profile as owner of the Reds, shied from publicity, and slipped in and out of the ball park unnoticed. But Griffey and Barry Larkin knew Lindner liked to come to the park early on Sundays before day games, parking his white Bentley convertible outside the players' entrance. One Sunday when Lindner walked into the clubhouse, Griffey shouted, "Give me your keys." Lindner flipped them to him and Griffey and Larkin slipped out of the clubhouse, climbed into the Bentley and—with the top down and the players wearing their baseball uniforms—they took a tour of downtown Cincinnati. And when they returned the car, they removed the classical music tape in the car's stereo deck and inserted a rap music tape and turned it on its highest volume so it would erupt when Lindner started the engine.

Griffey was born on the same date (November 21) and in the same town (Donora, Pennsylvania) as St. Louis Cardinals Hall of Famer Stan Musial, certainly a harbinger of what was to come for Junior. The Griffey family moved to Cincinnati when Junior was six and his dad was playing for the Reds. And it seemed that every year on Father's Day, Junior Griffey did something special in honor of his father, none better than on June 20, 2004. He became the twentieth player to hit five hundred career home runs and when he did it in St. Louis his father was seated in the stands. Amazingly, that was his 2,143rd career hit, the exact total his dad had during his major-league career.

But he was not allowed to brag about it.

19 | ERIC THE RED

THE BEST ONE OF THEM ALL?

From the more than twenty-five thousand baseball stories I have written there is one that stands out, not because it was well-written or memorable, but because it was a piece I wish I had never written, one I wish I had pulled from my typewriter and swallowed immediately. It was about Eric Davis, the classiest, finest gentleman baseball player I ever encountered. To this day he remains my all-time favorite. My grandson, Eric McCoy, is named after him.

The story I wrote was total character assassination and totally without foundation. It was in the late 1980s and there was a rumor that the Philadelphia Phillies were interested in trading for the Cincinnati Reds outfielder. We were in San Diego when I caught whiff of the rumor. I had a good source in Philadelphia and I called him. The man told me, "Yeah, we were interested. But not anymore. We've heard he is into drugs."

Stupidly, without checking a second or third source, I rushed it into print, wrote a column about it, quoting my unnamed source. Davis was crushed. He called me into a corner of the visitor's clubhouse in San Diego-Jack Murphy clubhouse and told me how disappointed he was in me, told me it was untrue, that he had never done drugs in his life, never even considered it, and never would consider it.

I should have known better. Davis had an impeccable character, never caused anybody any trouble. And we had a great personal relationship, which should have been destroyed that day. Davis, though, never mentioned it again. Not once. Ever. He later wrote a book and used my name in it several times, always positively, and never mentioned how one untrue story written by me could have ruined his career.

146

Davis, a five-tool player who was at the top of the list in all five tools, came of age in 1986. He was twenty-four and he hit twenty-seven home runs and stole eighty bases—power *and* speed. And his outfield defense was sensational. The national media began calling him "the next Willie Mays," probably because he had all the all-around abilities of Mays. They didn't call him the next Mickey Mantle, probably because he was black. But Davis didn't want to be the next Willie Mays and resented the comparison. All he would say was, "I just want to be Eric Davis."

And being Eric Davis was more than enough. Injuries, mostly due to running into walls at full speed—including the brick wall in Wrigley Field—and making diving catches, prevented him from becoming the Hall of Fame player he could have been. His razor thin, well-sculpted body took a pounding and a beating.

My oldest son, Brian, came to spring training with me one year and Davis treated him as if he were his own son. He talked to him every day and went out of his way to do it. He so impressed my son that he named *his* first son, my first grandson, Eric. Davis is a roving minor league instructor for the Reds these days and our friendship remains. We hug each other whenever we cross paths. Call it a man crush if you wish, but that's the way I feel about Eric Davis, the best baseball player and the best man I've encountered in the game.

It is strange how friendships and mutual respect are formed. Tim Belcher is a case in point. He made his name as a pitcher with the Los Angeles Dodgers. On the night in 1987 when Cincinnati's Tom Browning pitched his perfect game, his opponent was Tim Belcher. The final score was 1–0, and Belcher gave up three hits.

It would have been easy for me to put an immediate disliking on Belcher. He came to the Reds in the winter of 1991 in a trade with the Dodgers— for Eric Davis. But Belcher's lively and outgoing personality won me over quickly. During spring training of 1993 the Reds played a road game in Vero Beach. Three writers, including me, stopped at a restaurant on our way back to Plant City. Belcher was already in the restaurant and stopped at our table to say hello and goodbye. When we asked for our check, the server said, "The gentleman you were talking to picked up your check." In forty-three years of covering baseball, Belcher was the first and last player to buy me a meal.

He bought pizza one day for *Cincinnati Post* beat writer Jerry Crasnick. The players were upset that owner Marge Schott paraded her St. Bernard, Schottzie, around on the Riverfront Stadium AstroTurf before games, doing her business the way dogs always do, wherever they pleased. Belcher expressed his displeasure and Crasnick wrote about it. The next day Belcher had a pizza delivered to Crasnick in the press box, and like the good guy that he is, Crasnick shared it with his working stiff compatriots.

Belcher was totally media savvy, knew how to handle the press. There was a game during which he gave up a lot of runs early and was removed. He showered and left quickly after the game. But he knew the media would want quotes about what happened. So before he left Belcher took a legal pad and wrote answers to ten questions he figured he would be asked and taped it to his locker for the media to find.

Belcher was 15–14 with a 3.91 ERA in thirty-four starts in 1992. He was 9–6 with a 4.47 ERA in twenty-two starts in 1993 when the July deadline arrived. General manager Jim Bowden was enamored of a young pitcher named Johnny Ruffin and traded Belcher to the Chicago White Sox for Ruffin. Belcher went on to win sixty-eight games over the next six years. Ruffin won a total of ten major leagues games for the Reds in four years, seven in one year, and disappeared from the game. Belcher is still in the game, a coach and consultant with the Cleveland Indians, and it is always a pleasure to run into him at spring training, during interleague games, and when he sometimes pops into Great American Ball Park as a scout.

When Kevin Mitchell came to the Reds for the 1993 season, he brought a lot of extraneous baggage, a reputation of being a bad guy, a troublemaker, somebody to avoid. And to make matters worse, general manager Bowden traded popular relief pitcher Norm Charlton to the Seattle Mariners for Mitchell. But what a delight Mitch was, and not just because in two of his three years with the Reds he hit forty-nine home runs, drove in 141 and hit .341 and .326. He was the exact opposite of his reputation. He was a media darling, an extremely humorous man with a dazzling smile that displayed a gold tooth. He told us funny stories about his friends, Big Fat Stinky Mike and Japanese Tony. He said Big

Fat Stinky Mike was so big that he took out the front seat of his Cadillac and drove it from the back seat.

Mitchell's sense of humor was sometimes threatening. The Reds called up a left-handed pitcher from the University of Kentucky in 1993 named Larry Luebbers, his first trip to the majors at age twenty-four, and he was starting that night. Mitchell had no clue who he was and when he walked by he asked us, "Who is that?" We told him his name was Larry Luebbers and Mitchell said, "Larry Lugers?" Then he said to Luebbers, "Hey, Lugers. I know you've heard about the German Luger gun. I'll use a Luger on you if you have me running all over the outfield chasing balls tonight."

Luebbers pitched only fourteen games for the Reds that year and was 2–5 with a 4.54 earned run average. Then he disappeared into the minors for six years and re-surfaced in 1999 briefly with the St. Louis Cardinals. He returned to the Reds in 2000 for fourteen bullpen appearances and was 0–2. Then he was gone. A few years later I was sitting at a blackjack table at the Belterra Casino near Florence, Indiana. A tall, gangly guy sitting at the table kept looking at me. Finally, he said, "You probably don't remember me; I'm Larry Luebbers. Of course I remembered him and I quickly asked, "Remember when Kevin Mitchell called you Larry Lugers and threatened you?" Luebbers laughed and said, "Oh, yeah. That guy scared the crap out of me. I didn't know if he might have been serious."

Mitchell loved to tell tales, some of them we felt might be taller than the Carew Tower in downtown Cincinnati. He told us he had five houses in San Diego. He told us he had rotating beds in all the houses. He told us he had twelve jet skis. He told us he had a nitro-fueled pickup truck. He told us that in one of his houses he had a sliding board from a door in his bedroom and emptied into the swimming pool. We all nodded and thought, "Yeah, sure."

In 1994, Jeff Horrigan of the *Cincinnati Post* flew to San Diego to do a piece, "A day in the life of Kevin Mitchell." Mitchell was not stretching the truth in any way. He had everything he said and Horrigan remembers, "We went out on Mission Bay on his jet skis and he took a friend who was a bail bondsman just in case he ran into trouble and needed immediate help." Everybody always said Mitchell was so good he could fall out of bed and hit for average and distance, and Horrigan found out it was true that he could also fall out of bed and go swimming.

Mitchell was a soft touch, too. When he left the stadium after games in San Diego, his hometown, he'd be greeted outside by fifteen to twenty guys, a group Mitchell called "my posse." Mostly, though, they were hangers-on looking for a handout, and Mitchell always complied, passing out $20 bills. It was suspected that one of his "posse," or somebody from a rival gang in San Diego, was so upset with him one day that they issued a death threat to Mitchell. The team was in New York when Mitchell received a message telling him that when the team played in San Diego there would be an assassin on the roof with a sniper's rifle. Extra security was provided and Mitchell played the series without incident.

Mitchell was so humorous that I began ending my daily Reds Notebook with a quote from Mitchell and I called it "Kevin's Korner." He caught on and began seeking me out to give me material. But he never could get the title correct. He would rush up to me and say, "Hey, Hal, I've got something for 'Mitch's Corner.'"

Every year the Cincinnati chapter of the Baseball Writer's Association of America gives out a Good Guy Award. The plaque goes to the player they consider most cooperative with the press over the season. Kevin Mitchell, the bad guy, the troublemaker, won it in 1992. When we walked up to his locker and presented the plaque, he began crying. "Nobody in my life has ever called me a good guy," he said.

Mitchell owned a bar in San Diego and the place was full of bright lights and chrome. The USA cable network had a crime show called *Silk Stalkings*, a show I loved and watched religiously. During a trip to San Diego he invited the four beat writers, Chris Haft of the *Cincinnati Enquirer*, Jeff Horrigan and Bill Koch of the *Cincinnati Post*, and me to come to his establishment where he fed us with mounds of hors d'oeuvres and snacks. I looked around and said, "I've never been here, but it sure looks familiar. It looks like the bar on *Silk Stalkings*." Mitchell smiled and said, "It should. This is where they film all their bar scenes."

Neon Deion Sanders was another player of whom Jim Bowden was enamored, another guy who seemed as if trouble followed him everywhere, a guy who was all flash and dash and cash. He was an NFL star, a defensive back with the Atlanta Falcons. As a baseball player, he was all speed and not much else. It was stunning to watch him run out a triple or score from first base on a single, his legs and feet a blur as he circled the bases. Bowden traded outfielder Roberto Kelly for Sanders on May 9, 1994. And like Mitchell, he was not as advertised. It became clear early that Neon Deion was pure shtick, a public persona.

Privately, in the clubhouse, he was quiet, polite, introspective. He was guarded with the press at first because, he said, he had been burned so often. But he learned to trust the easy-going Cincinnati media and opened up. He didn't last long in Cincinnati. Near the trade deadline in 1995 Bowden traded him and four other players to San Francisco for pitchers Mark Portugal and Dave Burba, a trade that clearly helped the Reds reach the National League Championship series in 1995. When the Reds visited San Francisco after the trade, Sanders had a press conference and told the Cincinnati media, "You guys were the most fair group of writers I've ever been involved with, the fairest and the most honest."

Hal taking notes at Great American Ball Park.

There was a game during which a fly ball was hit to left field, near the wall. Sanders drifted back to catch it but misjudged it slightly, and the ball bounced off the top of his head and over the wall for a home run. When Sanders arrived at the ballpark the next day, he found a special item in his locker. Teammate Barry Larkin had taken Deion's plastic batting helmet and glued Deion's glove on top of the helmet, pocket up. A note said, "Maybe this will help you catch a ball that hits the top of your head."

Sanders befriended singer MC Hammer and there were times when Hammer traveled with the team. He was accompanied by a huge, beefy bodyguard. The Reds provide a rooming list to everybody in the traveling party and one day I was scanning the list and came across the name, "Wee-Wee." I began asking around because some players used fictitious names so they wouldn't be bothered in their rooms by phone calls from fans. I thought it might be a fan. When I asked Sanders about it, he laughed and said, "Wee-Wee? That's Hammer's bodyguard." I didn't have the guts to call the guy "Wee-Wee" to his face.

Sanders dropped the Neon from his name, found religion, and wrote a book: *Power, Money & Success: How Success Almost Ruined My Life*. He autographed it for me with the inscription: "To Hal, one of the best and fairest writers I've ever known." It is a book I cherish.

Scouts are some of my favorite people—starting right at the top with Gene Bennett, who scouted for the Cincinnati Reds for sixty years and signed Barry Larkin and Don Gullett and many more. When Larkin, a Cincinnati native, was playing at the University of Michigan, the Reds wanted to draft him, but they weren't sure they wanted to take him in the first round. Bennett was sipping water at a cooler in a hall in the front office of Riverfront Stadium when club president/general manager Bob Howsam walked by. He stopped at the water cooler and asked, "Are you sure Larkin can make it as a player?" Bennett straightened up, swallowed his water, and said, "Barry Larkin can walk out there on that field right now and be a star." The Reds drafted him No. 1. Was Bennett right? Larkin played less than two years in the minors, only 673 at-bats, before he was promoted to the majors, a stopover on his way to the Hall of Fame.

They didn't listen to Bennett on another player. There was a kid who showed up at a baseball camp in Michigan wearing a Reds baseball cap. He was a shortstop. Bennett told him that the Reds already had a shortstop, a guy named Barry Larkin. So the kid said, "I can play anywhere. I can play center field." So they sent him out to center field. "And he looked like Willie Mays," said Bennett. The kid's name was Derek Jeter.

Bennett recommended that the Reds draft him, but because they had Larkin they passed him over. Instead, they drafted an outfielder named Chad Mottola. Reds scout Julian Mock said of Mottola, "This kid is so big and so strong he could whip a bear with a switch." But he couldn't hit with a bat or a switch and never made it. And everybody knows about Derek Jeter.

While on the road I loved to have lunch with scouts to pick their brains and talk baseball. One of my favorites was a scout for the Minnesota Twins named Wayne Krivsky. He loved the Reds and dreamed of some day becoming the team's general manager and said, "Man, we'd have a lot of fun. The team is so full of tradition with the Big Red Machine and Joe Nuxhall and Marty Brennaman and you. It would be so much fun."

The dream came true. When general manager Dan O'Brien was fired, after starting a rebuilding program of the minor league system that Marge Schott destroyed, Krivsky was hired before the 2006 season. During spring training of 2006, Krivsky made three trades to add three significant players at the loss of almost nothing—trades that should have established his legacy. First, he obtained pitcher Bronson Arroyo on March 20 for outfielder Wily Mo Peña, an unbelievably strong human specimen who could hit balls out of sight, especially during batting practice, but not so much in games. His defense was deficient and I once wrote, "Wily Mo Peña couldn't get his skillet-like glove through an airport metal detector." I saw him reading my story in the clippings the club provided of everything the writers wrote, and I thought, *Oh, oh*. But Peña looked at me and said, "That's very funny."

Arroyo went on to win 105 games in six years with the Reds, made the All-Star team in 2006 and pitched two hundred or more innings in five of those six years, missing two hundred innings all six years by one inning in 2012. He was one of the more intelligent players I ever dealt with. He was a great interview, never using a cliché, and always furnishing incisive and honest appraisals of his performance and that of the team. And the other pitchers migrated to his locker for advice and insights. Wily Mo Peña? He is playing in Japan.

On April 7, just before Opening Day, Krivsky traded with the Cleveland Indians for second baseman Brandon Phillips, who had problems with manager Eric Wedge. The Indians dumped him for a player to be named later. That player wasn't named until June and it was minor league pitcher Jeff Stevens, who hung around the majors for a few years but accomplished little. Meanwhile Phillips became an All-Star/Gold Glove player and a fan favorite who communicated with them through his Twitter account, *DatDudeBP*.

There was a third trade that spring that escaped much notice because of the acquisitions of Arroyo and Phillips. On March 21, one day after the Arroyo trade, Krivsky made a deal with San Diego, acquiring catcher David Ross for minor-league outfielder Bobby Basham. Ross was a significant contributor to the Reds for a couple of years and is still playing, winning a World Series ring with the Boston Red Sox in 2013. Basham? He never made it to the majors.

In December after the 2007 season, when Krivsky decided the team needed pitching, it was a perfect time to trade Hamilton. He dealt him to Texas for pitchers Edinson Volquez and Daniel Ray Herrera. It was a trade good for both teams—for a year. Volquez won seventeen games and made the All-Star team his first year and Hamilton won the American League MVP, hitting .302 with thirty-two home runs and 130 RBI. Both players then began fighting injuries and Volquez never won more than five games over the next three years.

The other pitcher involved in the Hamilton trade was a left-handed pitcher named Daniel Ray Herrera, who served the team well in the bullpen. He was listed at 5-foot-9, but he had to have been measured while standing on a pile of rosin bags. He actually was about 5-foot-6. The Reds were in Philadelphia when Herrera arrived on Sunday. On Saturday, The Preakness Stakes horse race had been run in Baltimore. When Herrera walked into the clubhouse, carrying a bag bigger than he was, Ken Griffey Jr. looked up and said, "Hey, didn't I just see you riding a horse in The Preakness?"

There was a controversial trade in July of 2006, which involved Krivsky and former Reds general manager Jim Bowden, who was then working for the Washington Nationals. It was an eight-player deal, the Reds receiving five for three. They acquired pitcher Gary Majewski, infielder Royce Clayton, pitcher Bill Bray, infielder Brandon Harris, and pitcher Darryl Thompson. Krivsky sent three No. 1 draft picks—outfielder Austin Kearns, pitcher Ryan Wagner and shortstop Felipe Lopez—to the Nationals. Amazingly, not one of those eight players contributed much to their new teams. In addition, Krivsky and the Reds thought Majewski was damaged goods and had received a cortisone shot for a tired arm just before the trade. The Reds filed a grievance, but Major League Baseball never acted upon it and the grievance was dropped.

20 | NEW DIGS
THE OLD LADY GOES DOWN

It was finger-numbing cold on December 29, 2002, as I stood on the concourse of Paul Brown Stadium, home of the NFL's Cincinnati Bengals. There was a fast-chilling cup of Sweet 'n Low-diluted coffee in my left hand, but I wished it was a plunger. They were about to implode Riverfront Stadium—I never adjusted to calling it Cinergy Field. And I wanted to blow up the old lady myself. But they wouldn't let me.

I was three blocks away from Paul Brown Stadium but when the walls came tumbling down, the dust and the dirt and the grime enveloped us. The only thing good about Riverfront Stadium was its deep tradition injected by The Big Red Machine. The stadium itself was a crumbling dump, although it was less than thirty-two years old. It was one of those multi-purpose stadiums built in the late 1960s and early 1970s to serve both football and baseball. That meant they had to accommodate a 120-yard football field and it made the baseball playing area too large, especially foul territory. The cliché description of those stadiums was "cookie cutters."

The Reds hoped to begin writing a more positive franchise history with a new ball park, a 42,319-seat $290 million edifice stuffed between old Riverfront Stadium and U.S. Bank Arena on property called The Wedge. The insurance company owned by Carl Lindner, Jr., who also owned the Reds, was called the Great American Insurance Company. Lindner bought the naming rights to the new park and it became Great American Ball Park. To baseball people, though—and the Associated Press stylebook, as well—"ballpark" is one word. But the Reds didn't want the place to be called "The GAB" (Great American Ballpark), so they split "ballpark" to make it Great American Ball Park.

General manager Jim Bowden wanted the right field corner to be 315 feet from home plate, to take advantage of the team's two power hitters, left-handers Ken Griffey Jr. and Adam Dunn. Major League Baseball refused to permit a Griffey–Dunn Corner and the distance to the right field fence was placed at 330 feet. It didn't matter to Griffey or Dunn because the park still played small and was nicknamed "Great American Small Park."

The park opened on March 31, 2003, and Griffey recorded the first hit, a double against the Pittsburgh Pirates, a game the Reds lost, 10–1, a quick indicator that new digs would not help bad baseball teams. And the small park was not needed by Dunn. On August 10, 2004, Dunn hit one off Los Angeles Dodgers eccentric right-hander Jose Lima that left the stadium. It cleared the right-field bleachers, landed on two-lane Mehring Way, and hopped onto a splintery piece of driftwood on the north bank of the Ohio River. It was measured at 535 feet, the longest ball ever hit in Great American. There, Dunn was also tied for ninth (479), thirteenth (474), and seventeenth (471). Most of the other times, he struck out. But he was always a jolly fellow and very self-deprecating. When he broke the major-league strikeout record in 2004 with 195 strikeouts, he smiled and said, "Well, it is always nice to be remembered for something, to hold some kind of record."

Dunn, a mammoth man at 6-foot-6 and 285 pounds (he called himself "The Big Donkey"), was a monster at the plate. From 2004 through 2008, he hit forty or more home runs all five years, drove in a hundred or more runs in four of the five years (ninety-two in 2006) and walked more than a hundred times all five years.

He grew up in New Caney, a small Texas town, and was a football star, the biggest high school quarterback in the whole damn state. Don't they always grow things bigger in Texas? The University of Texas recruited him and he signed a scholarship. He was also a baseball star and the Reds drafted him No. 2 in 1998, behind another outfielder, Austin Kearns. It was stipulated that Dunn could leave his minor-league team in August so he could begin football practice with the Longhorns. Dunn was red-shirted his freshman year and the quarterback was Major Applewhite. Then Texas signed another quarterback, Chris Simms, son of former NFL quarterback Phil Simms. Texas decided to turn Dunn into a tight end and he wanted no part of that. So he turned to baseball fulltime.

One day, when Dunn endured a miserable day at the plate—0-for-5 with four strikeouts—he left the shower with a beach towel wrapped around his waist and a hand towel in his hand, removing shaving cream from his right ear, and he said for all to hear, "To think I could have played football." After hitting a game-winning walk-off home run one day, the entire team waiting for him at home plate, poised to pummel him in a scrum, Dunn sprinted through the players massed at the plate and bolted into the dugout and up the ramp to the clubhouse, as though running for a touchdown through an entire high school team. Asked about it afterwards, he said, "I didn't want to get whacked and buried under a pile. It was easy to get through. There were only twenty-four of 'em."

As a kid in his hometown of Porter, Texas, Dunn frequented a Mexican restaurant called La Casita and his favorite dish was chicken fajitas. The restaurant is still there and the chicken fajitas are called "The Adam Dunn special," still on the menu.

Left hander Kent Mercker gave up one of the top ten distance home runs in GABP on April 45, 2008, to Philadelphia's Ryan Howard, a 479-footer that is the fifth-longest ever. Mercker didn't mind and said, "If you have to give them up, you might as well give them up in historical fashion. They don't count any more for distance."

The new park, though, was not home sweet home for the Reds. After finishing 66–96 in 2001, their last season at Riverfront, the Reds played nearly a decade, nine years, without putting together a winning season, never finishing higher than third in the National League Central. They went through managers like dirty sliding pads—Bob Boone, Dave Miley, Jerry Narron, and Dusty Baker.

Bob Boone replaced Jack McKeon as manager for 2001, under a cloud of controversy. General manager Jim Bowden had talked with former Reds second baseman and Cincinnati native Ron Oester about taking the position and actually offered it to him. Oester asked for a day to think over the offer. In the interim, Boone, a special assistant to Bowden, convinced Bowden that he, Boone, could do the job and Bowden gave it to him.

Bowden announced that Boone was the new manager without ever calling Oester back, never giving him a chance to accept or reject the job that he'd offered to Oester first. Oester never spoke to Bowden again.

Oester was part of the 1990 World Series championship team, and the Reds honored them at a twenty-year, on-the-field celebration. When the team lined up down the first base line and each player was introduced, Bowden moved down the line shaking hands. When Bowden reached Oester and stuck out his hand, Oester turned to gaze into the outfield, perhaps symbolically turning his back on the man whom Oester thought had turned his back on him.

Boone came from a famous baseball family. His father, Ray Boone, was a better-than-average infielder, and when he played third base for the Cleveland Indians from 1948 to 1952 and my dad was taking me to Cleveland Municipal Stadium, he was one of my favorite players. Bob was an exceptional catcher, a Gold Glover for the Philadelphia Phillies, and both his sons, Bret and Aaron, played infield for the Reds.

While most managers conducted post-game media sessions in their offices, Boone took to meeting the press and TV cameras in a small room that was the entrance to the clubhouse, a room that contained a desk for the security guard, the walls covered with photographs depicting the more glorious past. Boone would walk out the door from the clubhouse and stand in front of the cameras for a brief press conference and say things like, "We didn't score enough points," and "We stranded enough people to populate a small Vietnam village."

The Reds lost ninety-six games in Boone's first season, 2001, and finished fifth. They lost eighty-four the next year and finished third before the club moved into Great American in 2003. That team lost ninety-three games and finished fifth again, next to last in the National League Central and one game ahead of the last-place Milwaukee Brewers, and in the middle of the season Boone was fired. His son, Aaron, was on the team at the time and there were tears in his eyes as he talked to the media after his dad was fired.

The home clubhouse in Great American Ball Park is palatial, one of the largest in baseball. The main room is the size of a basketball court and has black leather couches and chairs sprinkled throughout and four flat screen TVs dangling from the ceiling in mid-room, each one facing a different direction on the compass—north, south, east, and west. The clubhouse has a players' cafeteria, a game room, offices for the manager, coaches, and the clubhouse attendant, a chapel, four indoor batting cages, and a large state-of-the art training room with a swimming pool for rehabilitation purposes.

Jose Guillen, an outfielder with one of the all-time best arms in the game, was a moody guy with a hot temper that boiled close to the surface. He had been told on a Saturday night that he would be in the starting lineup on Sunday. But when he arrived at the park, whistling as he walked toward his locker, he spotted the lineup card. His name wasn't on it. He picked up three of his bats and flung them against the wall. The bats went through the wall like spears, leaving two gaping holes in the pristine clubhouse. Guillen paid for the repairs but not long after, he was traded to the Oakland Athletics for pitcher Aaron Harang.

The 2003 team used twenty-six pitchers, including Danny Graves, who was 4–15 in twenty-six starts with a 5.33 earned run average. He was later converted into a closer, where he earned his niche as one of the Reds' all-time best. The Opening Day pitcher that year was Jimmy Wayne Haynes, whom the Reds had signed as a free agent prior to the 2002 season and he had his best season in '02 with a 15–10 record. But he went 2-and-12 with a 6.30 earned run average in eighteen starts in '03.

Opening Day? He gave up six runs, five hits, and three walks in four innings and the Reds lost, 10–1. It was a harbinger for both him and the Reds. Haynes lost his first five starts, and started the sixth game, which the Reds also lost, although a relief pitcher was credited with the loss because Haynes left when the game was tied.

The Reds had another Jimmy on the staff—Jimmy Anderson, another free agent signee. He was a portly 200-pound left-hander and his six-year career record was 25–47, and in seven starts for the 2003 Reds he was 1-and-5 with a 6.30 earned run average. One day somebody was looking for Ryan Freel, a diminutive outfielder, and yelled in the clubhouse, "Anybody seen Ryan Freel?" From his dressing cubicle, standing face-in, Adam Dunn said, "I think Jimmy Anderson ate him."

At one point, because Dunn drew so many walks and always had a high on-base percentage, Boone made Dunn his leadoff hitter, the world's tallest and biggest leadoff hitter, but the experiment was quickly scrapped.

Dave Miley replaced Boone in mid-season, promoted from within. He was a darling of the organization as a minor-league manager, winning championships everywhere he went. And after he was fired in the middle of the 2005 season he returned to the minor leagues as a Triple-A manager for the New York Yankees. In 2014 he was inducted into the International League Hall of Fame. He was a catcher, drafted by the Reds in 1980, but never made it to the majors, playing until 1988. When he retired, the Reds immediately made him a manager and he managed at all levels from 1988 until he was named Reds manager in 2003, with one year as the Reds bench coach in 1993.

Hal observes from behind home plate.

He was always a favorite of mine, a fun-loving guy with a moon-shaped face and a permanent smile and an impish sense of humor. In the 1990s the *Dayton Daily News* put out a poster of me to place in the newspaper racks for street sales, promoting my upcoming trip to spring training. The poster displayed a picture of me wearing a Panama hat, a Tommy Bahama shirt, sun glasses, cigar in my mouth, and I was holding a baseball in front of me.

Miley had me autograph the poster and he had it taped on the front of his desk when he managed at Triple-A Indianapolis.

During spring training of 2005, a large entourage of Reds people frequented a dive bar in Sarasota called The Banana Factory. It was Karaoke Night and nearly every member of the Reds group got up to sing, including Miley. Freelance writer Gary Schatz recorded the entire night on a CD, including Miley's very good rendition of Johnny Cash's "Ring of Fire." During the season, Schatz slipped the CD into the hands of the person who played the music over the public address system during batting practice and there it was, reverberating all over Great American Ball Park, manager Dave Miley singing "Ring of Fire." And local disc jockey, Jim LaBarbara, known as The Music Professor, played it often on his shows. Miley was not amused.

Miley changed when he became manager of the Reds. He was ultra-cautious, feared that what he said or did wouldn't sit well with general manager Dan O'Brien. His pre-game press conferences were a lot of sitting and staring at each other. To break the ice, Miley would tell his joke of the day and that would be the highlight of the meeting. He had a favorite expression when he couldn't think of a name or an object and would call it, "Shum-shum." When asked pointedly about things, he would smile and say jokingly, "What do you want me to do? I'm only one man." It was said in jest but when it appeared in print it didn't look so good, and O'Brien ordered him to stop saying it.

Both broadcaster Marty Brennaman and I warned Miley, "Start being your own man. Run the team the way you ran your minor-league teams. Do things your way. Don't worry about what they might think upstairs. If you are going to get fired, get fired doing things the way you want to do them." He never heeded the advice and in the middle of the 2005 season he was fired. He managed half of 2003, all of 2004, and half of 2005.

His one full season his team lost eighty-six games and finished fifth. Miley was a lame duck. The Reds only gave him one-year contracts and very few major-league players. They had Adam Dunn and Ken Griffey Jr. and not much else. Aaron Harang was the winningest pitcher with eleven wins and left hander Brandon Claussen with ten, but both lost more than they won. The team, though, had a fan favorite in Ryan Freel, a gutsy little guy who was on top of the world one day and in the depths of hell the next. It only came out after he retired—and committed suicide—that his reckless play had caused a plethora of concussions.

He ran into walls to catch balls, fell into the stands to catch balls, knocked down infielders to break up double plays. He never finished a game without mud caked on his uniform, often the knees torn out. The Reds had a giveaway one night—a Ryan Freel tee shirt with dirt stains all over it.

During an interview one day he told me he had a friend who accompanied him at all times. "When I'm in the outfield, my friend Farney sits on my shoulder and talks to me," he said. Every spring training, near the end of camp, Freel thought he was on the bubble, wouldn't make the team, and he would call me aside in some small cramped clubhouse in Dunedin, Florida, or Winter Haven, to ask me, "Am I going to make it?" I would assure him that his place was safe, because it was. But he was insecure and told me, "I'm small, I don't have a lot of talent, so I have to play the way I play to stay up here."

When Miley was fired in mid-season of 2005, a long, tall baseball lifer with a slow North Carolinian drawl named Jerry Narron replaced him. Narron was an easy-going, soft-spoken guy who had an expression when he made a decision: "Hal, it is not written in cee-ment." Amazingly Narron was the fourth straight former catcher to manage the Reds—Jack McKeon, Bob Boone, Dave Miley, and Narron. Narron, though, was the first with big-league managerial experience, a short stint with the Texas Rangers.

Like Miley, Narron only had one full season with the Reds, 2006. He finished the last half of 2005 after Miley was fired, and he himself was fired on July 1 of 2007. In 2006, the team nearly became the first since Jack McKeon's 2000 to finish above .500. They finished 80–82, They lost the opener to the Chicago Cubs, 16–7, but were 7–3 after ten games. With two games left in the season they were 80–80, but were shut out twice in Pittsburgh in their last two games, 3–0 and 1–0.

Narron's major accomplishment was in helping the Reds pull off a shocking move during the baseball winter meetings in 2007. The Tampa Bay Rays, then known as the Devil Rays, had drafted a five-tool super-stud named Josh Hamilton in 1999 with the first overall pick. But injuries and a drug addiction stopped Hamilton cold and he was placed on baseball's restricted list for three years, unable to play. In 2007 he was eligible for the Rule 5 draft—any team could pick him up for $50,000. Nobody expected any team to pick up a problem-child.

But Narron and his brother, Johnny, were well-acquainted with Hamilton, a native of Raleigh, North Carolina, which was not far from Goldsboro, home to the Narrons. They convinced the Reds to take a flyer on Hamilton and the Reds acquired him in the Rule 5 draft. They hired Johnny Narron to be Hamilton's personal babysitter and constant companion, to keep him out of trouble on the road.

One night I encountered Hamilton and Narron heading toward the team hotel, the Westin on Chicago's Magnificent Mile. Just a block over there were blocks and blocks of excellent restaurants on Rush Street. I was coming back from Carmine's, a great Italian restaurant.

"Where have you been?" I asked.

Hamilton said, "Oh, we just had a great meal."

I asked where and he said, "McDonald's."

Hamilton was beset by injuries in 2007 and only played ninety games, but he hit nineteen home runs and drove in forty-seven. He was extremely popular with the media because of his story and his cooperation. He was not so popular with many of the players because of the attention he drew and the special attention he received from the Reds. I approached second baseman Brandon Phillips one day and started to ask him a question and he said, "Why don't you go talk to Hamilton like you dudes always do."

After the 2007 season Hamilton was traded to the Texas Rangers for pitchers Edinson Volquez, who won seventeen games in 2008, and relief pitcher Daniel Ray Herrera. Hamilton was named the American League's Most Valuable Player.

21 | ANOTHER BEGINNING

BAKER, THE WRITER'S DOZEN

Dusty Baker was leaning on the batting cage in Chicago's Wrigley Field, his arms crossed on a support bar, his head on his arms as he intently watched his Cubs take batting practice. It was April 15, 2003, and Baker wore his blue Cubs jacket with the collar turned up because a lip-numbing wind knifed off Lake Michigan and into Wrigley.

Baker saw me approach and turned quickly, a smile breaking out. "I see you," he said. "I know what you did and I appreciate it. You predicted that we would win the division, the only guy in the country to do that. Thanks, dude." Although I probably wasn't the only guy, I did predict the Cubs would win it and win it they did.

Baker never forgot it. And every time the Reds visited Wrigley or the Cubs came to Cincinnati, I made certain to stop by and say hello. I also became friends with Cubs general manager Jim Hendry and during the winter meetings for the next few years Baker, Hendry, and I had lunch together at least once during the week.

After Jerry Narron was fired in mid-2007, coach Pete Mackanin was named interim manager for the rest of the season. During a trip to San Francisco, my niece, Meghan Tomczak, was working in Los Angeles and wanted a getaway weekend and joined me in San Francisco. She bore an amazing resemblance to movie start Eva Longoria. After a game in San Francisco, Meghan met me in the press box after the game and we were leaving the stadium. We passed general manager Wayne Krivsky and he nearly walked into a wall when he saw me with Meghan. The next day he asked me, "Hal, how do you know Eva Longoria?"

That night Meghan and I went to Lefty O'Doul's bar across the street from the Westin St. Francis Hotel and I immediately spotted Mackanin. I said to Meghan, "Go along with me on this," and she agreed. Keep in mind, I'm sixty-seven at the time and Meghan is in her twenties and gorgeous. We walked up to Mackanin and I said, "Pete, I'd like you to meet my fiancée Meghan." He looked at her, looked back at me, looked at her again, and said, "Good for you, Hal."

When Mackanin took over, the Reds were twenty games under .500 at 31–51. For the rest of the season under Mackanin, the team was 41–39. Although it was a small sampling, Mackanin was the first Reds manager with a winning record since Jack McKeon in 2000. It was thought that surely Mackanin would have the interim title removed and become the fulltime manager. He certainly had earned it, but it was not to be.

Bob Castellini, a Cincinnati fruits and vegetables wholesaler, among many other businesses under the Castellini Group of Companies umbrella, put together a group in late 2005 to purchase the Reds from Carl Lindner. His stated mission was to return the Reds to the glory days, to the times of the Big Red Machine. He promised the fans he would do everything in his power to make it happen, and he has tried extremely hard to accomplish that mission.

He decided the team needed a name manager, a manager with a track record. After taking the San Francisco Giants to a World Series and the moribund Cubs to the National League Championship Series, Baker was out of baseball, working for ESPN as a baseball analyst. He was the man Castellini wanted, and he was the man he hired.

General manager Wayne Krivsky had started the reclamation project with the rebuilding of the depleted farm system and made some astute trades in acquiring pitcher Bronson Arroyo, catcher David Ross, and second baseman Brandon Phillips for not much more than a couple of broken bats and a used second base. The process was slow and agonizing and the Reds were no better in 2008 than they had been under Boone, Miley, and Narron. They lost eighty-eight games and finished fifth. On April 23 of that season, just twenty-two games into the season when the Reds were 9–13, Krivsky was fired and Castellini named former St. Louis Cardinals general manager Walt Jocketty as director of baseball operations and general manager.

Hal with Reds owner Bob Castellini at spring training, Goodyear, Arizona, 2010.

Krivsky should have read the handwriting on the clubhouse wall, but he didn't. Unlike most managers and general managers who are fired, Krivsky had a press conference to express how crushed he was to lose his dream job. He shed tears. He admitted he did some things wrong, didn't delegate enough authority, and that if given the chance he would do things differently. But in his short stay Krivsky made four outstanding deals, in three of which he acquired very good players and gave up nothing. And he put the Reds' farm system back in working order. It was a tough way to see a good friend go.

As a friend of Krivsky's I was not pleased. He had worked hard, things were moving in the right direction, and, as far as players, he had been dealt a short hand. Castellini, as was his right, wanted quick results. At the press conference after Krivsky was fired and Jocketty was introduced I asked Castellini, "When is the team going to start showing some continuity?" He looked me straight in the eye from behind the podium, adjusted his red tie, and said, "We are just not going to lose any more."

Castellini became rather cool toward me after that and once even tried to have me removed as a writer for *FOXSportsOhio.com* because he thought I was too negative. With FOXSportsOhio as the team's television outlet, he carried that kind of power, and Fox told me they weren't bringing me back the next year. I penned a hand-written note to Castellini and it had enough passion in it that he invited me to a meeting. We had a convivial chat and he relented. I understood where he was coming from. He is a man who wants to turn things around in Cincinnati, and he certainly showed that when the fans thought he couldn't possibly keep Joey Votto away from free agency. He displayed what he is all about when he signed Votto to a ten-year $225 million contract and followed that up by signing pitcher Homer Bailey to a six-year $105 million contract. Castellini is willing to do what he thinks it takes to return to those days of glory.

The Reds only improved by four games and one place in the standings in 2009, losing eighty-four games and finishing fourth. But it was mostly a young team, future stars like Johnny Cueto, Homer Bailey, Aaron Harang, Joey Votto, Jay Bruce, Brandon Phillips, and Edwin Encarnacion just getting their feet wet in the majors. Jocketty realized, though, that something was missing. There was no leadership in the clubhouse and on the field, no veteran presence for all the young talent to emulate and from whom they could learn.

So at the trade deadline Jocketty traded twenty-six-year-old third baseman Edwin Encarnacion to the Toronto Blue Jays for thirty-four-year-old Scott Rolen, a Gold Glove third baseman for the Philadelphia Phillies, St. Louis Cardinals, and Toronto Blue Jays. Encarnacion, a player with all the tools but unable to grasp the handles on those tools, was hitting .206 at the time of the trade. And his throws from third base to first base endangered the health and well-being of fans sitting in the lower deck behind first base.

Rolen was hit in the head by a pitch as soon as he arrived in Cincinnati and didn't play much that season, only 162 at-bats. But he took over the clubhouse for the 2010 season and the transformation so desperately wanted by Castellini began to take place. Under Baker, the team put it together in 2010, with Rolen leading the way and Joey Votto putting together an MVP season. They won the division with ninety-one victories.

Baker was a writer's delight. He never lied. He answered every question posed to him, and he answered with honesty and expansiveness. He sprinkled his media sessions with references to his former teammate, Hank Aaron. He was always surrounded by an army of friends from all walks of life and could talk intelligently about wine, singer Jim Morrison, and especially about baseball.

The Reds were in first place on August 8, but the St. Louis Cardinals were so close the Reds could smell the toasted ravioli on their breaths. And the Cardinals were coming to Cincinnati for a three-game series. Second baseman Brandon Phillips had missed a few games, and as I entered the clubhouse before the first game of the Cardinals series I stopped at his locker.

"I assume you will be in the lineup because I can't see you missing this series," I said to Phillips, recorder in hand.

"Oh, yeah, I'm going to play against those guys," he said. "I can't stand them. They are all a bunch of whiny little bitches, all of them." And he continued a lengthy disparaging discourse of the Cardinals. I wrote it all in my blog and a St. Louis writer Joe Strauss saw it and asked, "Did he really say all that?" Indeed he did. The Cardinals read it and, of course, were furious.

Phillips was batting leadoff for the Reds and as he approached the plate for his first at-bat, he tapped catcher Yadier Molina on the shin guards, something he did to all catchers. But Molina whipped off his mask and got into Brandon's face. Pushing and shoving began and the benches emptied. Most baseball fights are GMA, general milling around. This one, though, was for real. During the course of the brawl, Reds pitcher Johnny Cueto was pinned against a wall in front of the backstop. He kicked out with his spikes, injuring St. Louis catcher Jason LaRue, a former Reds catcher, and pitcher Chris Carpenter.

In the aftermath, both Dusty Baker and St. Louis manager Tony LaRussa were suspended, along with Phillips, Cueto, Carpenter, and Molina. They all were fined and Phillips paid Cueto's fine.

I expected Phillips to come into the clubhouse the next day and get in my face, yell at me, claim he was misquoted or it was off the record or taken out of context. No sooner had I arrived in the clubhouse, standing in front of a black leather couch, when Phillips walked in and headed my way. *Oh, oh*, I thought. *Here it comes.* Phillips walked up to me with a smile, gave me a fist bump, and continued on by. Clearly he was happy with the way it all turned out. He wanted to send a message to the Cardinals.

The message was clear in that three-game series. The Cardinals won all three games easily. But after that, the Reds won eight of their next nine and the Cardinals went on a losing streak. The Reds grabbed first place by a comfortable margin and on September 28 in Great American Ball Park, right-fielder Jay Bruce hit a game-winning walk-off home run against Houston left-hander Tim Byrdak to clinch the division and send the Reds to the postseason for the first time since 1995.

Hal in the press box at Great American Ball Park.

Up in the owner's box, Bob Castellini smiled broadly. But the smile didn't last long. In the first round of the playoffs, the Reds lost three straight games to the Philadelphia Phillies, including a no-hitter by Roy Halladay in game one, a 4–0 Phillies win. The Reds lost game two in Philadelphia, 7–4, then they were shut out again in the final game in Great American Ball Park, 2–0. There were no smiles in the owner's box.

With the success of the young 2010 team, the Reds figured they didn't need to do much in the off-season, just some tinkering, a minor tune-up. They signed a couple of veteran outfielders, Brian Barton and Jeremy Hermida, to minor-league contracts. They signed pitcher Dontrelle Willis, shortstop Edgar Renteria, and outfielder Fred Lewis to major-league contracts. None contributed much—Willis was 1-and-6 with a 5.00 ERA when he was released. Renteria hit .252 in ninety-eight games and Lewis hit .231 in eighty games.

The team regressed dramatically. After a 5-and-0 start, it was 42–40 after June and still in contention. But the Reds staggered through July with an 11–15 record and lingered between third and fourth place before and eventually finished third with a 79–83 record, seventeen games behind the Milwaukee Brewers, the tenth time in eleven seasons that they finished under .500. Mike Leake, pitching in his second season after coming directly to the Reds from Arizona State University— without playing in a single minor-league game—led the pitchers with twelve wins.

Fans expected more. Fans always expect more. They thought the 2011 team should have been as good or better than the 2010 team, but it doesn't always work out that way. And as the 2011 season progressed and the team sputtered, manager Dusty Baker fiddled with the lineups and the batting orders, trying anything he could to jump-start the team. He didn't make out the lineup card by pulling names from a hat. He came to the park early each morning for night games and sat by himself at his office desk, dressed in a polo shirt and golf slacks studying statistics, poring over numbers. He checked match-ups—how each hitter on his team did against that night's pitcher. He would say, "I try to give all of my players their best chances to succeed." And he protected players who were not likely to succeed against that night's pitchers.

But fans mocked his lineups and questioned his batting orders. Some of the media constantly questioned his lineups and batting orders and Baker patiently explained nearly every day why he was playing this player over another player. Chris Heisey, "The People's Choice," became fourth outfielder and pinch-hitter, a potent weapon against a fastball pitcher but a popgun against breaking ball pitchers. Baker would play him against a fastball pitcher and he might get three hits. The next day the opposing team would feature a breaking ball pitcher and Baker wouldn't have Heisey in the lineup. The fans would howl and the media would ask, "Why isn't Heisey playing?"

Baker loved Heisey, loved his hustle and his work ethic and his positive attitude, but fans thought Baker didn't like him and that was the reason he didn't play regularly, even though he played in 120 games and batted three hundred times. He hit .254 with eighteen homers and fifty runs batted in. "I used Heisey in the best situations for him to succeed and I'm protecting him in those in which he has little chance to succeed," said Baker. And Heisey agreed, never complained, never asked why he wasn't playing more.

At one point the frustrated Baker said, 'I'm really tired of having to explain my lineups and batting orders every day," he said. "I've been in this game a long time and I think I know what I'm doing." He had been in the game long enough to win two National League Manager of the Year awards, one in San Francisco and one in Chicago. He missed by one vote of being National League Manager of the Year with the Reds in 2010.

It got worse. One day after all the other media had left his office following his pre-game meeting with the press and broadcasters, Baker asked me to stay behind. When everybody else was gone Baker pointed to a large cardboard box he kept tucked against a wall behind his swivel chair. It was stuffed with mail. When he pointed to it, I said, "Fan mail?"

He smiled and said, "Not exactly. Pull one out."

I selected one at random and handed it to Baker. He opened it and showed me. It was hate mail. This particular randomly chosen letter was filled with venom and invectives. It used the "n" word several times. I was dumbfounded and asked, "Do you get a lot of this trash?"

He nodded his head and said, "Every day."

This is a man who doesn't have a racist tissue in his body and, in fact, seems to have more white friends than black friends, although he has an army of both. But that was the environment under which he was trying to win baseball games for Cincinnati fans.

It never got better, either, even though Baker guided the 2012 Reds to the National League Central Championship with ninety-seven wins, and the 2013 Reds to a wild card spot with ninety wins. But after winning the first two National League Division games in San Francisco in 2012, the Reds lost the next three. Then in 2013 they lost the one-game wild card playoff in Pittsburgh. The reason? Fans said Baker couldn't win the big games. Couldn't win in the postseason, as if the manager threw the pitches and swung the bats.

In the 2012 division series against San Francisco, everything blew up in the bottom of the first. Johnny Cueto struck out the first batter, Angel Pagan, and was 0-and-2 on Mark Scutaro. But on the second pitch, Cueto grabbed his back and doubled over. He suffered back spasms and had to leave the game. Sam LeCure took over, pitched masterfully, and the Reds won, 5–2. Game two was a Reds blowout, 9–0, as Bronson Arroyo held the Giants to two hits over seven innings with his assortment of slow, slower, and slowest pitches, some of which he made up as he went along.

That gave the Reds a two-games-to-one lead heading home. They needed only one win in three in Great American to advance to the National League Championship Series. They never got it when they should have finished it in three. Homer Bailey, who had pitched a no-hitter against Pittsburgh just two starts previous, held the Giants to one run and two hits over seven innings and struck out ten. But it was 1–1 after nine and in the 10th inning Scott Rolen, one of baseball's all-time best defensive third basemen, bobbled a ground ball and the winning run scored.

It would have been Johnny Cueto's turn in game four but his back didn't recover. Mike Leake, a starter all season, was not included on the post-season roster because the team only needed four starters for the NLDS. He was added to replace Cueto and started game four. The Reds were never in it and lost, 8–3. Now it was down to one game and it was started by Mat Latos, a young guy who was still perplexed over why a team would trade four guys for him. In the off-season, the Reds traded pitcher Edinson Volquez, once a seventeen-game winner and No. 1 draft pick; first baseman Yonder Alonso, No. 1 draft pick; catcher Yasmani Grandal and No. 2 draft pick; and pitcher Brad Boxberger for Latos. The Giants only scored in one inning, but they scored six—four on catcher Buster Posey's grand slam—and the Giants won the game and the series, 6–4.

Of course, it was Dusty's fault.

The Reds won ninety games in 2013, but finished third behind St. Louis and Pittsburgh. But under a new system, the Reds made the playoffs. Each league permitted two wild card teams to enter the playoffs—the two teams with the best records who didn't win their division. As it so happened, both teams came from the National League Central, Pittsburgh and Cincinnati. The wild card team with the best record would get home field advantage, and the Reds were in command for the home field heading into the final week. They lost their last six—including four straight at home—to the Pirates to end the regular season and lost the home field advantage.

Before the Pittsburgh series, Baker was asked if the team had a "sense of urgency" to beat the Pirates to capture the home field for the one-game post-season playoff and Baker said it didn't, that he felt no sense of urgency. He meant that his team just needed to play its game, do its best, and matters would take care of themselves. But fans reacted passionately, feeling that the manager was not lighting a fire under its team.

For the one-game playoff in Pittsburgh, Baker selected Johnny Cueto to pitch, even though he was pitching only his third game since coming off the disabled list. The Pirates hadn't been in the playoffs since 1992, hadn't had a winning season since 1992, and Cueto and the Reds were facing a blackout. Nearly every fan that stuffed PNC Park was clad in black and it was raucous. It chanted Cueto's name, "Cue-to, Cue-to," from the first pitch. In the second inning, as he started his wind-up, with the fans chanting, Cueto dropped the ball and it rolled along the grass to the left of the mound. Cueto denied it but every fan in Pittsburgh believes the crowd unnerved him. He gave up two runs during the inning he dropped the ball and lasted only three and two-thirds innings, giving up four hits. It was enough for Francisco Liriano, like Cueto a fellow Dominican. He shut down the Reds for seven innings and the Pirates won, 6–2.

For the third time in four years, the Reds had made the playoffs but had not one win in the first round. Of course, it was Dusty's fault. He had taken the once moribund Reds, who hadn't made the playoffs since 1995 and hadn't had a winning season in a decade, to the playoffs three times in four years and won ninety or more games in three of these four years.

But shortly after the season, Baker was fired. After the Pittsburgh defeat he was told that hitting coach Brook Jacoby would be fired. Just as Sparky Anderson had done when he was told some of his coaches would be fired, Baker said, "If you fire him, you might as well fire me." The Reds took him up on it.

During a meeting after the season, Baker said he was asked if he would resign. He said no. He said he was asked if he would retire, and he said he was not ready to retire. He was asked if he would leave by mutual agreement, and he said no.

So they fired him.

22 | SPRING TRAINING
SUN, GAMES, AND PRANKS

Spring training is the highlight of the year for a baseball writer. It is six weeks of a paid vacation in the Florida or Arizona sunshine with four or five hours of baseball mixed in every day. It is all downhill after spring training ends and the regular season begins because it becomes serious to the manager, coaches, and players. No more fun in the sun. It is time for work.

During spring training, however, where else can you sit by a hotel swimming pool in your bathing suit, slathered in sun block, doing your work with a portable typewriter or laptop computer in your lap, a beverage within easy reach? That's spring training.

Legendary Indiana University basketball coach Bob Knight was a close friend to Jim Ferguson, Reds Director of Publicity (the position is called Director of Media Relations these days). Ferguson introduced Knight to manager Sparky Anderson and they became friends.

One spring after the basketball season, Knight took a few days off and came to spring training. I had covered a few Indiana-Ohio State basketball games and became acquainted with Knight. I was seated close to the pool at the Tampa International Inn, spring home of the Reds at that time, pounding out a story on my Underwood Olivetti portable typewriter, my wife seated next to me.

Knight stopped at my wife's chair and said, "You know, your husband wouldn't be such a bad guy if he'd take that damn typewriter and throw it into the pool."

"He can't do that. That's how he makes his living," said my wife.

"Well, it's a horseshit way to make a living," Knight said as he sauntered off.

How wrong he was.

In 1979, I was in the same seat with the same typewriter, doing an interview with new manager John McNamara. McNamara was in his first year as manager, replacing Sparky Anderson. As we talked, a beautiful blonde in a bikini walked in front of us and said, "Hi, Hal." McNamara looked at me, looked at her as she walked away and said, "Who was that?"

I said, "That's Connie Bair, relief pitcher Doug Bair's wife."

Said McNamara with a sly grin, "Well, damn, he just made the team."

When exhibition games began, the Reds played games all over Florida. Publicity director Jim Ferguson always rented a station wagon and hauled the writers to the road games—Earl Lawson of the *Cincinnati Post & Times-Star*, Bob Hertzel of the *Cincinnati Enquirer*, Paul Meyer of the *Dayton Journal Herald*, Jim Selman of the *Tampa Tribune*, and me.

Selman was the official scorer for home games at old Al Lopez Field where the Reds trained. He had a deep southern drawl and when a player made an error, he would say, "That's ah erra." Everybody loved kidding Selman, an easy-going southern gentleman. There was always talk that Tampa would get a major-league team, but it didn't materialize until 1998 when the Devil Rays were born.

Time and again the city was tantalized with rumors of a team moving to Tampa—the Chicago White Sox, the Seattle Mariners, the San Francisco Giants. It never materialized.

And we kidded Selman about it and he always laughed and said, "Well, we still get all the tourist money from Yankee tourists. In fact, when we get a team, we're going to call it the Tampa Yankee Swindlers."

One of the longest trips the Reds made was from Tampa to Vero Beach, where Los Angeles trained. It was across Route 60, a narrow two-lane road that wandered for miles and miles through nothing, mostly swamps. It was not unusual to spot an alligator sunning itself at roadside.

A game started one day and Bruce Schoenfeld, beat writer for the *Cincinnati Post* at the time, decided to drive from Tampa on his own. He was missing at game time, and showed up about the fourth inning. He had driven his rental car off the road and into the swamp. He wouldn't let us search his pockets for water moccasins.

The ball park at Vero Beach did not have an outfield fence and neither the dugouts nor the press box had a roof. You sat in the sun and cooked. So the writers sat on a bank that served as the outfield fence because the clubhouse was in the right field corner and we could catch players walking in and out for interviews. Of course, we wore shorts and didn't wear shirts. We could work on our stories and our suntans at the same time. We never sat in the press box at Al Lopez Field, either. Attendance at games was sparse and the left-field bleachers were seldom occupied. We writers used it as our auxiliary press box, sitting in the sun with our shirts off.

In fact, those were much looser times, and the Reds' bullpen was directly in front of the left-field bleachers. So I began sitting on the bench with the relief pitchers in the bullpen during games. Once in a while, I would grab a glove and warm up the left fielder between innings. One day I picked up a baseball and autographed it. Between innings George Foster ran to his position in left field and I began tossing the ball back and forth with him. On the fourth toss, he looked at the ball, spotted my signature on it, turned and lobbed the ball over the left field wall.

In 1982, I had a pacemaker installed for a minor heart problem. I was seated in the grass next to the bullpen bench when relief pitcher Tom Hume began tossing pebbles at me. He hit me on the chest with a pebble and I grabbed my chest and began writhing on the ground.

"My pacemaker," I stammered. "You hit my pacemaker and my heart is racing." Hume's face turned purple and he ran to my side, apologizing profusely, until he saw me laughing and realized he'd been had.

I took my sons, Brian and Brent, to spring training with me for a week when they were on spring break. Brent was about ten at the time and the writers would send him into the clubhouse to fetch us soft drinks. Outfielder Paul O'Neill was in his first spring training camp and one morning, before a game, Brent went into the clubhouse to do his duty. When he came back, he said, "Paul O'Neill is in the clubhouse throwing things everywhere, throwing everybody's shoes and stuff, everything he can get his hands on." O'Neill was unhappy that he had been told he was being sent back to the minors and thanks to Brent we had a story.

Hal with sons Brian and Brent at Hal McCoy Day.

When the team played in St. Petersburg or Sarasota, we had to cross Tampa Bay on the fifteen-mile long Sunshine Skyway and in the middle of the bay was the Sunshine Skyway Bridge. It was mammoth and scary. The two-span behemoth's roadway went almost straight up to the center of the span so that ships could go under.

Both Earl Lawson of the *Cincinnati Post* and I were dubious about that bridge and the two of us always grabbed the seat in the back of the station wagon, a seat that faced backward, looking out the back window. That way we couldn't see the bridge until we were on the down side. Our apprehension came to fruition in May of 1980, just a week after spring training ended. A twenty-thousand-ton 609-foot-long freighter, the *Summit Venture*, rammed into a southbound bridge support and knocked it down. Six cars, a truck, and a Greyhound bus plunged into the water and thirty-five people died.

They've replaced the bridge with a beautiful span that glows golden in the Florida sunshine, but it still raised goosebumps when I had to cross it. One of the few good things about the Reds moving to Arizona was that I didn't have to cross the Sunshine Skyway any longer.

Spring training is the best time of year because access to players is so easy and they are always in a good mood. Nothing counts. Strikeouts and errors and runs given up don't count, so the atmosphere is totally relaxed.

In 1988, the Reds moved from Tampa to Plant City, Florida, and if fans want to see the real inland Florida, Plant City is the place to go. It might not be in the middle of nowhere, but you can see it from there. Even though it is the strawberry capital of the world, there is nothing in Plant City but pickup trucks with gun racks. None of the writers stayed in Plant City. Most of us remained in Tampa, civilization, and drove the forty-five minutes across Interstate 4 to Plant City.

When they built Plant City Stadium in the middle of a cow pasture, city officials told the Reds that restaurants and hotels would pop up near the stadium. That never happened. Not one new structure was built near Plant City Stadium during the ten years the Reds were there.

Owner Marge Schott was upset about it. Orlando and Disney World were trying to lure a team to a new spring training site. They built Champions Field, a magnificent facility, and Schott was angry.

"We could have moved to Happyland," she said, meaning Disney World.

Plant City Stadium remained surrounded by pastures and when the wind was right, fans were treated to the odor of cow manure. There was a retainer pond behind the right-field wall at the stadium and soon it became home to a ten-foot alligator, which liked to sun itself on the far bank on the other side of the clubhouse.

Clubhouse personnel named the gator "Schottzie," and Mrs. Schott, being an animal lover, wanted to see her namesake. The gator was sunning itself one day on the far bank and Mrs. Schott walked around the pond and was headed in the gator's direction before she was stopped and informed that the gator was not part of a petting zoo. Shortly after that, the gator was "processed," which means it was removed, relocated, or became a pair of alligator shoes.

Relief pitcher Rob Dibble pitched in a game one night and could neither throw strikes nor get anybody out. So he was removed. To get to the clubhouse he had to walk down the right-field line, out a gate, and past the retainer pond to get to the clubhouse. Bob Hunter of the *Columbus Dispatch*, a close friend and the best man at my wedding to Nadine, had his son, Gordy, with him. Gordy wasn't watching the game. He was skipping rocks across the retainer pond. There were five or six metal folding chairs on the banks of the pond, used by players while they fished. Dibble, one by one, tossed every chair into the water.

If Hunter's son hadn't witnessed it, we never would have known. But he told his dad and we asked Dibble about it and he confirmed it. He didn't fish the chairs out of the pond—too many water moccasins—but he paid for them.

One of Dibble's bullpen buddies, Randy Myers, was an off-the-wall guy. He loved military stuff. He kept a machete in his locker, along with a grenade. Nobody was ever certain if the grenade was live, but it was always there. One day, Myers went water moccasin hunting, beating the poisonous snakes with a shovel. He put six of the dead snakes on the shovel and, holding the shovel in front of him, walked into the clubhouse. Some of those present never moved faster in their lives, and at least two climbed atop their lockers, coiled into the fetal position, and screamed like babies.

I might have been one of them.

In the early 1990s, the Reds had a pitcher named Jack Armstrong and one spring he was not happy with his contract offer. So he refused to report to camp, although he was ensconced in a condo in Plant City not far from camp. Mike Paolercio, the *Cincinnati Enquirer* beat writer, and I decided to pay him a visit to get his side of the story. During the interview he told us, "I could make more money as a tuna boat captain than what they want to pay me."

After the story ran, several players loaded up Armstrong's locker with a yellow rain slicker, fishing nets, high rubber boots, fishing poles, a stuffed and mounted swordfish, and a large nautical compass. Armstrong later signed, laughing heartily when he reported to camp and found his locker turned into a fishing boat. From that point Armstrong became known as Captain Jack Armstrong.

Spring training pranks were rampant. Players had a lot of time on their hands. It was raining one day and practice was canceled. While pitcher Scott Scudder showered, pitchers Rob Dibble and Norm Charlton slipped into the parking lot and removed all four wheels from Scudder's Jeep and placed them atop the vehicle. Payback? Oh, there is *always* payback. A few days later Charlton walked into the clubhouse and found his baseball spikes frozen solid in a bucket of ice.

Pitcher Pete Harnisch was one of the funniest guys ever to put on the wishbone-C hat worn by the Reds. He was especially humorous during spring training. One day he walked stark naked across the clubhouse, a toothbrush tucked between the cheeks of his buttocks. He stopped in the middle of the room, put his hands on his hips, the toothbrush protruding from his butt cheeks, and said loudly, "Some asshole stole my toothbrush."

Harnisch liked to work the *USA Today* crossword puzzle every morning in the clubhouse and one day he approached a group of writers and asked, "What's a six-letter word for the French?" Somebody furnished an answer and Harnisch said, "Oh, good. I knew 'chicken-shit bastards' wouldn't fit."

There are some games during spring training, especially on the road, when the regulars stay home and the minor leaguers and rookies make the trip. MLB has a rule that teams must play at least five regulars in every game. When the Minnesota Twins came to Ed Smith Stadium, the Sarasota home of the Reds in the early 2000s, manager Tom Kelly's lineup card consisting of a bunch of names that were household words only in their own households.

Hal during spring training at Sarasota, Florida, 2006.

I kiddingly said to Kelly, "The commissioner isn't going to like it that you're not playing your regulars."

Kelly flashed a quick smile and said, "If the commissioner can tell me who my regulars are, I'll gladly let him fill out my lineup card."

Once, when pitcher Pete Harnisch was scheduled to pitch a spring exhibition game, manager Bob Boone posted a lineup filled with no-names. Harnisch checked the card on the wall and said, "Hey, Skipper, are we trying today?"

Harnisch spotted me once on a back field of the spring training complex, a cell phone stuck to my ear. He shouted for everybody to hear, "Hey, Hal, who you kidding? You don't have any friends to talk to. We all know you're listening to the time and weather guy."

Well, not quite. I wasn't talking to the time and weather guy. Nor was I on any important call trying to get a scoop. I was talking to my wife.

It is usually easy to get in-depth interviews during spring training because players are so accessible and there is a lot of down time. But not always. During the winter of 1993 the Reds signed thirty-two-year-old free agent shortstop Tony Fernandez, who was coming off knee surgery. The stipulation was that Fernandez would move from shortstop to third base. He was not pleased about the move, but he had no other options when he signed with the Reds.

Every day after practice hc would sit quietly, facing his locker, bent over a bowl of vegetable soup. I approached one day and asked, "How's you knee?" His answer was one word: "Fine." So the next day I tried again. "How's your knee?" I asked. Without raising his head, slurping his soup, he said, "Don't want to talk about it. Talked about it yesterday." Fernandez, though, was a great find for the 1994 Reds. He played 154 nearly flawless games at third base and hit .279.

When the Reds trained in Sarasota, one of the highlights of the spring was to see Mike DeWine, the U.S. senator from Ohio, and his father sitting behind the Reds' dugout. The DeWines were huge baseball fans, particularly the Reds. The family owned a minor league team in Asheville, North Carolina, a Class A affiliate of the Colorado Rockies, and the Tourists are one of the more successful minor league franchises.

When I was elected to the baseball Hall of Fame, Senator DeWine read a proclamation into the Congressional Record on my accomplishments as a baseball writer and presented me with a framed copy. On one trip to Washington, Senator DeWine invited me to take a personal tour of the Capitol Building. We started with a visit to his office, stuffed with Reds trinkets and memorabilia. One of his young aides walked into the office and when he saw me he said, "So nice to see you in person. I feel as if I know you personally. During baseball season my first job every morning is to get on the internet and make a printout of your Reds stories so the senator can read them."

183

We toured the Senate Chamber and visited some venues off-limits to the general public. When we left the building, we posed together for a photograph on the top steps of the Capitol Building, with the dome in background. After the photo shoot, we walked down the steps and started up the street when Senator DeWine spotted an elderly man walking ahead of us. He had two dogs and carried a tennis racket.

"Hey, Ted," Senator DeWine shouted. The man stopped and turned. It was Senator Edward Kennedy from Massachusetts, on his way to a park across the street to bat tennis balls for his dogs to retrieve. Senator DeWine introduced us and told Senator Kennedy that I covered the Cincinnati Reds. "Oh, no," he said. "I don't like you. I still remember the 1975 World Series and I'm a big Boston Red Sox fan."

For the years the Reds trained in Sarasota, I rented a condominium on Siesta Key, the Palm Bay Club. I could walk out the front door, make a right turn, and walk fifty feet onto the pure white sand of the Gulf of Mexico beach and it was like walking on sugar. Nadine loves the beach, loves the water. When the Reds shifted their spring training site to Goodyear, Arizona, Nadine quit coming to spring training.

"There's no beach," she said.

And I said, "Oh, yes there is. It's *all* beach. There's just no water."

23 | SCOUT'S HONOR

PLAYING THE FIELD

My favorite group of baseball people is the scouts. Scouts from nearly every team follow the baseball trail, watching games played by other teams and keeping copious notes. In Great American Ball Park they gather, five to ten at a time, in a corner nook of the third row in the press box, right next to my seat. Just before games begin, they troop to their choice seats behind the home plate screen to watch.

They are either gathering intelligence on the Reds or the visiting team to turn in scouting reports to their teams—how good the players are and how their team can best beat the Reds, or their opponents when the scout's team plays them. Or they are there to scout individual players their team might be interested in acquiring via trade or free agency. They are, in a word, spies. But they are *accepted* spies because they are given free tickets and choice seats behind home plate. In fact, Great American Ball Park has a section called 'Scout's Alley,' and that's where they sit.

But they are gushing fountains of information, and they are willing to share it with writers as long as their names and the names of their teams aren't used, which is why baseball fans often read in their newspapers, "according to one National League scout."

I once stupidly made the mistake of identifying a scout, and to this day I don't know why. It just slipped. Former Reds pitcher Kevin Jarvis was scouting for the San Diego Padres, and he told me he was there to watch outfielder Chris Heisey because his team was interested in him. I wrote it and identified Jarvis and the Padres. Jarvis and I had a solid relationship when he pitched for the Reds, but my stupid faux pas ruined it and Jarvis doesn't talk much to me, and I don't blame him.

My relationship with scouts began after I met George Zuraw, a scout for the Reds during The Big Red Machine era. During spring training, scouts are as thick as marching fire ants in the Florida sand. Before every spring training game, a dozen or so show up and they all eat lunch in the media dining room. In Sarasota, the lunch room and the media work room were one and the same and the room actually was called, "The Hal McCoy Media Room." My picture was on the door and one day a scout stopped at the door, looked at my picture, and said, "I didn't know Hal McCoy died." I was standing just inside the door.

Zuraw always invited me to slather some mustard on a salami sandwich and to sit at one of the long picnic tables with the scouts. And he introduced me to everybody. It was one of the best things a baseball guy ever did for me. Even if you don't get anything to write, it's a delight to listen to the stories of these long-time scouts, most of whom have been in the game for decades and know how to tell a story. And, of course, there are a lot of lies and tall tales included. Embellishment is also a staple.

So when the scouts gather every day near my seat in the Great American Ball Park press box before games, I take time to greet each one and listen to some of their stories. One who visits the most is long-time Los Angeles Dodgers scout Carl Lowenstine and Great American is a frequent stop for him because he lives in Hamilton. He is everybody's favorite, including mine. If there is a nicer man on the face of this earth I'd like to meet him, because that man has to be on the far side of sainthood.

Lowenstine has battled cancer for several years but it seldom stops him from being at the ball park, and it never stops him from asking you how you feel and how your family is doing. He knows my eye situation and looks out for me. During the winter baseball meetings one year in New Orleans I came down an escalator into the lobby. Lowenstine was at the bottom of the escalator and noticed my shoe was untied. Instead of telling me about it, he dropped to his knees and tied it for me.

He is such a nice guy that he is an easy target for kidding and practical jokes. He takes a lot of grief because of his love of soft ice cream and he constantly raids the soft ice cream machine in the Great American media dining room. Tim Naehring, a Cincinnati native who was a solid major-league player, mostly with the Boston Red Sox, likes to point out that Lowenstine once scouted him in high school and turned in his report, marking "NP" next to Naehring's name. NP in scouting parlance means, "No Prospect."

Lowenstine was at a game in Louisville one night and while scribbling some notes, a foul ball was lofted over the scene and hit him in the head. The next time Lowestine visited Cincinnati, Reds director of professional scouting Terry Reynolds presented him with a Reds batting helmet to wear as protection from errant baseballs.

I make my own contributions to the stories the scouts share, most of which are in this book. They particularly like the one about what happened to me after a game in Milwaukee. I had a lot of work to do that day, a Sunday, and I was the last one out of the press box. I entered the elevator to leave the stadium. I boarded, the door shut, I pressed the button and nothing happened. And the door wouldn't open. I was stuck. I picked up the emergency telephone and nobody answered. What to do, what to do? I was panicked, even though I'm not claustrophobic. I dug my cell phone out of my pocket and called my wife, Nadine, back in Dayton to tell her of my plight—as if she could immediately come to my rescue.

I thought about calling 911, but my phone went dead. I kept pushing the buttons. Nothing. I began pounding on the door for several minutes. Suddenly a voice outside said, "Who's in there?" I said, "Hal McCoy and I'm stuck." The voice laughed and said, "This is Jim Fregosi and as far as I'm concerned, you can rot in hell."

Fregosi, a long-time scout for the Atlanta Braves and former manager of the Toronto Blue Jays, Philadelphia Phillies, California Angels, and Chicago White Sox, had been in Friday's restaurant in the left-field corner, indulging his love for the product of hops. After telling me to rot in hell, he said, "Hold on, don't go anywhere." Very funny. He located a maintenance man and I was extricated. I had an airplane to catch and even though Fregosi wasn't leaving town that day he drove me to the airport in his rental car and when he dropped me off he said, "Stay out of elevators."

Fregosi was one of everybody's favorite scouts, a guy whose personality, booming voice, and endless stories, dominated the room. When Fregosi was in the house, the house belonged to him. He constantly kidded and chided me and the other scouts said, "He must really like you. The more he rides a person the more he likes them." Fregosi was an excellent big-league infielder before becoming a manager and then a scout for the Braves. Every time he walked into the press box he looked at me and said, "Are they still paying you?" And I'd answer, "At least I've worked for the same people for forty-two years. You've had so many different positions you obviously can't keep a job."

I earned his respect one day when there was a trade rumor involving the Braves. I asked him about it and he said, "I can't tell you the names unless you already know them." I boldly told him I could get the names with one telephone call. It was a bluff. But I did make a call to a friend in the Braves organization and he gave me the names. I went back to Fregosi and spouted the names. He gave me a quizzical look and said, "You ARE good."

One of Fregosi's scouting companions was Chicago White Sox scout Bill Scherrer, who pitched for the Reds in the early 1980s. Scherrer, a Buffalo native, loved to bowl as much as pitch and I always told him that bowling was the second best thing to do in Buffalo to keep warm during the winter. He once missed a start for the Reds when he came up with a swollen pitching thumb from bowling the night before.

Scherrer and I were waiting for a cab one year during the winter meetings in Orlando and we decided to share the ride. As I got into the cab, I conked my head on the corner of the car door, gashing my head, and the blood flowed. It was rolling down my cheek and Scherrer thought we should go to the hospital, but I didn't want to miss my plane home and said no. Scherrer was nervous about my wound. He was a chain smoker and could stand it no longer, so he paid the cab driver an extra $20 to let him smoke in the cab. He didn't need to worry, though. The bleeding stopped by the time we reached the airport.

One of my most loyal blog readers is Milwaukee scout Ben McLure. Other scouts told me that if I miss a day or two Ben worries that something is wrong with me. When my grandson, Beckett, was born McLure sent him a Milwaukee Brewers contract. When Beckett comes of age I intend to produce that contract and ask McLure, "How much are you going to give him?"

One of the highlights of my year arrives in mid-November when Wyomania rolls around. Wyomania is a weekend gathering of veteran scouts and baseball writers in Cheyenne and Laramie. It began in the early 2000s when Wyoming native Tracy Ringolsby, a Hall of Fame baseball writer, invited three other writers to attend a University of Wyoming football game in Laramie, an area where the state tree is the telephone pole. Laramie is more than seven thousand feet above sea level and one of the local hobbies is gasping for air.

The Original Four was Ringolsby; Bob Elliott from Toronto; Bob Dutton, then of Kansas City; and Rick Hummel of St. Louis. They sat in a blizzard at the football game. As the years passed, Ringolsby invited more and more writers and scouts and baseball people and attendance now is near forty. Phil Rogers calls the gathering, "a hunting trip without guns." Beer bottles are the weapon of choice for this group—not to throw but to empty.

Ringolsby keeps hoping another blizzard strikes during the football game but so far I've been lucky. Cold? Yes. Snow? Not yet. I was first invited in 2009, the year I retired as a traveling beat writer. I was guest of honor and they presented me with a University of Wyoming football jersey, number 37 (the years I was a traveling beat writer), with my name on the back.

The gathering is an amazing group of people. Ringolsby, Elliott, Hummel, Paul Hagen of Philadelphia, and myself are all members of the Baseball Hall of Fame. And there are others who belong or soon will be voted in—Bob Dutton, Bob Nightengale of *USA Today*, Mark Gonzales and Phil Rogers of Chicago, and Evan Grant of Dallas. Some of my favorite scouts are there, too—Gary Hughes of the Red Sox, Marv Thompson of the Brewers, and Pat Murtaugh of the Diamondbacks, a connoisseur of cowboy boots, which is another passion of mine.

Hughes worked for a while with the Reds and we were inseparable during spring training. We visited the Sarasota Kennel Club greyhound track almost nightly. At the time, Minnesota manager Tom Kelly was involved in greyhound breeding and named a dog after us—Gary's Real McCoy. The dog raced at the Fort Myers track and was an All-American sprinter. As a favor to Hughes and me, they sent Gary's Real McCoy to Sarasota for one race so we could see him run. He was a favorite in the eight-dog field and I put $50 on him to win. He finished seventh, only because the eighth-place dog fell. When I told the trainer I'd lost $50 on my namesake, he said, "I could have told you he wouldn't do well here. It's a strange track and he wasn't used to the surroundings."

Deion Sanders played for the Reds at the time and had never been to a greyhound track. He showed up one night and they put him and his family in a private booth to keep the masses away from him. Hughes and I kept slipping into his booth to give him racing tips. When his wallet emptied he wished we had stayed away from him.

Hughes and I dined out often during spring training, and I always picked up the tab because I was on a generous expense account. Two women, the Cox sisters, owned the *Dayton Daily News* at the time, and every time I paid the bill, Hughes would say, "Thank you, the very lovely Cox sisters."

Once we went to the Melting Pot restaurant in Sarasota and Hughes kept ordering very expensive fine wine. The evening cost the very lovely Cox sisters $350. I didn't eat for a week so I could spread the damage over seven days on my expense account.

But the hot chocolate over strawberries was worth it.

24 | ONCE AROUND THE PARK
THE WONDERFUL WORLD OF SPORTSWRITING

During my fifty-two years of sportswriting I have spent more than 67,500 hours in baseball parks across America (and one three-game series in San Juan, Puerto Rico) covering more than 7,500 games—the equivalent of 2,813 days or 7.7 years of my life. Those are years I'll never get back, but those are also years I'd never want to get back.

Adventures in press boxes and stadiums began with my first assignment as a sportswriter. It was the fall of 1962 and I was sent to cover a high school football game in Troy, Ohio. I wanted to make that story something Jim Murray would be proud to call his, even though Murray probably never spent a minute in a high school press box.

So after the game, I took my time crafting my story—way too much time. As I worked I didn't notice the press box emptying, didn't realize I was the only person left until the lights went out. I had to dictate my story back to the office by telephone. Cell phones were years and years away so I had to use a land line from the press box. But with no lights I couldn't read my copy. I stretched the telephone cord outside the press box so I could use the illumination from a streetlight in the stadium parking lot to read my story. Then I packed my gear and headed for the parking lot. Now I was not only the last guy standing in the press box, I was the last human being inside the stadium. And the gates were all locked. I had to climb over a ten-foot high gate to get out.

Welcome to the world of sportswriting.

There was even a day when I stood in a press box wondering if it might be the last day of my life. It was October 17, 1989, and I was covering the

World Series in San Francisco's Candlestick Park. It was 5:04 Pacific time before Game Three and I was standing in the press box talking to my office. Suddenly, the press box began shaking. A cup of coffee on my work space toppled, covering my scorebook with brown liquid. I looked up and the light towers in the outfield were swaying like hula dancers.

I knew what it was. I said into the phone, "We're having an…" Then the telephone went dead. They didn't hear my entire sentence: "We're having an earthquake." It was the Loma Prieta quake, a major quake along the San Andreas Fault that registered 6.9 on the Richter Scale. I swear the press box bent forward and I was staring out the window straight down on the field. I thought the press box and all its inhabitants, including me, were headed for a splattered death on the field. After fifteen seconds, the shaking stopped. Pieces of concrete fell off Candlestick Park and cracks developed all over the stadium. Players from the San Francisco Giants and Oakland A's milled aimlessly on the field.

The quake killed sixty-three, injured 3,757 and left close to twelve thousand people homeless. The game, of course, was called off and the World Series was delayed for several days. After writing my story—my first and only earthquake story—I climbed into my rental car for the thirty-minute drive to my hotel in downtown San Francisco. The drive took three hours. Bridges were down. Pieces of highway had crumbled. All lights were out. People were directing traffic at intersections where traffic lights did not work. I wandered back streets, trying to find my way downtown. I figured I'd find the city lights. There were none. It was totally black.

For the next few days I wandered the city doing human interest stories about the earthquake. But after a few days, the paper called me home and I didn't return for the finish of the World Series, known after that as The Earthquake Series.

Fans love Chicago's Wrigley Field, home of the Chicago Cubs, as well they should. The place was built in 1914 and it hasn't changed much since. It still has a manually-operated scoreboard, and there is very little advertising blighting the friendly confines with the ivy climbing up the brick outfield walls.

It is a wonderful place to watch a baseball game, if you are a fan. But it is not so friendly to baseball writers. When I first began inhabiting Wrigley in the 1970s the press box dangled under the upper deck, a narrow single row. Once you were in your seat, you were in your seat. If you had to get up to go to the bathroom, everybody between you and the end of the press box had to stand to let you pass. At the far end of the box was a griddle where they cooked hot dogs and hamburgers for the writers and the greasy smell permeated the entire area.

They eventually built a spacious press box at the back of the upper deck, but after games writers had to travel down the two decks to the clubhouses on the concourses with the fans, a logistical nightmare. But that's nothing compared to the challenge of working in the visitor's clubhouse, which is about the size of a walk-in closet. There is no place to run, no place to hide. As you walk from dressing stall to dressing stall, you have to step over strewn equipment and pray you don't step on a superstar's toes.

One day I was leaning against a huge pillar plopped in the middle of the clubhouse, trying to stay out of the way. Pitcher Joey Hamilton tried to squeeze past me to get to his locker and said for all to hear, "Why does the media have to hang out in here?" Hamilton's best friend on the team was fellow pitcher Gabe White, one of my all-time favorite guys. He earned that when he said to Hamilton, "Hal can stand anywhere he wants. He can sit in my chair if he wants. Hell, he can put on my uniform if he wants." Thanks, Gabe.

There was a similar clubhouse calling-out in Cleveland. The Reds bullpen was having a rough spell and after a game against the Indians I wrote, "The Reds don't have a bullpen. It's a pigpen." The next morning, mild-mannered, always-cooperative relief pitcher David Weathers came into the clubhouse waving a printout of my story and yelling, "So, we're a pigpen, huh?"

Kent Mercker, a close friend with Weathers, stepped up and said, "Hal's right. We are a pigpen. All I ask is that I be the Head Hog." Thanks, Kent.

Mercker was one of the most intelligent baseball players I ever covered. He raced through the Sunday *New York Times* crossword puzzle as if it was a beginner's puzzle. And he was one of the most humorous. He once said that he knew it was time to retire, "Because when I run from the bullpen to the mound my tits jiggle." Asked what he planned to do during retirement, he said, "I plan to do something scientific—like turn vodka into urine."

There was a pitcher for the Reds named Chris Hammond, a very religious young man who read the Bible every day in the clubhouse. Mercker noticed. About halfway through the season Mercker walked past Hammond, still reading his Bible, and Mercker said, "Haven't you finished that book yet?" When Mercker pitched in Atlanta he was in a rotation that consisted of two Hall of Famers, Greg Maddux and Tom Glavine, plus John Smoltz. Only one of those guys ever pitched a no-hitter and it was Kent Mercker.

One of my favorite Wrigley Field incidents involved Reds pitcher Tom Browning, Mr. Perfect after pitching a perfect game against the Los Angeles Dodgers in 1988. Browning was not expected to pitch in the series and was bored. A member of the Cubs told him, "You need to get inside the scoreboard and watch the game from there. It's the best view in the ballpark." Browning and fellow starting pitcher Tim Belcher wanted to do it but couldn't get permission. So Browning looked around and spotted the brownstone apartments across Sheffield Street, behind the right-field bleachers. The apartments had flat roofs and fans sat there watching the games for free.

"I thought that would be a great place to watch the game," Browning told me. "I asked the Cubs' clubhouse guy, Tim Hellman, about it and he set it up with one of the apartment owners." So, during the game, there was Tom Browning, in his road gray Reds uniform, sitting on the roof parapet, his feet dangling over the edge. "I would have been all right, but Tim Belcher alerted the television cameramen that I was there and they showed me."

Manager Davey Johnson thought it was funny, but his sense of humor also permitted him to fine Browning $1,000, which he donated to a charity operated by his fiancée. "That made owner Marge Schott really mad because she wanted to donate that money to the Cincinnati Zoo," said Browning.

There were only two occasions during my thirty-seven years on the road with the Reds when I nearly missed a game. One was in St. Louis and the other was in San Diego. The Reds stayed at the St. Louis Marriott, which was right across the street from Busch Stadium. After a Saturday game, I spent too many hours enjoying the St. Louis nightlife, even though

I knew Sunday was a day game. I was sleeping soundly in my room Sunday morning, with the window open, when I was awakened by the public address announcer across the street in Busch Stadium when he said, "Now batting for the Cardinals, No. 23, catcher Ted Simmons."

It was the bottom of the first inning. I set a record for getting dressed and sprinting across the street in time to see the top of the third inning." I couldn't believe none of my traveling cohorts noticed my absence and gave me a call.

St. Louis was involved in the other incident, too. After a series against the Cardinals, the Reds flew west for a series in San Diego, a night game. *Cincinnati Enquirer* beat writer Chris Haft and I had a non-stop morning flight to San Diego, but the flight was canceled. The best thing we could do was fly to Los Angeles and rent a car to drive from LA to San Diego.

We arrived at the stadium about fifteen minutes before the first pitch. But after the game, on the way to the hotel, I had a flat tire on the rental car. I still wonder what might have happened if we had the flat tire while speeding south on I-5 from Los Angeles to San Diego.

San Diego was where I was nearly arrested for the only time in my life. It was the 1998 World Series between the San Diego Padres and New York Yankees. The Yankees completed a four-game sweep as Andy Pettitte beat Kevin Brown, 3–0, in San Diego–Jack Murphy Stadium. My long-time good friend, Joe Henderson of the *Tampa Tribune*, and I finished our stories quickly, departed the ballpark, and scrambled into my rental car, hoping for a quick escape.

Egress from the Padres ballpark is not easy, always a traffic snarl. And it was still snarled as we tried to snake our way out. Suddenly, a horse reared in front of us and its hooves landed on the hood. It was a San Diego mounted policeman. There appeared to be no damage to horse or car so we spotted an opening and gunned it. Then red lights were flashing everywhere and the car was surrounded by police. An officer tapped on my window and when I rolled it down he said, "Do you know you hit a police horse back there? That's the same as assaulting a police officer. You could be in big trouble."

I was envisioning some hard time in San Quentin and wondering what Johnnie Cochran would cost when the officer's radio crackled. It was another officer saying he had talked to the mounted policemen and both the horse and the mounted policemen were okay and that the officer said it was his fault, not mine. The policeman let me go and actually shook my hand, probably wondering why it was soaked in perspiration and shaking as if I'd just been using a jackhammer.

Visiting Montreal was a love-hate proposition for most players, managers, coaches, and media. For one thing, nearly everybody in the traveling party despised going through customs, a long, arduous task. In the early 1990s, the Reds had a young pitcher named Steve Foster who hadn't done much traveling and had never been out of the country. The first time he made the trip north with the team, he stopped at the desk occupied by a Canadian customs agent in the airport and was asked, "Do you have anything to declare?"

Foster was stumped. He thought a moment and then said, "Yes, sir. I'm proud to be an American." The agent was not amused.

The team loved the Sheraton-Centre hotel, where they stayed in Montreal. Was it because the rooms were so great? No, it wasn't. In fact, one day when several teammates boarded an elevator already occupied by Pete Rose, he looked at all the players crowding into the elevator and asked, "What's everybody doing in my room?" Was it because the hotel restaurant was Mobil quality? No, it wasn't. Was it because the hotel bar was dazzling? No, it wasn't. It was because right next door to the Sheraton-Centre was the Chez-Paree, a club that featured totally nude dancers. The Chez-Paree served lunch, complete with the naked dancers. There were nights after games when there could have been a team meeting held on center stage and most of the team would have been in attendance.

The ballpark, Olympic Stadium, was a drab and dreary monstrosity built for the 1976 Olympic Games as Man's Monument to Concrete. It was converted to baseball and football after the Olympics and the playing surface was huge. And the bowels of the stadium were the world's largest catacombs with corridors here, there, and everywhere. If an unfamiliar visitor made one wrong turn trying to find the visitor's clubhouse, he could be like the guy in the Kingston Trio song who rode forever under the streets of Boston on the BMT, never to be found again. When it was designed, it was supposed to have an innovative removable roof, a parachute-type fabric that could be lifted off the stadium by grapples dangling from an immense tower built behind center field. It never worked. Eventually they sealed over the stadium with a permanent roof, leaving the useless tower sitting outside the stadium.

The best thing about Olympic Stadium was that the clean and efficient subway system, the Metro, ran directly under the stadium. You could board the Metro two blocks from the hotel—and the Chez-Paree—and disembark under the stadium in the Pie-Neuf station. In French, that's pronounced *peenoof*, but the players always called it "pie-nine." Montreal is predominately French-speaking, but most residents are bi-lingual. They prefer French, however, and some act as if they don't understand when you speak English. The Reds had a team bus driver on one trip that either didn't speak English or didn't want to. It was uncharacteristically hot the summer of 1977, and on the ride from the game to the hotel the bus was sweltering hot.

Reserve infielder Rick Auerbach yelled, "Hey, driver, turn on the air conditioning." Nothing. He waited a couple of minutes and yelled again, "Hey, driver, turn on the air conditioning." Nothing again. Finally, after a few more minutes, Auerbach yelled, "Hey, driver, the pizzas are done." Laughter enveloped the bus but the driver never did switch on the air conditioning.

When they built Riverfront Stadium in 1970, they made a slight miscalculation in the press box. The windows were too high. When seated, writers couldn't see the field. So they laid some boards on the concrete floor to raise our sight level and called it "a temporary fix." Those boards were still in place when they imploded the stadium after the 2002 season. When they lifted the boards they found a dead rat under them, right where Associated Press writer Joe Kay sat.

Well, at least it was dead. When they first opened the Houston Astrodome in 1965, it was called The Eighth Wonder of the World, the largest multi-purpose domed stadium in the world. But it was an ugly place to play baseball. Adjustments had to be made right away. The roof was glass and the glare was so bad that fielders couldn't find fly balls and pop-ups. So they had to paint the glass panels, making the place dark and dreary. And they discovered that grass wouldn't grow, forcing them to come up with an artificial plastic surface they called AstroTurf. It was lightning fast and turned baseball into the world's largest billiards game. With the gagging Texas humidity, they had to install the world's largest air conditioning system and the Astros were soon accused of turning the units on high when the visitors batted, blowing in to hold up fly balls from becoming home runs. And when the Astros batted they were accused of turning the units off so the ball would fly farther.

As the years passed, the place became infested with rats. After games, when fans departed, they would turn loose a dozen or so hungry cats to thin the rat population. They apparently didn't do a great job. One night after a game I was busily pounding out my game story in the press box when I felt something nuzzling my shoe. When I looked under my work table, I spotted a rat that probably could have devoured any cat in the house. I finished my story in my hotel room.

There are times when more pleasant things show up in the press box. There was a night in Philadelphia when one of my favorite singers at the time, Meat Loaf, sang the National Anthem before a game in Philadelphia. As the game began, I was writing a pre-game sidebar in the press box. I have a sixth sense. I can feel when somebody is looking over my shoulder. I hate it when somebody does that. I looked over my left shoulder and there was Meat Loaf standing there reading my screen as I wrote. Did I mind? Heck, no. It was Meat Loaf. He said, "I always wished I could have been a baseball writer." And I said, "I always wished I could be a recording artist, but even the soap in the shower tells me to shut up."

During the 1996 World Series I was seated in the Yankee Stadium press box when Derek Jeter fouled one back. I caught it. I have caught four foul balls in the press boxes over the years. Three of them I threw back to kids in the stands. I kept that one.

At another Yankee Stadium World Series, my seat was in the third row. Seated next to me was a portly white-haired man who just sat and watched. No notebook. No pen. No laptop. He just watched. On the other side of a partition was owner George Steinbrenner's private box, and he was seated next to Billy Crystal. Several times, when Steinbrenner wasn't pacing behind us cursing the umpires and his players, he would say something to the gentleman next to me. I had to ask. "I'm Bill the baker," he said. "I give chocolate chip cookies to Mr. Steinbrenner all the time and he gave me this seat." Bill Stimers was a close friend to Steinbrenner and a Yankee Stadium fixture since 1970.

When I was on the West Coast, there was a three-hour time difference that always played havoc with my deadlines and I usually had my face buried in my laptop throughout the games. One night in Los Angeles, there was an empty seat next to me in the Dodger Stadium press box. I was pounding away on the keys when somebody sat down. He began asking me all sorts of questions about the Reds, about Barry Larkin, about Rob Dibble, about Eric Davis, about Lou Piniella. I kept grunting one-word and two-word answers, never looking up. Finally the guy asked, "Would you like a cup of coffee or a soft drink?" Just to get rid of the guy I snapped, "Yeah, coffee."

The guy said he'd get me one and departed. After he left, a writer sitting two seats down leaned toward me and said, "Do you know who you're talking to, the guy you are ignoring." I told him that I didn't and he said, "That's Charlie Sheen." Whoops. When he returned with my coffee I thanked him profusely, quit typing, and politely answered all his questions. And it made for a pretty good sidebar story, too.

Hal with actors and Dayton, Ohio, natives Martin and Charlie Sheen.

Charlie Sheen's father, actor Martin Sheen, was born in Dayton, so Charlie became a huge Reds fan and entertained some of them with parties at his Hollywood home when the Reds were in town. I was never invited, darn it. But I did become semi-friends with him. When Barry Larkin was inducted into the Hall of Fame in 2012, Sheen attended the ceremony in Cooperstown. I had heard that he even read a lot of my Reds stories.

Before the ceremony, he was doing a television interview on a stage and my wife, Nadine, suggested I go say hello. I didn't want to do it but she insisted. I went behind the stage and tried to get his attention. But a very large bodyguard said, "He ain't talkin' to nobody." I said okay and walked away. But Nadine spotted Sheen walking from the stage toward a private tent and said, "There he is. Go say hello." I didn't want to do it, but again she insisted. By the time I caught up with him, he was in the tent. Nadine said I should go in, but I wouldn't. She spotted a window in the back of the tent and suggested I pop my head into it and get Sheen's attention.

I didn't want to do it, but again she insisted. When I reached the window, the same super-pituitary bodyguard was there to stop me. I told him, "I am a baseball writer and have covered the Cincinnati Reds for forty years. I understand Charlie sometimes reads my stories and I'd just like to say hello." The bodyguard told me to go around front and he would check with Sheen. I went back to the front of the tent in time to see the bodyguard whispering to Sheen. Sheen looked at me and said something. The guard came out and said, "Stay here, he'll be out in a couple of minutes." Yeah, sure.

But he did. He walked out of the tent and approached Nadine and me. We chatted for several minutes and at one point Nadine said, "Do you mind if I give you a hug." Sheen said, "Sure," and they hugged. At that point, Nadine said, "Holy shit, my mother will never believe this." Then she blushed and apologized for the bad language. Sheen laughed and said, "I've heard worse." Yeah, he sure has.

Not long after, Sheen was in Cincinnati for a game, inhabiting a private box. This time I was the bold one and went to the box and walked in. Sheen greeted me and introduced me to his father, Martin Sheen, and his brother, actor/director Emilio Estevez. Somebody snapped a picture of Charlie, Martin, and me.

But he didn't offer to get me a cup of coffee.

STADIUM INDEX

The fifty-two stadiums where I covered major league baseball games.

TEAM	STADIUM
CINCINNATI	Crosley Field, Riverfront Stadium, Great American Ball Park.
ST. LOUIS	Busch Stadium I, Busch Stadium II, Busch Stadium III.
MONTREAL	Jarry Park, Olympic Stadium, Hiram Bithorn Stadium (Puerto Rico).
ATLANTA	Fulton County Stadium, Ted Turner Field.
NEW YORK METS	Shea Stadium, Citi Field.
PITTSBURGH	Three Rivers Stadium, PNC Park.
PHILADELPHIA	Veterans Stadium, Citizens Bank.
MILWAUKEE	County Stadium, Miller Park.
SAN FRANCISCO	Candlestick Park, AT&T Park.
SAN DIEGO	San Diego/Jack Murphy Stadium, Petco Park.
HOUSTON	Astrodome, Minute Maid Park.
COLORADO	Mile High Stadium, Coors Field.
WASHINGTON	RFK Stadium, Nationals Park.
NEW YORK YANKEES	Yankee Stadium I, Yankee Stadium 2.
BALTIMORE	Memorial Stadium, Camden Yards.
CLEVELAND	Municipal Stadium, Progressive Field.
CHICAGO WHITE SOX	Comiskey Park, U.S. Cellular Field.
DETROIT	Tiger Stadium, Comerica Park.
LOS ANGELES DODGERS	Dodger Stadium.
ARIZONA	Chase Park.
CHICAGO CUBS	Wrigley Field.
BOSTON	Fenway Park.
TORONTO	Rogers Centre.
TAMPA BAY	Tropicana Field.
MINNESOTA	HHH Metrodome.
LOS ANGELES ANGELS	Edison Field.
KANSAS CITY	Kauffman Stadium.
TEXAS	Ball Park at Arlington.
OAKLAND	Oakland/Alameda County Stadium.
SEATTLE	Safeco Field.
FLORIDA	Dolphins Stadium.

25 SHAMU IN SHAPE
SPORTSWRITER FINDS NEW RACQUET

One of the most frequent questions I'm asked is, "What did you do with your free time on the road for those thirty-seven years you covered the Cincinnati Reds?" Sleeping in plush hotel room Perfect Sleepers and eating in five-star restaurants come quickly to mind. Drinking and carousing were possibilities, too.

For me, though, what I did mostly on the road was born on the sands of Daytona Beach, Florida, in July of 1970. I was vacationing and someone snapped a photograph of me and my son, Brian. I looked like Shamu in a Lacoste golf shirt. I weighed 250 pounds, most of it in my face and a beach ball stomach.

When I returned to work, I ran into a *Dayton Daily News* reporter named Rex Broome. At one point, his girth matched mine. But on this day he looked like a pencil wearing a tie. "How did you lose all that weight," I asked. He gave me the name of a doctor on Salem Avenue on Dayton's northwest side. I quickly made an appointment.

The doctor put me on a diet that consisted of a lot of grapefruit and lettuce. And during my weekly visits he injected me with something to curb my appetite. I never asked what, but it worked. In less than a year I dropped seventy-five pounds and was down to 175. When I reached that level, the doctor asked, "Now do you want to keep that weight off?" Of course I did. "So why don't you take up tennis?" he said. Tennis? Hey, I played baseball, basketball, and football. Tennis is a sissy sport. No way.

At about the same time, fellow sportswriter Marc Katz approached me and said, "I'm putting together a company tennis tournament. We have fifteen entrants. I need one more." I asked if he was entered and he said he was. I knew he didn't play much tennis, either, so I said, "Okay, if I can play you in the first round." Amazingly, he agreed and I borrowed a tennis racquet. Even more amazingly, I beat him in a match of bloop balls and moon balls that set tennis back to the dark ages.

I lost the next round, but I was hooked. I loved it. I bought a racquet and shoes and a tennis outfit and began playing every day. It became an obsession, and I quickly got pretty good at it. I used to go every day to the Jim Nichols Tennis Center in Triangle Park close to downtown Dayton. My wife was working during the day, so I took my infant son, Brent, with me and placed him in a playpen under some maple trees while I played whoever walked into the park looking for a game. The pro at Nichols was a pretty redhead named Sue Press. Brent was a redhead, too, and she guarded him for me, even changed his diapers while I banged serves and volleys.

When I began covering the Reds in 1973, I was an above-average player, even won a few club tournaments and my local city tournament in West Carrollton. I took a set off Martina Navratilova, one of the all-time best women's professional players. Well, it was by osmosis. I was a practice partner at the Dayton Indoor Tennis Club for Beth Herr, a state-ranked high school player. When the women's tour made a stop in Cincinnati, she received an invitation to play. The week before the tournament, I beat her 7–6, 6–4. Then she played Navratilova in the first round a few days later and lost, but she did win a set. Hence, I took a set off Martina, too.

I was covering the University of Dayton basketball team in 1972 and we made a trip to Miami to play Biscayne College. There were tennis courses at the hotel and I was playing UD Athletic Director Tom Frericks. When we finished, a young man approached me and said, "Would you like to play a little longer? I have a young woman here who would like to hit some balls."

I looked toward the sidelines and spotted a tall, leggy blonde in an extremely short white tennis skirt holding a tennis racquet. "Sure," I said eagerly. We were introduced and I didn't recognize the name. Only later did I realize that I had hit tennis balls with movie actress Cybil Shepherd, who was twenty-two at the time. She already had a dinner date, and I didn't even get her telephone number.

Hal playing tennis, 1978.

One of my off-and-on opponents at Dayton Indoor was a local attorney named Chuck Lowe, an extremely handsome guy. But I never made the connection because the last name was a common last name, even though I knew professional actors Rob Lowe and Chad Lowe were from Dayton. After a match one day Chuck said, "Aren't the Reds going to New York next week?" I told him they were and he said, "Would you mind if my son, Chad, gave you a call?" I said I'd be honored. I was sitting in my room in the New York Grand Hyatt when my phone rang. "Hal, this is Chad Lowe. Can we make a trade? If you get me four good tickets to tonight's game I'll leave you tickets to the show I'm in." Of course, I did it and had great seats at his off-Broadway show, *Grotesque Love Songs*.

When I went on the road with the Reds, I packed a tennis bag and tried to play every morning. In 1973 Al Michaels, who would become a broadcasting legend, was the Reds' radio broadcaster. Early that first year he told me he played a little bit and wondered how good I was. I brashly said, "I'll play you two sets and bet you $50 that you won't get more than one game off me." He took the bait and set up a match. He won the first game and I thought, "Man, there goes two days of meal money." But I managed to win, 6–1, 6–0, and I'm still waiting for the $50.

Most of the time, I just picked out a tennis club and wandered in. I'd sit in a lawn chair, sunning myself, waiting for somebody to ask me to play. Some days all I got was a deeper tan and no opponent. But gradually I became enough of a regular that people began asking me to play.

One of my favorite stops was the Bitsy Grant Tennis Center in Atlanta, a public facility that had twenty-one artificial clay courts. Bitsy Grant was a touring pro and Davis Cup player in his younger days, and he still played at the place named after him. They had a rule that players must keep their shirts on. But as soon as Bitsy arrived he took off his shirt to play. And shirts all over the place were peeled off. He had a regular group that included legendary Georgia Tech football coach Bobby Dodd, a drop-shot artist named Pinky Bowers, and a hustler named Hugh Manning. When one of them didn't show up, I would be invited to complete the foursome.

When Bitsy wasn't there and I wasn't playing, I'd sit on the veranda overlooking the courts, waiting to play. If there was somebody sitting close to me, Hugh Manning would walk in, point at me and the other guy, and say, "I'll take the next guy who walks through the door and we'll beat you two to death." Manning was not that good, just a big talker, and he just wanted a game.

And what was my entry fee? Usually it cost me four tickets to that night's game. That was the method I used all over the country to gain entrance to private clubs—free baseball tickets. I would go to a private club on Hotel Circle in San Diego, down the street from the Town & Country hotel where the Reds stayed. I met a burly left-hander named Bruce Barker. He had a wicked serve that I could never handle and he beat me to death. But he owned the Aztec Car Rental in downtown San Diego, near the airport, and when I was in town he gave me free use of a new Camaro, to assuage the pain of my constant beatings on the tennis court.

At the time, the biggest name in tennis was Jimmy Connors and I bore an incredible resemblance to him. I played it up to the maximum, adopting his Prince Valiant haircut, his Wilson T-2000 racquet, and the white shirt he wore with red and blue stripes on the shoulder. Like Connors, I was left-handed. I was dressed one day in my Jimmy Connors outfit, carrying my tennis bag, when I stepped onto the hotel elevator in the Philadelphia Hershey Hotel. Two women were on the elevator and they looked me up and down and one said, "Mr. Connors, may we have your autograph?" I told them I wasn't Jimmy Connors, that I was four inches taller. They didn't believe me and kept insisting. I didn't give in and when they got off the elevator I heard one say to the other, "I told you he was an asshole."

Reds manager Sparky Anderson even called me Jimmy Connors and always asked me, "Who'd you whip up on today, Jimmy?" Within a couple of years, though, I convinced a few members of our traveling party to slide out of bed early every morning to play. There was team trainer Larry Starr and *Cincinnati Enquirer* beat writer Bob Hertzel, both of whom I taught how to play. There was Reds TV broadcaster Bill Brown, now with the Houston Astros, and there was *Cincinnati Post* beat writer Greg Hoard.

We played for years, pairing off for singles matches all over the country. I never lost a singles match to any of them except Starr. He beat me one time in Houston when we played at noon and it was 105 degrees. Starr was a marathon runner. In San Francisco we played at Golden Gate Park, about five miles up and down hills from the St. Francis Hotel. Starr would hand me his tennis gear and run to the park (I drove my rental car), play four or five sets, then hand me his gear and run back to the hotel.

How nutsy were we about this? Greg Hoard and I played on different coasts on the same day. The team was in Atlanta and we played that morning before the game. After the game we hopped a plane and made it to Los Angeles in time to play again. In Los Angeles we usually played in Echo Park on some extremely seedy courts in a nefarious part of town.

At one point, I bounced an overhead over the fence and Hoard went to retrieve the ball, which came to rest in a pile of trash. Hoard came running back to the court screeching, "There's a dead body back there!" There was a body, but it wasn't dead. It was a street person taking a nap.

During the 1986 Boston-New York Mets World Series, Hoard and I set up a doubles match on the MIT courts in Cambridge, Massachusetts. It was against former New York Yankees third baseman and American League President Bobby Brown and former Pittsburgh Pirates slugger and Mets broadcaster Ralph Kiner. Hoard and I were playing well, beating them badly. Brown was clearly agitated over the whipping we were giving him and Kiner. At one point Hoard turned to me and said, "Man, I can see what a competitor Brown is. He is not having fun." But *we* were.

The best baseball-playing tennis player I knew was outfielder Paul O'Neill. He often hit with touring pro Jim Courier, and O'Neill's serve was a cannonball that ripped through the opponent's racquet strings. I hit with him but couldn't get more than two or three games off him. But he knew I could play a little bit.

The Reds had a utility player named Skeeter Barnes and he heard O'Neill and me talking tennis one day. He said he wanted to play me, "Because no writer can beat a baseball player in any sport." O'Neill told him, "You won't get a game off him." So we set up a match for Echo Park in twilight, just as darkness was setting in. I beat him 6–0, 6–0, 6–0. O'Neill wasn't there and asked about the match and Barnes said, "There were no windscreens and car headlights kept getting in my eyes." O'Neill laughed and said, "Didn't those same headlights get in Hal's eyes?"

Hertzel of the *Enquirer* was a fierce competitor, a high school catcher in Wilmington, Delaware. He didn't mind losing, but he hated to play poorly. We were playing doubles at Bitsy Grant one day when Hertzel laid his racquet down on the baseline during a changeover. We thought he was going to get a drink. But several minutes passed and he didn't return. We looked up toward the clubhouse and there was Hertzel climbing into a cab. He left his racquet and we hid it from him for several days. Another time we were playing in Los Angeles, this time on some outdoor courts on the fourth floor of a downtown building. Hertzel missed a shot and flung his racquet toward the back fence. It helicoptered over the fence and plunged four stories to Figueroa Boulevard.

Richie Ashburn, one-time leadoff hitter for the Philadelphia Phillies and Hall of Fame broadcaster, was an excellent tennis player. We played often, either in Philly or in Cincinnati when the Phillies were in town. But he knew I was a hard-court serve-and-volley player, and he was a clay court retriever. So he would only play me on soft surfaces, never on a hard court. And for three years he beat me to death. But I kept getting better and he advanced in age and when I beat him two straight times, he wouldn't play me any more. I only played on grass once and that was when Ashburn took me to the Merion Cricket Club early one morning. The grass still had dew on it when I hit my first serve and headed for the net. My feet went out from under me and I slid head-first into the net, my tennis whites now a grassy green from my shirt collar to my shorts.

When I wasn't playing Ashburn in Philadelphia, we played on some public courts under the I-95 viaduct in South Philly. Every morning before we played we had to sweep broken glass off the courts. Once in a while, we picked up shell casings. At most courts, players used three tennis balls. But not at Golden Gate in San Francisco. The courts were so close together they only permitted two balls at a time. But there certainly was no dress code. We saw players in Army fatigues, a player with a necktie tied around his head as a sweat band, players dressed in lumberjack plaid shirts, and players in sport coats.

Finding a place in Montreal was a challenge. Usually we played on cracked courts with nets full of holes at McGill University atop Mount Royale, overlooking downtown Montreal. One day Starr said, "I know a club where we can play." We boarded a bus, rode it to the end of the line, then hopped a cab. Two hours later, we were still looking for the place. When we found it, it was closed. I did play a few times at a private club in

Montreal with Reds general manager Murray Cook and assistant general manager Branch Rickey III, the grandson of baseball's great emancipator, the man who broke the color barrier by signing Jackie Robinson. Cook and Rickey were excellent players and we had close matches.

We played in exotic places, too. We played in an old Hollywood movie studio with a wooden court that made the ball rocket around like a jai-alai pelota. We played at a posh Los Angeles private club and a member said, "If Joe Morgan plays tennis, bring him out. We accept his kind, too." We never went back. We played at the U.S. Tennis Center in Flushing, New York, home of the U.S. Open. It's a public facility when the tournament isn't being played, but you can't play on the stadium court. Trainer Larry Starr and I sneaked onto the stadium court one day and played a few games before we were caught and evicted. We rode the 7 subway from Manhattan to Flushing. Hoard perspired profusely when he played and after one match he was soaked head to toe when we boarded the maroon 7 train for the ride back to Manhattan. I looked at Hoard and said, "It looks as if you pissed your pants." He smiled and said, "That's good. Anybody who has ideas about mugging me isn't going to come close."

During the days of The Big Red Machine, some of the players sneaked out the side doors of the hotel to join us on the tennis courts, guys who knew they wouldn't be playing and savored the exercise. There was catcher Bill Plummer, who seldom played because of Johnny Bench, and there was Ray Knight and Joel Youngblood. Plummer became fairly adept, but Knight and Youngblood never got the hang of it. There were days when we played near the team hotel and some of the players actually watched us. The courts at the Shamrock Hilton in Houston were right in front of the hotel. Tom Browning, Mr. Perfect, sat on a bench one day and watched Hoard and me play. Afterward he said, "Hey, you guys can really play. I thought you would be a bunch of hit-and-giggle guys pushing the ball around."

I was playing tennis almost daily when I was sixty-two, until my eye problems surfaced. Although I would have been great on line calls with my diminished vision, I had to give it up. I had to give up driving, too. But I miss tennis more than driving.

26 McCOY, UP

SPORTSWRITER HEADS FOR THE HALL

The best thing surrounding my induction into the Baseball Hall of Fame in Cooperstown, New York, on July 27, 2003, was that my father was there. My sister, Beverly, told everybody I was being indicted, but I really was inducted.

My father was the person, the only person, behind my passion for baseball. I played catch with him at an early age to please him. I played the game to please him. I played it to the best of my ability to make him proud.

I know he was proud, but he knew how to bring me down. He was a loyal fan of the Cleveland Indians and read about his Tribe every day in the *Akron Beacon Journal* and particularly the writing of *Beacon Journal* columnist Terry Pluto. When the Cincinnati Reds went to Cleveland to play the Indians in an interleague series, my father was not feeling well, welded to his recliner rocker in his Akron home. Terry Pluto was at the first game and I told him that my father read all his stories and that he wasn't feeling well.

Terry said, "Okay, when are we going to see him? Let's go see him before tomorrow night's game." Pluto picked me up at the Marriott Key Center in downtown Cleveland the next morning and we rode the forty miles to my father's house. We walked in the back door and there was my dad sitting in his chair reading the *Beacon Journal*. I said, "Dad, do you know who this is?" Without pause, my father, the man who taught me the game and the man who I thought was so proud of my accomplishments, quickly said, "Yes, I do. That's Terry Pluto, the best baseball writer in America." Thanks dad, I love you, too.

On the day of my induction, a scorching hot day in a grassy meadow on the outskirts of Cooperstown, my father sat in the front row with twenty thousand people behind him. I spotted him easily from the stage. He was wearing his ever-present straw hat and the white buck shoes he purchased after he saw Pat Boone wearing them in the 1970s. He wore them only for special occasions, so he thought this was special.

As I walked to the podium for my induction speech, I scanned the stage and saw Willie Mays and Bob Feller and Johnny Bench and Joe Morgan and Tony Perez and Whitey Ford and Brooks Robinson and Frank Robinson—all the Hall of Famers in attendance—and thought, *What in the world am I doing here?* My eyes get even weaker under stress and this was about as stressful as it gets. But I looked down and I could clearly see the tears streaming down my father's cheeks and I could see my oldest son, Brian, his shoulders bobbing up down as he sobbed. I felt as if I was at a funeral attended by twenty thousand people. *My* funeral.

Then I glanced at the index cards on which I had outlined my twelve-minute acceptance speech, a speech I fortunately had rehearsed in front of a mirror several times, including once that morning in the hotel bathroom. Nadine wanted to hear it ahead of time, but I wouldn't do it. I looked at the cards as I stood in front of the baseball world, and they were a blur. I couldn't read a word. I looked at Nadine, seated in the front row, shrugged my shoulders and shook my head. She smiled and gave me a thumbs-up, just as a photographer snapped her. The photo of her, smiling broadly with her thumb up, appeared the next day on the front page of the *Dayton Daily News*.

So I winged it. And I pretty much said it the way I wanted it said and got through it until near the end when emotion got the better of me and I joined my father and son in a tearfest. My father was eighty-five, but rode seven hours in a car with my sister to get to Cooperstown. He was alert at eighty-five. How alert? During a party that weekend he was approached by Baseball Commissioner Bud Selig who told him, "You should be proud of your son. We all are." And my dad looked him in the eye and said, "I don't always agree with every decision you make, but thanks a lot." When he said that, I was looking for a loose plank so I could climb under the porch of the Otesaga Hotel, where the party was held.

Hal giving his Hall of Fame acceptance speech.

At the same party, Hall of Fame catcher Johnny Bench approached my dad and me. He took his Hall of Fame credential, handed it to me, and asked, "Will you sign this, please?" My dad was incredulous and asked me later, "Why would Johnny Bench want *your* autograph?" That was an excellent question, but Bench certainly knew how to make a guy feel good—not just my dad, but me, too.

During that same party, Bench advised me, "Write down everything that happens to you this weekend. If you don't, you'll forget a lot of it because so much happens." It was good advice, but advice not taken. I didn't write it down, and the weekend was a blur of activities, all of them highlights. Bench also said, "And I will tell you right now. You no longer are Hal McCoy. From now on you will always be, 'Hall of Famer Hal McCoy.'" He was right again. Even my best friend, Murray Greenberg, calls me "The Famer."

I wasn't voted into the Hall of Fame the first time I was on the ballot. I was first on the three-man ballot in 2001. A committee of baseball writers puts together the three-man ballot every year. At the time, the voting was done during the annual Baseball Writers Association of America meeting at the World Series. All writers at the meeting get to vote. I was in the room when the secret ballot was cast. They counted the ballots and announced, "It's a tie between Joe Falls and Hal McCoy." Peter Gammons of the *Boston Globe* and *ESPN* was the third person on the ballot.

They were about to vote again between Falls and me, when a writer for *USA Today*, Chuck Johnson, walked into the room. They immediately put him on the spot by saying, "We need your vote." Johnson, a truly nice guy and a good friend, said, "Who is on the ballot?" With me sitting right there, they told him Joe Falls and Hal McCoy. Unbeknownst to most in the room, Johnson had worked with Falls in Detroit and he immediately said, "Joe Falls."

I lost. But I was thrilled to be on the ballot. I had worked in Detroit with Falls, too, and he was a legendary baseball writer for a wire service in Detroit and later with the *Free Press*. He deserved it. And I never, ever held it against Chuck Johnson. He was put in an impossible situation, but he made the right call. They changed the voting procedure the next year. The committee still picked the three candidates, but instead of voting at the World Series they sent ballots to every member of the BBWAA. In 2002, I won.

The results were announced at the winter baseball meetings in Nashville at the BBWAA meeting. After it was announced that I had won, I walked on a cloud to the media workroom and sat down at my workspace. Ten minutes later my cell phone rang. When I answered, a voice said, "Hey, Hal, do you know who this is?" I said, "Sure, I recognize your voice, Junior." It was Ken Griffey Jr. "I'm just calling you to congratulate you on going into the Hall of Fame." To this day I don't know how he found out so fast, but what a class thing to do.

A little while later, my phone rang again and this time it was Aaron Boone, the person most influential in stopping me from walking away from baseball writing when my eyes went bad. Without preamble, without identifying himself, Boone said "Man, they'll let anybody into the Hall of Fame these days." Then he, too, offered his sincere congratulations. As they say, class always surfaces.

Along with players Eddie Murray and Gary Carter, broadcaster Bob Uecker—one of the world's funniest men—was being inducted that same year. To see how funny he is, one only has to watch the movie *Major League*.

Uecker played a broadcaster, Harry Doyle, and his lines were hilarious, most of them of which he did ad lib, no script.

On Saturday morning before the ceremony *ESPN* had a meeting to plan its telecast. One man said, "Bob Uecker will go first and then you'll go on, Hal." I interrupted quickly and said, "Time out. Time out. If I have to follow Uecker, I'm just going to get up and say, 'I agree with everything he just said,' and then I'll sit down."

Fortunately, *ESPN* permitted me to go first and then sit down because Uecker, winging it all the way, was hilarious. During my speech, I recalled how I almost quit due to my eye problems and thanked all the people who talked me out of quitting. Uecker had no idea what I was going to say, but when he stood at the podium the first thing he said was, "I, in deference to Hal McCoy, was asked to quit many times."

During the two days leading up to the induction ceremony, my family and friends wandered around Cooperstown, in and out of shops, up and down Main Street. I was stopped every few steps by people asking for my autograph and asking to snap my picture. I had never been asked for an autograph in my life and it was heady stuff.

On Saturday night, there was a huge party at the baseball museum, attended by all the Hall of Famers in attendance. They had a red carpet from the front door to the street. When we got out of our vehicle, a spotlight was aimed at me and over the public address system came my name. It was baseball's version of Oscar Night in Hollywood. After I was introduced and headed up the red carpet, somebody across the street from behind a barricade yelled, "We love you, Hal McCoy." Yes, very heady stuff.

After Sunday's ceremony, my family and a few friends were walking up a side street toward Main Street, headed toward Nicoletta's, an excellent Italian restaurant. As we passed a bed-and-breakfast, an elderly woman came running across the lawn, waving a program. "Mr. McCoy, Mr. McCoy. Will you please sign my program?" I stopped and said of course I'd sign it. As I now do when I'm asked for my autograph, I asked for the person's name. And she said, "Oh, I'm Babe Ruth's daughter." Are you kidding me? Babe Ruth's daughter wants *my* autograph? As I told her, "I should be getting *your* autograph." I didn't get it then, but a few years later Julia Ruth Stevens sent me a signed copy of her book, *Babe Ruth: A Daughter's Portrait*.

We had rented the back room of Nicoletti's restaurant, and the main dining room was jammed. As I walked through the front door the patrons obviously remembered me from the induction ceremony and the entire restaurant pushed away from their tables and gave me a standing ovation. Real, real heady stuff.

Johnny Bench was absolutely correct. The weekend was the highlight of my professional life and remains the best thing to happen to me, other than my marriage to Nadine and the birth of my two sons, Brian and Brent. My life *did* change. I am always referred to as "Hall of Famer" Hal McCoy. Incredibly, hardly a week goes by that I don't receive a baseball or index cards in the mail, asking me to sign them. I am asked for my autograph at any function I attend, plus in the grocery store and in restaurants. Fans outside Great American Ball Park stop me before and after games to ask for my autograph and to pose for pictures with me.

Athletes seem to get tired of the constant attention and the requests for autographs. Not me. Not ever. I am so honored that people think enough of me to want my autograph and photograph. I have never turned down a single request and never will. It is real, real, *real* heady stuff for a guy who grew up in near poverty in a house with no indoor plumbing, riding in the family car when I could see the pavement through holes in the floorboards, walking to school wearing shoes on which the soles came loose and flapped as I walked.

During the course of my career I had several offers to leave Dayton for bigger papers in larger cities. I was tempted, but I remembered the Detroit experience and always remained in Dayton. There was a job offer from the *Philadelphia Bulletin* and I interviewed for it, believing they wanted me to cover baseball. I was stunned when sports editor Tim Kelly said, "We want you to cover the Philadelphia Flyers hockey team." The Flyers at that time were known as The Broad Street Bullies because they may not have always won the games but they always won the fights. I told Kelly, "I don't know a hockey puck from a Betty Crocker biscuit." He said he didn't care. He liked my stuff because I always wrote about people and didn't get technical and that's what he wanted for his Flyers coverage. I quickly declined.

Then I had an offer from the *Houston Post* and it, indeed, *was* to cover baseball. When the Reds were in Houston for a series, I interviewed with sports editor John Wilson and he asked me what I was making in Dayton.

When I told him, he snapped his head back and said, "Tell you what. I'll trade you jobs." Obviously, I did not take that job, either. There were also offers from the *Cleveland Press*, the *Washington Star*, the *Kansas City Times*, and the *San Francisco Examiner*.

I am thankful I never took any of those jobs and for two reasons: each and every one of those newspapers was an afternoon paper, and each and every one of those newspapers is dead and buried. And if I had left Dayton in mid-career I am certain I never would have my picture hanging in the Cooperstown Hall of Fame.

27 | GAME STILL ON

McCOY SIGNS WITH NEW TEAM

Newspapers are struggling, losing advertising and circulation. They are trying to reinvent themselves but can't figure out a way to beat the internet. So advertising keeps shrinking, the news hole keeps shrinking, and news staffs keep shrinking. On August 6, 2009, a day that shall live in infamy for me, the *Dayton Daily News*, trying to save money, offered buyouts to staffers over fifty-five. Although I was sixty-eight, past retirement age, I didn't want to retire. I loved what I was doing. When people asked me when I would quit I said, "When my head hits my laptop in some baseball press box."

So the paper was offering buyouts and the editor, Kevin Riley, called me in to discuss it. Riley is a great guy. We both went to Kent State University, and we both are lifelong sufferers of the Cleveland Indians. The Indians were in the 1997 World Series against the Florida Marlins and I covered it. It went to Game Seven and our beloved Indians led 2–0 going into the seventh inning. Rookie Jaret Wright, just twenty-one and three years out of high school, had given up one hit.

Deadline was approaching, so I began writing. I wrote a complete story about how the Cleveland Indians had finally shaken the demons and won their first World Series since 1948. I completed the story and waited for the game to finish. But the demons hovered over Pro Player Stadium.

Bobby Bonilla hit Wright's first pitch of the seventh inning over the wall. No big deal, though, because the Tribe still led, 2–1, going into the bottom of the ninth against Cleveland closer Jose Mesa—Joe Table for those who are Spanish-challenged. Florida's Moisés Alou led with a single and I shifted nervously in my chair. Charles Johnson singled Alou to third and sweat beads popped out on my forehead. Craig Counsell hit a sacrifice fly to right field and tied the score, 2–2. And deadline was approaching. I began writing again. I saved the "Cleveland Wins" story and began putting together a "Florida Wins" story. Because deadline was minutes away, I sent both stories to the paper and would insert the score in the correct story after the game.

It happened in the 11th inning against Cleveland veteran Charles Nagy. Bonilla led the inning with a single. With one out, Counsell hit a perfect ground ball to second baseman Tony Fernandez, a double play waiting to happen. But Fernandez, known for his glove, missed it for an error. The demons swirled around Fernandez's head. Edgar Renteria singled home the winning run, and the Indians still haven't won a World Series since 1997. And editor Kevin Riley kept the story I wrote about the Indians winning the 1997 World Series—even though they didn't—and he has it to this day.

So I sat comfortably in front of Riley's desk with Nadine at my side, ready to tell him I would not take the buyout. I wanted to continue forever. Then came the bombshell. He told me the *Dayton Daily News* not only would no longer cover the Reds on the road, they weren't going to cover them at home, forty-five miles down I-75. He said I could stay, but the paper would not cover the Reds. I quickly said, "I'll take the buyout. What am I going to do, cover high school? I'll retire."

I was in shock, benched after thirty-seven years of covering the Reds, covering more than seven thousand games and writing more than twenty-five thousand stories. Nadine took me home and I sat on the back patio gathering my thoughts, a beer in my hand. I figured it was time to give my version of what happened in my blog. And this is what I wrote:

The hammer fell today and it hurts like hell.

They're putting the ol' baseball scribe out to pasture, and if there are teardrops on your screen, well, that's from me, just an old softie.

My run is over—thirty-seven years of bliss, doing a job that wasn't a job. It was pure joy and pure fun.

And I wanted you, all my loyal readers and followers over the past three and a half decades, to be the first to know. The run is nearly over.

The newspaper told me today that it will no longer cover the Cincinnati Reds the same way it has in the past, beginning next season. And don't blame the paper. It is the economic times, and we're all suffering. They just can't afford the more than a quarter of a million dollars a year to send me coast-to-coast.

The Dayton Daily News has been nothing but great to me. How many companies would keep a legally blind employee and furnish that employee with a driver and/or a car service to get him to and from games? The paper did that for me and it certainly didn't have to do it.

The DDN didn't have to do that, but it did, and I'm so forever grateful, just as I am for the thirty-seven years they permitted me to do what I love to do so much.

So it is off to retirement after this season ends. It isn't early retirement. I'm sixty-eight, soon to be sixty-nine. But it isn't something I want to do. I feel like I still have my fastball at the keyboard and can deal with the curves thrown my way.

I feel as if my fingers have been cut off, but the economic times are harsh and I understand and I'm not angry. I just feel as if something good has ended prematurely, something I'm not completely ready to accept but must.

It was a great run and I thank all of you from the bottom of this decrepit old heart for feeding me the energy to keep doing what I love to do.

I'll miss the feedback from all of you. I'll miss going to the ballpark every day, seeing something every week that I never saw before. I'll miss so many friends I've made doing this job. I'll miss my peers in the press box and the so many people in baseball who have crossed my path and have been so great to me.

I'll miss sitting down at the laptop every day and reporting on the Reds and major-league baseball. I would list them, but it would be longer than George Carlin's list of words you can't say on television and even then I'd miss too many people who have been part of my career.

Right now, I'm on the back patio, enjoying a Tanqueray and tonic with my beautiful and supportive wife, Nadine. I'm sure it is the first of many tonight, so I wanted to get this down before I became incoherent.

My miniature schnauzer, Barkley, is looking at me, wondering why his old man is sniffling. Well, it's time to get out the old scrapbooks and read of better times.

So many times over the years, I've dealt with surly ballplayers who never say hello until it's time to say goodbye.

I'll finish the season covering the Reds and baseball, the last hurrah, then say my final goodbyes. They're putting me out to pasture. I only wish it was center field.

I was miserable and feeling sorry for myself. What was I going to do with myself? Sitting around doing nothing was not an option. With my eyes, tennis was not an option, although I would be great at calling the lines. I couldn't drive, so what was I going to do?

The Reds had a "day" for me to celebrate my retirement from being a beat writer. They chose a day when the Houston Astros were in town and offered to let me throw out a first pitch. That was perfect. Aaron Boone, the player most influential in me continuing to be a beat writer was with the Astros then, and I chose him to catch the pitch.

I had thrown out three other ceremonial pitches before games and always went to the top of the mound, stood on the rubber to make the pitch so the players wouldn't call me a wussy. The first two times were after I was elected into the Hall of Fame. The Class A Dayton Dragons honored me and invited me to throw a pitch. Donnie Scott, a longtime friend and a baseball lifer, managed the Dragons and I asked him to catch the pitch. I threw a strike. The Reds also permitted me to throw the ceremonial pitch after my induction into the Hall of Fame. Once again I chose

Aaron Boone caught Hal's ceremonial first pitch, 2009.

to stand on the rubber, and I chose Barry Larkin to catch the pitch. I threw a strike again. Catcher Jason LaRue watched from the dugout and later said, "I was impressed. You looked like you actually played the game. Not many writers ever played the game." I threw a pitch in St. Petersburg when the Tampa Bay Rays honored me. I chose Rays coach Billy Hatcher to catch it. He was a Rays coach and had played for the Reds, starring in the 1990 World Series. I threw a strike and was three-for-three.

Then came the throw to Boone. Reds Hall of Fame broadcaster Marty Brennaman always threatens people who throw ceremonial pitches: "You better not bounce it. You better get it all the way to the catcher or everybody listening to Reds broadcasts are gonna know about it." And I bounced it. It kicked right in front of Boone but he short-hopped it easily. He gave me the ball and there was a dirt smudge on it. And bless his heart, Brennaman never mentioned it. Maybe he didn't see it. In those days, I used to do the second inning on the radio with Brennaman and I just knew he was going to get all over me for bouncing the pitch. He didn't mention it.

On that night, the Reds graciously granted me use of the Frontgate outdoor private box, right behind home plate. It holds about a hundred and I had family and friends with me, plus writers from all over the country showed up. And every media relations director I had worked with on the Reds showed up.

There was Jim Ferguson, the long-time *Dayton Daily News* beat writer who left to become the Reds media relations director, giving me my chance to be the paper's beat writer. There was Jon Braude, who became every Cincinnati beat writer's hero when during an argument he slapped Reds general manager Jim Bowden in the face. There was Mike Ringering, a great guy and a published novelist. I said something to him one day that I thought was funny but was cruel. We were in Milwaukee and Ringering was glum that day. I asked him what was wrong and he said, "One of my cats killed my parrot." I said, "Why didn't the parrot yell for help." He didn't take it kindly and I don't blame him. He had an extremely tough job working for owner Marge Schott but endured with as much aplomb as possible and always did all he could to help the writers.

And there was Joe Kelly, a humorous, soft-spoken, hard-working guy. He, too, worked for Schott. But he quit one day to take another job. He went from the big-league Cincinnati Reds to the Cincinnati Cyclones, a minor-league hockey team. And he received a raise in pay. Kelly was the public relations director on April 15, 1991, the night in San Diego when manager Lou Piniella kicked over a bucket filled with beer and ice in his office after a 3–2 eleven-inning loss. When writers walked into his office and saw that a hockey game could be played on the floor Piniella merely said, "Watch the ice, guys." Then he said, "It was a tough way to lose a game and that's all I have to say." And he walked out of the room. He was angry because it was his team's fourth straight loss and angry over the way they lost it.

San Diego's Shawn Abner was on second base with one out and Bip Roberts was batting against Cincinnati relief pitcher Ted Power, usually a reliable guy, with a good fastball and a nasty slider. On his first pitch, a slider, he threw a wild pitch and Roberts took third. His next pitcher was a fastball and it eluded catcher Jeff Reed, another wild pitch, and Abner scored. Game over, Reds lost, 3–2. And Piniella kicked over the ice bucket. As the writers left Lou's office, PR man Joe Kelly said, "Here's the line score on this game: wild pitch, wild pitch, ice bucket."

Reed was a good hitter but a bit shaky on defense. Legendary umpire Bruce Froemming didn't like working behind the plate when Reed caught because Froemming was hit by pitches several times. Froemming kiddingly called Reed "Mr. Magoo."

Rob Butcher, the current media relations director, came from the New York Yankees and acquired a tough skin and a no-nonsense demeanor. He is one of the legions of people fired by George Steinbrenner. Butcher went home to Wilmington, Ohio, for the Christmas holidays, but Steinbrenner called him to come back to New York for a press conference. Butcher said no and Steinbrenner fired him. Steinbrenner later asked him back but Butcher said no and became the Reds PR person. And he is one of the best in the business.

After I announced my retirement, and after the farewell party in Great American Ball Park, I received a telephone call from Commissioner Bud Selig, whose office is in Milwaukee. He asked if I was coming to Milwaukee with the Reds on an upcoming trip there. I said yes and he asked me to stop by his office to see him. His office is near the top of the tallest building in Milwaukee, a corner office that is mostly glass on two sides, a magnificent and sweeping view of Lake Michigan.

We chatted for nearly forty-five minutes, mostly about his negative feelings about Pete Rose. Near the end of the conversation, he asked if I still wanted to write baseball and I said, "With all my heart." He picked up a telephone and called baseball's offices in New York to Rich Levine, MLB's Vice President of Public Relations. Selig said, "I have Hal Mc-Coy in my office and, as you know, his paper is no longer going to cover

Hal waves to his fans prior to giving a speech.

the Reds. But he wants to continue. See what we can do for him." I thought I had a shot. Several times when I saw Rich Levine, I gave him an expensive hand-rolled cigar. That was in late August and I left Selig's office with my head in the clouds and not just because I was more than thirty stories up.

But the season ended and the days passed. Thanksgiving came and went. Christmas came and went. New Year's Eve came and went. Then in early January, the phone rang. It wasn't MLB. It was *FoxSportsOhio.com*. They asked if I would be interested in working for them, doing feature stories on the Reds for all home games and doing an in-game chat on-line with the fans. They didn't offer much money, but I didn't care. It meant going to the ballpark and it meant writing. I said yes.

The next day the telephone rang again. This time it *was* MLB. It was Carlton Thompson, executive editor at *MLB.com*, a former beat writer and sports editor for the *Houston Chronicle* and a good guy whom I knew well. He offered me a job. I told him, "You are one day late. I just took a job with *FoxSportsOhio.com*." He graciously said, "Well, that's great. But if that doesn't work out, give me a call." So now I had a job that I accepted and another job that I could have accepted. I was back in business—and now, five years later, thanks to *FoxSportsOhio.com*, I'm still in business. They send me to spring training for three weeks every year and they pay the mileage from Dayton to Cincinnati and back for all home games.

And I am loving it. Still at it after all these years. And I'll be at it as long as Fox wants me. If they don't, *MLB.com* will receive a telephone call. After all, baseball is in my blood, in my DNA.